Developing Strategic Writers through Genre Instruction

Resources for Grades 3–5

Zoi A. Philippakos
Charles A. MacArthur
David L. Coker Jr.

FOREWORD BY STEVE GRAHAM

THE GUILFORD PRESS
New York   London

© 2015 The Guilford Press
A Division of Guilford Publications, Inc.
370 Seventh Avenue, Suite 1200, New York, NY 10001
www.guilford.com

Printed in the United States of America

This book is printed on acid-free paper.

Last digit is print number: 9   8   7   6   5

Library of Congress Cataloging-in-Publication Data
Philippakos, Zoi A.
  Developing strategic writers through genre instruction : resources for grades 3–5 /
Zoi A. Philippakos, Charles A. MacArthur, and David L. Coker Jr. ; foreword by Steve Graham.
    pages cm
  Includes bibliographical references and index.
  ISBN 978-1-4625-2032-9 (paperback)
  1. Language arts (Elementary) 2. Education—Standards—United States.   I. MacArthur,
Charles A.   II. Coker, David L., Jr.   III. Title.

LB1576.D457 2015
372.6—dc23   2014047284

DEVELOPING STRATEGIC WRITERS THROUGH GENRE INSTRUCTION

Also Available

Best Practices in Writing Instruction, Second Edition
Edited by Steve Graham, Charles A. MacArthur, and Jill Fitzgerald

Differentiated Reading Instruction in Grades 4 and 5:
Strategies and Resources
Sharon Walpole, Michael C. McKenna, and Zoi A. Philippakos

Effective Read-Alouds for Early Literacy:
A Teacher's Guide for PreK–1
Katherine A. Beauchat, Katrin L. Blamey, and Zoi A. Philippakos

Teaching Beginning Writers
David L. Coker Jr. and Kristen D. Ritchey

*To all writing teachers
who strive to make a difference every day—
this book is for you!*

About the Authors

Zoi A. Philippakos, PhD, is Assistant Professor of Reading and Elementary Education in the College of Education at the University of North Carolina at Charlotte. Previously she worked as a researcher and instructor at the University of Delaware. Her research interests include reading and writing instruction for students in the elementary grades, strategy instruction and self-regulation, and approaches to professional development for classroom teachers. Her dissertation research examined the effects of reviewing using genre-specific criteria on fourth- and fifth-grade students' persuasive writing. With Charles A. MacArthur, Dr. Philippakos developed a writing curriculum for basic college writers in 2014. She has worked as an elementary school teacher and literacy coach and provides professional development to teachers on effective reading and writing strategies. Dr. Philippakos is coauthor of the books *Differentiated Reading Instruction in Grades 4 and 5: Strategies and Resources* (with Sharon Walpole and Michael C. McKenna, 2011) and *Effective Read-Alouds for Early Literacy: A Teacher's Guide for PreK–1* (with Katherine A. Beauchat and Katrin L. Blamey, 2012). She has published several articles and chapters on strategy instruction in writing.

Charles A. MacArthur, PhD, is Professor of Special Education and Literacy in the School of Education at the University of Delaware, where he teaches courses on literacy problems, writing instruction, and educational research. A former special education teacher, his major research interests include writing development and instruction, development of self-regulated strategies, adult literacy, and applications of technology to support reading and writing. Dr. MacArthur is currently coprincipal investigator of a study of writing instruction in first grade, and he completed a research project developing a writing curriculum for college basic writing courses in 2014. His major funded research projects have focused on the development of a writing curriculum for students with learning disabilities, writing strategy instruction, decoding instruction in adult education, speech recognition as a writing accommodation, and project-based learning in social studies in inclusive classrooms. He is coeditor of the *Journal of Writing Research*, was previously editor of *The Journal of Special Education*, and serves on the editorial boards of several journals. He has published over 100 articles and book chapters and has coedited several books, including the *Handbook of Writing Research* and *Best Practices in Writing Instruction, Second Edition.*

David L. Coker Jr., EdD, is Associate Professor in the School of Education at the University of Delaware, where he teaches courses on writing and reading development and instruction. His research focuses on writing development, early writing assessment, and effective approaches to writing instruction. A former classroom teacher, Dr. Coker is the principal investigator of a federally funded study to examine the impact of writing instruction on first-grade literacy outcomes. He is coauthor of the book *Teaching Beginning Writers* (with Kristen D. Ritchey) and has published articles in leading journals of literacy, educational psychology, and learning disabilities.

Foreword

When I first began to look at the academic literature on writing and its development, I came across a book about the writing of freshmen at one of the most prestigious colleges in the United States. The authors of the book, two members of the Department of English at Harvard College, complained that many students entering the university could not distinguish a sentence from a phrase or even spell the most simple of words. Their analyses took place well over 100 years ago (Copeland & Rideout, 1901).

While much has changed in the ensuing years, concerns about students' writing have remained. Not surprisingly, these concerns have not been limited to college students. In 1975, for instance, Merrill Sheils published an article in *Newsweek* entitled "Why Johnny Can't Write." She began her article by boldly asserting:

> If your children are attending college, the chances are that when they graduate they will be unable to write ordinary, expository English with any real degree of structure and lucidity. If they are in high school and planning to attend college, the chances are less than ever that they will be able to write English at the minimal college level when they get there. If they are not planning to attend college, their skills in writing English may not even qualify them for secretarial or clerical work. And if they are attending elementary school, they are almost certainly not being given the kind of required reading material, much less writing instruction, that might make it possible for them eventually to write comprehensible English. (p. 58)

Not surprisingly, these extraordinary claims were challenged as over-the-top and too broad and as based on a hodgepodge of distortions and misconceptions (Englin, 1976). Despite refutations then and today (see TamuCLiC, YouTube video, 2009) about the veracity of the assertions made in Sheils's 1975 article, concerns about the writing of students in the United States have not disappeared. This was evident in a 2003 report by the National Commission on Writing, which stated that "it would be false to claim that most students cannot write. What most students cannot do is write well."

The National Commission based these statements on data collected by the National Assessment of Educational Progress (NAEP; U.S. Department of Education, 1998), showing that only about one out of every four students in grades 4, 8, and 12 were proficient or advanced writers. Similar conclusions can be drawn today, as the most recent NAEP data reveal that most students in the United States still do not acquire the skills necessary for proficient or grade-level-appropriate writing (National Center for Education Statistics, 2012).

The NAEP findings and long-standing concerns about students' writing inevitably lead to the question of why? While this is a complex and not easily answered question, one culprit is likely the quality of writing instruction our children receive. To illustrate, teachers in the upper elementary grades indicate that their students spend only about 25 minutes per day writing, and they spend only 15 minutes a day teaching students how to write (Gilbert & Graham, 2010). It is highly unlikely that many students will learn what is needed to master this complex skill with such little instruction. Although there are pockets of excellence in school-based writing instruction at both the lower and upper grades (Applebee & Langer, 2011), middle and high school students do little writing and maybe even receive less instruction (Gillespie, Graham, Kiuhara, & Hebert, 2014). Perhaps just as important, teachers infrequently reported applying evidence-based practices when teaching writing in any grade.

When I share these findings with others, many are quick to blame teachers. This is a mistake. In my experience, teachers want their students to succeed and do the best they can for them. Unfortunately, teachers do not receive the preparation they need or deserve from the teacher education programs they attend. The majority of teachers indicate that they receive little to no preparation on how to teach writing while attending college (Gilbert & Graham, 2010; Gillespie et al., 2014; Graham, Cappizi, Harris, Hebert, & Morphy, 2014). Although they are more positive about the inservice preparation given in the district where they teach, they overwhelmingly acknowledge that they acquire the needed knowledge and skills that best prepare them to teach writing through their own personal efforts.

That is why *Developing Strategic Writers through Genre Instruction* is so important. This book is an excellent resource for teachers, showcasing evidence-based practices that have been shown to improve the writing of all students. It is a resource that they can learn and draw from on their own. It is also a teacher-friendly guide to quality writing instruction as well as classroom-ready resources for teaching students the process involved in writing different types of text using the highly effective Self-Regulated Strategy Development Model developed by Karen Harris (Harris & Graham, 1999). This approach has been studied in over 100 investigations and, in all but one, it has resulted in improved student writing (Graham, Harris, & McKeown, 2013).

This book is also important because it focuses on third to fifth grade. The third grade is right at the juncture where teachers start devoting less attention to teaching writing (Cutler & Graham, 2008; Gilbert & Graham, 2010), even though students are a long way from becoming skilled at this point and still desperately need teacher instruction and guidance.

I hope you enjoy and benefit from this book as much as I did. I am certain your students will.

Steve Graham, EdD
Arizona State University

REFERENCES

Applebee, A., & Langer, J. (2011). A snapshot of writing instruction in middle schools and high schools. *English Journal, 100,* 14–27.

Copeland, C., & Rideout, H. (1901). *Freshman English and theme-correcting in Harvard College.* New York: Silver, Burdett.

Cutler, L., & Graham, S. (2008). Primary grade writing instruction: A national survey. *Journal of Educational Psychology, 100,* 907–919.

Englin, S. (1976). Why *Newsweek* can't tell us why Johnny can't write. *English Journal, 65 (8),* 29–35.

Gilbert, J., & Graham, S. (2010). Teaching writing to elementary students in grades 4 to 6: A national survey. *Elementary School Journal, 110,* 494–518.

Gillespie, A., Graham, S., Kiuhara, S., & Hebert, M. (2014). High school teachers use of writing to support students' learning: A national survey. *Reading and Writing: An Interdisciplinary Journal, 27,* 1043–1072.

Graham, S., Cappizi, A., Harris, K. R., Hebert, M., & Morphy, P. (2014). Teaching writing to middle school students: A national survey. *Reading and Writing: An Interdisciplinary Journal, 27,* 1015–1042.

Graham, S., Harris, K. R., & McKeown, D. (2013). The writing of students with learning disabilities, meta-analysis of self-regulated strategy development writing intervention studies, and future directions: Redux. In L. Swanson, K. R. Harris, & S. Graham (Eds.), *Handbook of learning disabilities* (2nd ed., pp. 405–438). New York: Guilford Press.

Harris, K. R., & Graham, S. (1999). Programmatic intervention research: Illustrations from the evolution of self-regulated strategy development. *Learning Disability Quarterly, 22,* 251–262.

National Center for Education Statistics. (2012). *The nation's report card: Writing 2011.* Washington, DC: Institute of Educational Sciences, U.S. Department of Education.

National Commission on Writing. (2003, April). *The neglected R: The need for a writing revolution.* Retrieved February 18, 2009, from *www.collegeboard.com.*

Sheils, M. (1975, December 8). Why Johnny can't write. Retrieved from *http://disdblog.com/wp-content/uploads/2012/12/sheils_johnnycantwrite.pdf.*

TamuCLiC. (2009, May 6). *Why Johnny can't write* [Video file]. Retrieved from *YouTube.com/watch?v=ykOtgK2sKy0.*

U.S. Department of Education, National Center for Education Statistics (1998). *The NAEP 1998 writing report card for the nation and the states.* Retrieved from *www.nces.ed.gov/nationsreportcard/naepdata.*

REFERENCES

Preface

Developing Strategic Writers through Genre Instruction is designed to support teachers in grades 3–5 in planning and delivering writing instruction that addresses the Common Core State Standards and develops self-regulated, strategic writers. The book includes three chapters with detailed lessons and materials for teaching writing in narrative, persuasive, and compare–contrast genres. Equally important, the book explains how to teach strategies in ways that develop self-regulated learners. A consistent instructional approach is followed for all the instructional units. Guidance is provided for teachers on ways to extend the lessons to any genre of writing and thereby develop their professional knowledge and skills.

Our instructional approach is based on strategy instruction with a strong emphasis on self-evaluation, on application across multiple genres, and on integration of writing with reading. Extensive research with students in elementary and secondary schools has shown that strategy instruction has strong effects on writing quality, especially with struggling writers, and especially when self-regulation strategies are included (Graham, McKeown, Kiuhara, & Harris, 2012; Graham & Perin, 2007). Research on teaching evaluation and peer review (Cho & MacArthur, 2011; Philippakos, 2012) has also shown positive effects on students' self-evaluation and the quality of their writing. Students also need to learn to write multiple types of texts (i.e., multiple genres) for many purposes. In this approach, students learn a consistent set of strategies for planning, drafting, evaluating and revising, and editing. Both the planning and revising strategies are based on knowledge of the elements of particular genres (e.g., opinion, reasons, evidence, and conclusion for persuasive writing). These elements are introduced through read-aloud activities and mentor–model texts that connect writing and reading. Evaluation is taught throughout the process, beginning with model texts and continuing through peer review and self-evaluation. Throughout instruction, teachers emphasize the development of independent, self-regulated learners. Students learn to set goals, use motivational strategies, monitor their progress, and reflect on their learning.

The book is intended to support teachers' professional development in writing instruction. After an overall introduction in Chapter 1, the core principles of our instructional approach and the specific instructional methods are described in Chapters 2 and 3. Detailed lesson plans for narrative, persuasive, and compare–contrast writing are presented in Chapters 4–6, and are meant to provide explicit instruction to teachers as they initially teach self-regulated strategies across the genres. Each chapter includes lesson plans for one main genre, followed by suggestions for extensions to related genres. For example, Chapter 4 focuses on story writing and then discusses extensions to personal narratives and other genres of fiction, such as mysteries. Across the three chapters, the role of reading increases in importance, with students using information from published sources for informative writing in the compare–contrast lessons. Chapter 7 discusses how teachers can apply the instructional approach in designing their own lessons. The goal is for teachers to be able to design writing lessons that are integrated with instruction in literature, science, and social studies.

This book would not have been possible without the support of many people. We would like to thank all the teachers, parents, and students with whom we worked and continue to work. We are grateful for our collaboration with them; their input was a catalyst in turning a project into a book and determining what was instructionally realistic. We would also like to thank our colleagues, Steve Graham and Karen Harris, whose decades of research on strategy instruction in writing and the Self-Regulated Strategy Development model provide the primary research support for the book. We express our thanks to Courtney Casperson and Sarah Munsell for reading the final lesson plans and for giving us their feedback as teachers, readers, and editors. We would also like to thank all our colleagues who teach and study writing for their commitment to the subject. Finally, we thank our spouses, Peter, Dorothy, and Cecilie, for supporting our work.

Contents

5 Persuasive Writing

6 Compare–Contrast Writing

7 How to Plan Your Own Genre-Based Strategy Instruction Lessons 238

Appendix. Study Guide 243

References 247

Children's Books 250

Websites 253

Index 254

Purchasers of this book can download and print
additional copies of the forms and handouts
from *www.guilford.com/philippakos-forms*.

List of Forms and Handouts

FORMS

HANDOUTS

Chapter 1

Writing Strategically

AN INTRODUCTION TO GENRE-BASED STRATEGY INSTRUCTION

"Let's talk about writing." Mr. Tragas is a third-grade teacher with whom we worked during our professional development work. He had been a teacher for 3 years, but this was his first year teaching third grade. Mr. Tragas's class of 25 young minds represented a range of writing abilities and instructional needs. Some of his students could write multiple paragraphs, others could complete a paragraph, and a few struggled at the sentence level. This last group of students also met with the special education teacher for additional (Tier 3) support in reading. Mr. Tragas shared with us that he did not feel as comfortable teaching writing as he did teaching reading. He also stated that he was not satisfied with the writing materials he pulled together from online teachers' sites or from books he had purchased himself, and that finding time for planning was difficult in an already demanding day. Mr. Tragas was able to meet with another colleague, but by the time they finished planning for math and reading, there was rarely time left to plan writing.

Mr. Tragas's classroom, instructional day, and challenges may echo yours. Classrooms often resemble mosaics of writing abilities, like Mr. Tragas's classroom. This pattern of students' writing performance can also be observed on a national scale. According to the 2003 National Assessment of Educational Progress (NAEP) report (Persky, Daane, & Jin, 2003), the overall writing performance of fourth graders was low; only 28% of fourth graders performed at or above the proficient level, and 58% performed at the basic level. The same picture emerged with eighth graders: 31% of eighth graders performed at or above the proficient level, and 54% performed at the basic level. Fourth grade was not included in more recent NAEP writing assessments, but the performance of eighth-grade students has not changed much (National Center for Education Statistics, 2012). These national results and Mr. Tragas's classroom feedback point to the need for attention to writing and writing instruction. Writing is an important component of literacy—but unfortunately a neglected one (National Commission on Writing in America's Schools and Colleges, 2003).

To meet the call for improved writing instruction, we designed this book to support grades 3–5 teachers in planning and delivering writing instruction that addresses the Common Core State Standards (CCSS) and that develops self-regulated, strategic writers. The book includes three chapters with detailed lessons and materials for teaching writing in narrative, persuasive, and informative genres, as specified in the Standards. Equally important, the lessons follow a consistent instructional sequence based on strategy instruction, which is an evidence-based approach with extensive research support (Englert, Raphael, Anderson, Anthony, & Stevens, 1991; Graham, McKeown, Kiuhara, & Harris, 2012). Students learn strategies for planning, drafting, evaluating, revising, and editing that are integrated with knowledge of genres.

A strategy is a conscious, cognitive process for completing complex tasks. For instance, good writers have strategies for planning their thoughts and for developing ideas. Some strategies that writers use to generate ideas include brainstorming ideas, asking questions, conducting an online search, reading additional sources, or asking others for information. People also use strategies in everyday life. For example, when meeting people at a party many of us use strategies to remember names. Some individuals may repeat the name of the person they meet several times, or they may make associations between the name and something memorable about the name or the person. In this book, students learn strategies to complete writing tasks and to manage their effort and motivation. Overall, the goal of this book is not only to assist preservice and inservice teachers in learning about and using genre-based strategy instruction, but to also support them in strategically designing their own writing lessons.

TEACHERS' CHALLENGES

Teachers can have strong, direct effects on students' literacy growth and motivation (Pressley, Mohan, Raphael, & Fingeret, 2007). However, teachers are also learners who face challenges in their profession. One of those challenges relates to teachers' preparation to teach writing. In nationwide surveys, teachers report that they have not been adequately prepared to teach writing. For example, two out of three teachers in grades 4–6 reported being ill-prepared to teach writing (Gilbert & Graham, 2010). Researchers have developed a solid base of knowledge about evidence-based practices for writing instruction, but those findings may not always find their way to classroom settings. Teachers are in need of professional development in writing instruction.

A second challenge is the limited time allotted to teach and plan for writing instruction. The Gilbert and Graham national survey (2010) found that fourth-, fifth-, and sixth-grade teachers taught writing, on average, only an hour and a quarter weekly, or just 15 minutes a day. Decisions about time may not always be under teachers' control, as many schools have specific time blocks for literacy. Even when individual teachers have the independence to allocate time among reading and writing lessons, the pressure for improved reading results often pushes writing to the side.

In our professional development work, we have witnessed an additional challenge that teachers face: collaboration with colleagues. Finding time to meet during the week to plan for writing instruction is challenging for teachers. In their professional learning communities (PLCs) and grade-level meetings, teachers often work on reviewing student data and planning for reading and math and may not have time to outline their instructional plan for writing. When they do discuss writing, they may share students' work and describe what they plan to teach; however, the instructional content and methods may not always be clear or consistent.

Another challenge that we saw teachers face was making instructional changes to address writing as a subject based on new policy guidelines. In particular, the Common Core State Standards Initiative (CCSSI, 2010) has brought increased attention to writing and set specific and challenging expectations about writing outcomes. However, the standards are silent about the instructional methods needed to achieve those expectations.

This book cannot address all of these challenges. However, it can support teachers in learning and implementing writing instruction that addresses the Standards. Additionally, the book is based on strong research evidence and is designed to support a wide range of students' abilities. Furthermore, the book aims to assist teachers in collaborating with colleagues to improve instruction and increase their professional knowledge.

THE CCSS FOR WRITING

Policy affects instruction, and the CCSS (CCSSI, 2010), with their guidelines for reading and writing, are already having an impact on how writing is taught in U.S. classrooms. The K–5 Anchor Standards for Writing (see Figure 1.1) address the types of writing that students should produce, the writing processes they should follow, and the importance of writing about the texts that students read.

First, the CCSS call for students to write narratives, persuasive, and informative/explanatory texts, including multiple genres within each category. *Genres* are types of writing designed for particular purposes and audiences with conventions for organization, content, and style (Hyon, 1996). Students need experiences writing in multiple genres because the writing demands in school, college, and the workplace are varied. Learning about multiple genres helps students learn what experienced writers know: that the organization and style of a paper is largely determined by its audience and purpose. This book directly addresses the challenges associated with genre-based writing. First, the lessons support instruction in multiple genres. In addition, the lessons support students as they learn to analyze writing tasks for topic, audience, and purpose in order to choose an appropriate organizational form.

Further, the CCSS include clear expectations about the use of the writing process, stating that by the end of grade 5, students should be able to apply the process to plan, draft, revise, and edit. Students need to learn strategies for engaging independently in each of these processes. Knowledge about genres must be integrated with strategies because proficient writers use knowledge about the organization of genres to generate

Text Types and Purposes
• Write arguments to support claims in an analysis of substantive topics or texts, using valid reasoning and relevant and sufficient evidence. • Write informative/explanatory texts to examine and convey complex ideas and information clearly and accurately through the effective selection, organization, and analysis of content. • Write narratives to develop real or imagined experiences or events using effective technique, well-chosen details, and well-structured event sequences.

Production and Distribution of Writing
• Produce clear and coherent writing in which the development, organization, and style are appropriate to task, purpose, and audience. • Develop and strengthen writing as needed by planning, revising, editing, rewriting, or trying a new approach. • Use technology, including the Internet, to produce and publish writing and to interact and collaborate with others.

Research to Build and Present Knowledge
• Conduct short as well as more sustained research projects based on focused questions, demonstrating understanding of the subject under investigation. • Gather relevant information from multiple print and digital sources, assess the credibility and accuracy of each source, and integrate the information while avoiding plagiarism. • Draw evidence from literary or informational texts to support analysis, reflection, and research.

FIGURE 1.1. Common Core Anchor Standards for Writing in K–5 (CCSSI, 2010, p. 18).

and organize content and also to evaluate their writing. This book explicitly discusses the ways in which the writing process is used across different genres.

Also, the CCSS call for integration of reading and writing instruction and for teaching students to become critical thinkers. For example, the Standards call for students to read text in order to use textual information in their own writing. Writing from sources is especially demanding as it requires the application of both reading comprehension and writing skills. The instructional approach in this book addresses these new demands across the lessons. We integrate reading and writing by using read-alouds and mentor texts to develop students' genre knowledge. In addition, in the informative lessons (compare–contrast), students learn strategies for taking notes on main ideas while reading and using those notes to write.

Overall, the CCSS call for students to be strategic, knowledgeable, and resourceful in using the writing process, determining the writing purpose, and writing for a specific audience. For students to be strategic, instruction should be, too.

RECOMMENDATIONS FROM RESEARCH ON WRITING INSTRUCTION

The CCSS set expectations for learning outcomes. However, they do not provide information about the instructional approaches that teachers should use to achieve those academic goals. For that, we turn to research on effective writing instruction, and in particular, to a number of reviews that have summarized findings on effective writing instruction (e.g., Graham, McKeown, et al., 2012; Graham & Perin, 2007).

A recently published practice guide (Graham, Bollinger, et al., 2012) provides evidence-based recommendations for writing instruction (see Figure 1.2) drawing on solid research studies. A panel of experts, convened by the U.S. Department of Education, reviewed the research and developed the following recommendations.

- **Provide daily time for writing.** The guide recommends allotting 1 hour a day to writing instruction and practice. However, it acknowledges the challenges in planning enough writing time and suggests meeting this goal by including writing across content areas.

- **Teach students to use the writing process for a variety of purposes.** This recommendation includes two parts that echo the CCSS guidelines for teaching students to write in multiple genres and to master strategies for planning, drafting, evaluating, revising, and editing. Extensive research supports the value of strategy instruction in writing, especially when combined with self-regulation strategies. The practice guide (Graham, Bollinger, et al., 2012) gave its strongest research rating to this recommendation. Also, a recent review of writing instruction in the elementary grades (Graham, McKeown, et al., 2012) found large effect sizes for strategy instruction, adding self-regulation components to strategies, and teaching text structure (organization)—all part of teaching multiple genres and strategies.

Strategy instruction has been found to support students across a range of ability and grade levels and in individual and classroom instruction, and the effects are increased when self-regulation strategies are included (Graham, 2006; Graham, McKeown, et al., 2012; MacArthur & Philippakos, 2013).

The Self-Regulated Strategy Development (SRSD) model (Graham & Harris, 2005; Graham, McKeown, et al., 2012; Harris & Graham, 2009) was found to be particularly effective. The SRSD model has been studied extensively as a way to teach strategies for planning and revising based on text structure, or genre. Instruction addresses the development of students' background knowledge (e.g., of text structure) and includes explicit explanation and think-aloud modeling of cognitive strategies. In addition, SRSD provides memorization routines, guided practice, and support for independent practice. Critically, throughout instruction, students also are taught strategies for self-regulation, including approaches for goal setting, self-evaluation, focusing attention, coping with problems,

---

1. Provide daily time for students to write.

2. Teach students to use the writing process for a variety of purposes.
   a. Teach students the writing process.
   b. Teach students to write for a variety of purposes.

3. Teach students to become fluent with handwriting, spelling, sentence construction, typing, and word processing.

4. Create an engaged community of writers.

FIGURE 1.2. Recommendations for effective writing instruction. Based on Graham, Bollinger, et al. (2012).

and self-reinforcement. Overall, it is an approach that has been found to increase students' writing quality, use of genre elements, writing length, and ability to self-regulate their performance.

 • **Teach students to become fluent with handwriting, spelling, sentence construction, typing, and word processing.** Writers are expected to record their ideas using correct spelling and punctuation and appropriate grammar. Limited fluency in handwriting or typing and problems with spelling can place high demands on working memory and interfere with writing quality (Coker, 2007). Students should be taught how to construct sentences and how to reach fluency in handwriting and typing. Instruction in handwriting, spelling, and sentence construction at appropriate ages contributes to an overall improvement in writing quality. The lessons in this book do not address such instruction directly; however, editing lessons include instruction to address common writing problems.

 • **Create an engaged community of writers.** Collaboration among writers can take place during all stages of the writing process, and it can have positive effects on students' writing. Research has shown the positive effects of peer collaboration on writing (Graham, McKeown, et al., 2012), and peer review has also shown positive effects when students are provided with adequate training on evaluation and giving feedback (Cho & MacArthur, 2011; MacArthur, 2012). The practice guide suggests that students should be given opportunities to collaborate throughout the writing process, including peer review. The instructional approach in this book offers regular opportunities for collaboration during planning, drafting, and revising. In particular, it includes extensive collaborative work to help students learn evaluation criteria in preparation for peer review (Philippakos, 2012).

GENRE-BASED STRATEGY INSTRUCTION

The CCSS (CCSSI, 2010) state that students should be able to write for three main text types and purposes; that they should engage in strategies for planning and revising; and that they should be able to write based on their reading. The practice guide (Graham, Bollinger, et al., 2012) provides evidence-based practices for teaching students to use strategies for planning, drafting, evaluating, and revising and to write in different genres. The instructional approach in this book addresses the CCSS and uses the recommended evidence-based practices described in the practice guide.

The CCSS clearly state that students in grades 3–5 should be able to write for three broad purposes: to narrate, to persuade, and to inform. In addition, they should learn multiple subgenres within each overall purpose. The approach in this book addresses these specific expectations in three units that teach students how to write fictional stories, how to write opinion essays, and how to write compare–contrast papers. We selected three representative genres and have provided all materials and lessons to support teachers' writing instruction. In addition, we have suggested ways to extend these lessons to related genres. For example, after the lessons on fictional stories, teachers could work on personal narratives, mysteries, or fables. Or after the lessons on opinion essays, teachers could work on book reviews in which students support their opinions about books. Guidelines about how to develop new lessons are provided in Chapter 7.

Teaching students to engage in the writing process is also central to both the Standards and the practice guide. The three instructional chapters of this book provide explicit and systematic instruction in the processes of planning, drafting, evaluating, revising, and editing. The instructional approach we use is based on successful models for cognitive strategy instruction, including SRSD (Graham & Harris, 2005; Harris & Graham, 2009; Harris, Graham, Mason, & Friedlander, 2008; Harris, Graham, & Mason, 2006) and the work of Englert and colleagues (Englert, Raphael, Anderson, Anthony, & Stevens, 1991), who integrated planning and revising strategies by basing them both on text structure.

In our approach, students learn how to plan by analyzing the written task, by considering the elements of the genre, and by using graphic organizers that reflect the genre elements. Then they learn how to evaluate and revise their writing by applying genre-specific criteria drawn from those same elements. For example, when writing an opinion essay, students plan by brainstorming and developing ideas *in favor of* and *against* their opinion. Next they organize those ideas using a graphic organizer structured as a genre-specific outline. The graphic organizer for an opinion text includes three parts: a *Beginning* with the *topic* and the *opinion*, a *Middle* with *reasons* and *evidence*, and an *End* with a *restatement* of the position and a *message* to the reader. Finally, they evaluate their work using a rubric with criteria based on the elements, such as "Does the *Beginning* introduce the *topic* and say why it is important?"

Furthermore, our approach strongly emphasizes the importance of learning evaluation criteria and self-evaluation. We draw on research on peer review practices (for a review, see MacArthur, 2012) and our own research (Cho & MacArthur, 2011; Philippakos, 2012) on the effects of learning to give feedback. Instruction in genre-specific evaluation criteria begins in the first lesson in each genre with evaluation of strong and weak papers. In addition, evaluation is modeled by teachers and practiced by students throughout the lessons. Extensive practice in applying evaluation criteria is provided in preparation for peer review.

In addition, the CCSS state that students should be able to write about what they read. In our approach, integration of reading and writing begins by introducing each genre and its elements during read-alouds of mentor texts. Research shows that learning text structure, an important aspect of genre, can improve reading comprehension as well as writing (National Institute of Child Health and Human Development, 2000).

Unfortunately, there is limited research on teaching elementary students to write using sources, although a few studies have found positive effects of structured note taking on reading comprehension (Graham & Hebert, 2011). The lessons in this book begin with writing from general background knowledge without any sources. The narrative writing lessons and the lessons on opinion essays draw on students' common knowledge. For informative writing, we introduce a strategy for taking notes from reading and using those notes as a basis for writing. This process is challenging but critical for informative writing in the content areas.

Finally, although the CCSS do not mention the components of motivation and self-regulation, the recommendations in the writing practice guide indicate that students should be able to (1) engage in problem solving, (2) manage writing tasks, and (3) regulate their writing processes. The lessons in this book provide specific strategies to support and promote students' self-regulation, progress monitoring, motivation, and reflection abilities. Overall, we offer preservice and inservice teachers specific lessons and materials needed to deliver and design high-quality writing lessons.

CLOSING THOUGHTS

Writing is challenging for writers of all ages; it is also challenging to teach. Teachers should be supported in their writing instruction in order to prepare students who are college and career ready. In our professional development work, we often tell teachers that the purpose of writing instruction is not only to develop effective writers and readers, but also to teach students the analytical skills necessary to write and read with a purpose. The evidence-based approach described in this book provides explicit guidance for teaching different genres, applying the writing process across genres, supporting students' self-regulation capacities, and developing effective learners.

In Chapter 2 we discuss the principles and instructional components of this approach. In Chapter 3 we share a *strategy for teaching strategies*, which is a blueprint for designing lessons based on this instructional approach. In addition, drawing from what we learned during our professional collaboration with teachers, we share some practical advice for managing common issues. Finally, we provide information about the organization of the lessons. Detailed lesson plans for narrative, persuasive, and compare–contrast writing are presented in Chapters 4–6, respectively. Chapter 7 provides a discussion of how teachers can apply the instructional approach in designing their own lessons. Finally, the Appendix includes a Study Guide for reading this book, which can be used independently or in small groups for professional development. We hope that the clarity of this approach and the inclusion of all materials for teaching your lessons will provide the resources you need as you help your students *become strategic writers!*

Chapter 2

Principles of Genre-Based Strategy Instruction

INTERVIEWER: What do good writers do when they revise?

ALISON: When we revise, we check to see that we have everything that goes in the Beginning, Middle, and End.

INTERVIEWER: Could you tell me exactly what good writers look for?

STUDENT: We look for an introduction to the topic and a clear opinion. Oh, and that will be in the Beginning of the paper. Then, in the Middle, we look for clear reasons and good evidence, you know, to make the reader *really* believe you. In the End of the paper, we look for a restatement of the opinion and for a message to the reader. Oh, and for transition words, and a title, and that we were not rude to the reader.

This excerpt is taken from an interview with Zach, a fifth-grade student who was learning about opinion essays. His class had completed the lessons on writing opinion essays, and Zach had just completed writing and revising his first opinion paper. His responses to the questions demonstrate a fairly sophisticated understanding of what it means to revise a text.

In this book, one goal is for students like Zach to learn the key elements and features of particular genres. Another goal is for them to learn how to use that genre-specific knowledge to plan, draft, evaluate, and revise their own papers. To achieve these goals, students learn a consistent set of strategies for approaching these tasks, and the strategies are then adapted to different genres. Also, throughout instruction, teachers emphasize the development of independent, self-regulated learners. Overall, students learn to set goals, use motivational strategies, monitor their progress, and reflect on their learning.

In this chapter, we first discuss the core principles of genre-based strategy instruction with self-regulation. Such a discussion is important in understanding the instructional methods and why certain instructional components are critical. Second, we explain the writing strategy and the self-regulation strategies. Finally, we discuss some of the key instructional methods used in this approach.

CORE PRINCIPLES OF GENRE-BASED STRATEGY INSTRUCTION

Strategies are conscious processes for solving problems or performing complex tasks (MacArthur, 2011). *Strategy instruction* is an evidence-based approach that draws on multiple theoretical sources and research evidence to address three instructional questions: (1) which writing strategies to teach, (2) how to help students use those strategies independently, and (3) what instructional methods to use in order to support student learning. First, to determine the best writing strategies to teach, we consider research on the cognitive processes of proficient writers and the genres that are important in schooling. Second, research on self-regulation is important when teaching the independent use of strategies across situations. Finally, extensive research on strategy instruction provides guidance on critical instructional methods.

Which Strategies to Teach: Cognitive Models of Writing

Cognitive strategy instruction in writing is designed to teach students the thought processes that effective writers use. The core idea behind cognitive strategy instruction is that it is possible to identify the cognitive processes of proficient learners and then teach those processes in some form to students (Graham & Harris, 2005; MacArthur, 2011). For example, proficient writers set goals for writing based on audience and purpose. They use strategies such as brainstorming or reading and talking to others to generate ideas. They have knowledge about how different types of text, or genres, are organized, and they use that knowledge to help generate and organize their ideas. Proficient writers also engage in a great deal of evaluation and revision both to fix problems and to identify opportunities to improve their writing. Overall, these writers have a wide range of resources they use to write clear and engaging texts.

However, this is usually not the case for developing or struggling writers. Proficient writers and developing writers have been found to differ dramatically in their use of strategies (Hayes, 1996). For example, developing writers do very little planning even when prompted (Troia, 2006), and their revising is limited primarily to minor word changes and error corrections (MacArthur, 2012). A primary goal of cognitive strategy instruction is to teach developing and struggling writers the strategies that proficient writers use to be successful. One thing that successful writers do well is to select specific strategies based on their writing purposes and knowledge of genres.

Which Strategies to Teach: Genres

Genres are types of writing designed to address certain purposes and audiences (Hyon, 1996; Martin, 2009). They are conventional forms that have developed over time for various purposes. Thus, when teachers ask students to analyze the topic, audience, purpose, and form of a text, they are essentially asking about its genre. The CCSS set expectations that students will learn to write for three broad purposes: to inform, to persuade, and to narrate. Each of these purposes can be achieved through multiple genres, some of which are conventionally assigned in schools (Martin & Rose, 2012). For example, persuasive writing is commonly taught as an opinion essay on a controversial topic. Students are expected to introduce the topic, give a clear opinion, support it with reasons and evidence, perhaps address counterarguments, and conclude with a summary. But persuasive writing can also include genres such as book or movie reviews, in which writers give reasons for their evaluations; write letters of complaint to a business; or analyses of themes in literature using evidence from the text.

Most research on writing strategies has included strategies for using knowledge of genres, or text structure, to generate and organize content during planning (MacArthur, 2011), which is what proficient writers do. Research has focused on persuasive essays, narratives, and several expository genres, including explanation and compare–contrast essays (Meyer, 1985a, 1985b). Although less research has focused on revising, recent work on SRSD has included strategies for both planning and revising (Harris et al., 2013). To our knowledge, research by Englert and colleagues (1991) on the Cognitive Strategy Instruction in Writing (CSIW) model was the first model to use text structure, or genre, to integrate planning and revising strategies. In the CSIW model, students chose an appropriate text structure for the topic, used a graphic organizer (GO) that represented that structure, and applied evaluation criteria appropriate to the structure during revision. The writing strategies in this book draw on this CSIW approach.

How to Support Independent Use: Self-Regulation

It is one thing to teach students to use a writing strategy when a teacher tells them to do so, but it is quite another for students to apply a strategy independently in appropriate situations. Research on the SRSD model shows that adding specific self-regulation strategies helps students internalize the writing strategies and use them independently (Graham & Perin, 2007; Graham, McKeown, et al., 2012). *Self-regulation* includes a range of techniques for setting goals, selecting strategies, monitoring strategy use, evaluating effects on performance, sustaining motivation and effort, and managing time and the environment (Harris, Graham, MacArthur, Reid, & Mason, 2011). Successful instruction in self-regulation strategies can help bolster students' motivation and the belief in their own ability to manage and complete a writing task. Both of these may help students persevere when writing becomes difficult. The self-regulation strategies in this book are based on SRSD (Graham, Harris, MacArthur, & Santangelo, 2018).

Instructional Methods for Teaching Strategies

In addition, the research has led to well-established methods for teaching strategies in a way that encourages self-regulated use (Harris & Graham, 2009; MacArthur, 2011). The most thoroughly developed and studied approach for teaching self-regulated strategies is the SRSD model (Harris & Graham, 2009). In this approach, teachers first develop the background knowledge students will need to use the strategies. In this book, that knowledge includes information about the purposes, organization, and other features of the genre. Students need to understand the purposes of the genre to make their writing meaningful. When a task is meaningful, students are more likely to see the value of strategies and generalize them to other tasks and settings. Second, teachers explain the strategies clearly and discuss their purpose and value. Third, teachers demonstrate the strategies using think-aloud modeling, an instructional approach in which the teacher demonstrates how to complete a task and verbally explains all the thinking processes involved. This think-aloud modeling is necessary to make the underlying cognitive processes used in writing visible to students. Teachers model how to use the strategies, and they also model self-regulation strategies for managing difficulties and maintaining motivation. Fourth, teachers guide students' use of the strategies, beginning with collaborative practice and gradually releasing responsibility to the students. In this guided process, teachers monitor student understanding and give feedback to students both on how they are using the strategy and on their writing performance. Students also monitor their own strategy use with self-regulation strategies. Fifth, teachers build motivation by helping students to see how the strategy improves their performance. Finally, teachers help students see how the strategies might be applied in a range of situations, discussing with students when and where they might use the strategy. Teachers provide ample opportunities for students to use the strategy, and may plan with other teachers to remind students about the strategy when appropriate. Throughout the process, teachers support students' use of self-regulation strategies.

Genre-Based Strategies for Planning and Revising

Drawing on the CSIW model (Englert et al., 1991) and consistent with SRSD recommendations (Harris et al., 2013), our approach systematically incorporates genre elements for *both* planning and revising. In our approach, students analyze the writing task for audience and purpose to determine which genre is best for that writing purpose. Then they use planning strategies and evaluation criteria specific for that genre. The genre elements, the elements of the GO, and the evaluation criteria used for evaluation and revision are all parallel. Our approach and materials make clear the genre-based connections between planning and revising since the same elements are used in the GO and in the evaluation rubric. For example, the compare–contrast elements are used to introduce the genre and to guide the format of the GO and also appear in the evaluation rubric (see Figure 2.1).

Integration of Reading and Writing

Our approach integrates reading and writing through the use of read-alouds and mentor texts in the various genres and through introduction to writing from sources for

Beginning
• **Topic:** What are the topics that are compared and contrasted? • **Purpose:** Why are the topics compared and contrasted?
Middle
• **Similarities:** Are the categories of similarities clear to the reader? • **Evidence:** Is the evidence clear and accurate? Is the evidence explained? • **Differences:** Are the categories of differences clear to the reader? • **Evidence:** Is the evidence clear and accurate? Is the evidence explained?
End
• **Restate purpose:** Why are the topics compared and contrasted? • **Think:** Did the writer leave the reader with a message to think about?

FIGURE 2.1. Elements of compare–contrast writing.

informative writing. Genre elements and writing purposes are introduced during readings and used to discuss the texts. Our approach is designed so that it can be applied to teach any genre of writing that is important for students to learn, including genres that require reading and using sources. Reading and writing connections are also supported through extensive practice in reading and evaluating good and weak papers, using evaluation criteria based on genre elements.

Learning Evaluation Criteria

Another important principle in our approach is the importance of learning evaluation criteria and applying them in peer review and self-evaluation. Research shows that teaching evaluation criteria and how to apply them during revision has a positive impact on writing (Hillocks, 1986; Graham & Perin, 2007). Research also corroborates the value of peer review (MacArthur, 2016; Harris, Graham, & Mason, 2006). However, peer review can be challenging because students often do not know how to evaluate each other's work. Our own recent research (Cho & MacArthur, 2011; Philippakos, 2012) indicates that the important ingredient in peer review may be "giving feedback" rather than receiving it. When we taught college students (Cho & MacArthur, 2011) or fourth- and fifth-grade students (Philippakos, 2012) specific evaluation criteria and gave them practice evaluating and giving feedback on papers written by unknown peers, their own writing improved significantly. We have incorporated this practice into our instructional approach. Students begin to learn evaluation criteria and apply them using model good and weak papers in the first lesson on each genre. They then receive additional practice in preparation for and during peer review. This practice prepares them for evaluating their own writing. Explaining and modeling evaluation criteria are excellent ways to teach students about the features of good writing. In addition, self-evaluation is critically important in creating independent, self-regulated writers.

WRITING AND SELF-REGULATION STRATEGIES IN THIS INSTRUCTIONAL APPROACH

The Writing Strategy Ladder

An integrated set of strategies for planning, drafting, evaluating, revising, and editing is presented as a *Writing Strategy Ladder* (see Handout 2.1). Each step of the ladder signifies tasks related to part of the writing process. The visual representation of the writing process as a ladder with steps supports students in multiple ways. First, it visually highlights that good writing requires the application of a process or series of steps. Second, the comparison to a ladder underscores the fact that writing requires effort and cannot be accomplished easily; however, it can be tackled in a systematic way. Third, it functions as a visual reference for students. When students are not certain about their next task, instead of asking their teacher, they can refer to the strategy. Fourth, the strategy ladder repeats across different genres. Therefore, through repeated application, it becomes familiar to students, who can then gradually use it independently.

Although these steps on the ladder are the same for all genres, the specific materials differ because the genre elements and writing purposes change. In particular, the GO changes to include the elements of each genre. Additionally, the evaluation criteria are modified to focus on the specific elements and features of the genre.

Steps on the Ladder

The *Writing Strategy Ladder* (see Handout 2.1) consists of five steps: Plan, Draft, Evaluate to Revise, Edit, and Publish.

Plan

Planning involves the generation and organization of ideas. It is an important step of the writing process as it helps writers stay focused and complete their work without "getting lost." Planning guides writers in the same way that a roadmap guides drivers as they go from point A to point B. Planning helps the writer get from "one point to the other" without getting lost, without delays, and by satisfying a specific writing purpose. Good writers spend considerable time planning before they write, and as part of planning they think carefully about the audience and the writing purpose. This process helps them generate and organize their ideas and thoughts in a meaningful way. In this approach the planning step consists of three tasks: FTAP, Ideas, and GO.

FTAP

The *F* in *FTAP* stands for *form* (e.g., essay), *T* stands for *topic*, *A* for *audience*, and *P* for *purpose*. The acronym FTAP refers to task analysis. Writers will use it to think about the task at hand and consider ahead of time the effort and time they need to devote to complete it. Identification of each part of the FTAP is important for writers' success. Knowledge about the *form* can help writers decide if they should write an essay, a letter, or a short paragraph. If writers know this information, they will have a better understanding of the length requirements or the format of their response. Equally important is the consideration of *audience* and how it affects planning, drafting, and revising. If writers ignore the audience and write only for themselves, they may not clearly explain information for readers, or they may adopt a style that is too formal or informal. The *purpose* in FTAP leads writers to a thoughtful selection of the appropriate genre, which writers need to determine early on in their work in order to successfully complete assignments. The purpose describes the writer's goal. Students may write to entertain, inform, or persuade their audience. Based on the purpose of the writing task, writers may select a genre that can help them accomplish their goal. As students learn to write for multiple purposes, the analysis of topic, audience, and purpose takes on additional meaning as it helps them decide what genre to use.

Ideas

The second task within planning is generating ideas. This approach includes *Brainstorming*, *Reading*, and *Note taking* to stimulate and develop ideas. Brainstorming occurs when students record what they already know about a topic. In other situations students need to read and find information from books or other sources. As they read, they take notes and record ideas for their writing. Note taking occurs when students write from reading sources. Generating ideas about a topic is important so writers can determine if they know enough about a topic to write about it. The process of generating ideas is also influenced by genre. For instance, in persuasion, students brainstorm ideas *in favor of* and *against* an opinion before they choose the side to support. However, in compare–contrast texts, students generate ideas that are both similar and unique to each topic (similarities and differences).

A common challenge for students is selecting a topic to write about. Often, writers select topics they like, but this does not necessarily guarantee that they have enough knowledge to write a detailed paper. One solution to this problem is to ask students to use the FTAP and Ideas tasks when selecting a topic. The completion of FTAP and Ideas tasks can help writers decide what topic to use in their work or even what information to search for in order to advance their knowledge about the topic. For instance, when writers are provided with a choice between two persuasive topics in a test, they could use the FTAP and Ideas parts of planning to determine the writing topic about which they have the most information.

Graphic Organizer

The third task in *planning* is called *GO* and refers to the graphic organizer that is used to logically arrange ideas from the brainstorming or notes. All the GOs share a common overall structure containing a Beginning, Middle, and End (BME). However, each genre has unique parts for BME because the text structure for each genre is different. For example, the persuasive GO includes a Beginning with an introduction to the issue and the writer's opinion, a Middle with reasons and evidence, and an End that restates the writer's opinion and leaves the reader with a message. The compare–contrast GO has a Beginning that states what is being compared and explains the purpose of the comparison, the Middle includes similarities and differences, and the End revisits the writer's purpose and leaves the reader with a message. As students learn about different genres, they are able to make connections between them and their components.

Draft

The second step of the Writing Strategy Ladder is to create a *draft*. Students are reminded to use the GO as they write and elaborate their ideas. In Chapters 4–6, there is also a chart with transition words that students can consult while drafting.

Evaluate to Revise

The third step is to *Evaluate to Revise*. Evaluation refers to the critical examination of written information with the purpose of identifying areas that need to be improved. Such improvements can include additions, deletions, substitutions, and/or organizational changes. Evaluation requires students to read critically and to diagnose problems in a written text. Reading critically with an evaluative lens requires training and practice. The evaluation criteria used in our approach are genre-specific, and they are introduced in the first writing lesson when students read and evaluate good and weak examples written by unknown writers. Then, in preparation for peer review, students sharpen their evaluation skills by giving feedback on additional weak papers. Practice giving feedback trains students to be effective reviewers during peer review and also during self-evaluation. The *Evaluate to Revise* step of the strategy is used both for self-evaluation and peer review.

Edit

The fourth step of the *Writing Strategy Ladder* is to *Edit*. *Editing* and *Evaluate to Revise* are not the same process even though sometimes the terms are used interchangeably. In both, writers reread their work with the purpose of identifying ways to improve it. However, when reading to evaluate and revise, writers examine the writing purpose, the genre elements, and the organization and content clarity. The focus of evaluating to revise is on the content. Editing refers to spelling, grammar, and word-usage issues that can make a text difficult to read and/or understand. Therefore, it is important that writers reread their work with editing goals in mind. For this step, we provide a basic editing strategy called SCIPS (see Handout 2.2). The acronym stands for $\underline{S}$pelling, $\underline{C}$apitalization, $\underline{I}$ndentation, $\underline{P}$unctuation, and $\underline{S}$entences. The instructional chapters do not contain lessons in these conventions, but we expect that teachers will draw on their own methods to teach the skills. For instance teachers may use sentence combining or sentence expansion to support their students' sentence writing (Saddler, 2012). We advise teachers to develop targeted mini lessons on the mechanics of punctuation and grammar to support their students' needs. Teachers should have students practice before holding them responsible for correcting these features in their essays. Following editing, students reflect on their skills in this area and set editing goals. Teachers can use the Editing Goals for Improvement form (see Form 2.1) or ask students to write a journal entry.

Publish

The final step of the Writing Strategy Ladder is to *Publish*. This is the sharing stage at which students celebrate the completion of a paper. Publishing can be done in several ways. Students can share their writing with peers in their classroom or in other classrooms and grades, and they can also take advantage of Internet applications to share their work with a wider audience. For example, teachers could create classroom blogs and websites for students to upload their work, or they could use Voicethread (see *www.voicethread.com*) for students to post their work, read it to the audience, and invite comments. Another alternative is Glogster (*www.glogster.com*), on which students can post their work and create a virtual poster that includes images and additional links that are relevant to the topic. Overall, *publishing* should be authentic, engage students, and motivate them to want to write again.

Self-Regulation Strategy

Be Strategic!

This set of strategies, based on SRSD (Harris & Graham, 2009), is designed to promote self-regulation and independence (see Handout 2.3). Be Strategic! provides students with a set of guiding questions to set goals, monitor their progress, sustain their motivation, and help them reflect on what specific strategies were helpful to them and could be generalized in other tasks. These questions can be used for all writing tasks for whole- and small-group discussions and for students' journal writing.

Self-regulation strategies require practice and extensive support in order for students to *believe* in the value of using these self-driven approaches. Therefore, in these lessons teachers need to provide extensive modeling of all the strategies for students. Teachers model goal setting, progress monitoring, problem solving, motivation/self-reinforcement, and reflection through self-talk. For example, during think-aloud modeling using the Writing Strategy Ladder, teachers deliberately model getting stuck or having other difficulties and using self-regulation strategies to solve problems.

Use Self-Talk

One way to support student self-regulation is through the use of self-talk. In Lesson 3 of Chapters 4–6, students are asked to think of things they could say to themselves to stay engaged, check their progress, and monitor their work. Teachers can ask students to record things they could say to themselves while working to help them complete the task instead of resorting to negative talk. For this purpose students could use Form 2.2 or develop their statements for self-talk on a blank sheet. Also, students can keep journals to record their goals and reflect on their use of strategies. The lessons also include prompts that can be used to encourage student reflection in the journals, but teachers are also encouraged to develop their own prompts.

CLOSING THOUGHTS

INTERVIEWER: So sometimes writers have a hard time when they write. What do you do if you have a hard time writing? Do you quit or do you keep going?

ALISON [a third-grade student]: I keep on going and try to think about it harder. You don't quit.

INTERVIEWER: What do you mean when you say "think about it harder" and "you don't quit"?

ALISON: If you are stuck and you don't know what to do, you should look at the ladder (*referring to the Writing Strategy Ladder*) and check what you should do next. If you can't think of ideas, you can meet with a partner and, if you are stuck, you should be positive and say good things to yourself.

INTERVIEWER: So what do you say to yourself to keep going?

ALISON: I can do this! (*Motions hand forward.*) Or, you know, the readers will learn a lot and will write good comments because I worked so hard to make those categories.

INTERVIEWER: Okay, does that help?

ALISON: Yeah. It gets me going, and I also say that when I finish, I can do something I like more.

INTERVIEWER: What do you mean? Could you give me an example?

ALISON: I could do other things that are easy and relax me. Like I could go on the computer or play hangman. (*Laughs.*)

In this chapter we discussed the core principles and instructional methods of genre-based, self-regulated strategy instruction. To be independent writers, students need knowledge about multiple types of and purposes for writing. They also need a repertoire of strategies for analyzing tasks, planning what to write, evaluating, and revising their work. The ultimate goal of this approach is to develop strategic writers who are able to regulate their performance, sustain their motivation, set goals, learn from their errors, and gain independence.

This approach provides clear guidelines for the application of the writing process and the use of mini-lessons and assessment procedures and is compatible with the writers' workshop approach. We discussed the principles of the approach in some detail because we think that teachers, as professionals, should be given clear explanations about the content and methods they use, so they can have interesting and informative conversations with their colleagues, students, and parents. Further, we believe that teachers should be given clear instructional models and lesson plans to get started with new approaches before they develop their own. This effort can support teachers in building their own writing curricula and authoring high-quality writing lessons that are based on the principles of self-regulated strategy instruction.

In the next chapter we describe the sequence of instruction that is used for all instructional lessons and that you will later use to design your own. Essentially, the sequence is a *strategy for teaching strategies.* We also provide practical suggestions gathered from the feedback and questions that teachers raised during our pilot work and professional development. Finally, we describe the organization of the instructional chapters so you can begin your teaching!

Writing Strategy Ladder

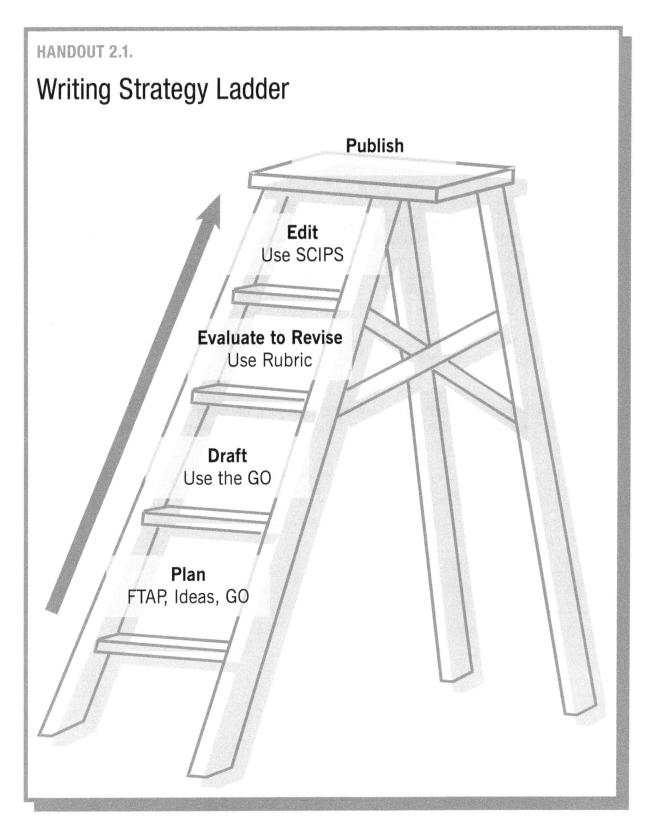

Publish

Edit
Use SCIPS

Evaluate to Revise
Use Rubric

Draft
Use the GO

Plan
FTAP, Ideas, GO

SCIPS for Editing

1. Read your paper out loud to find your errors.

2. Use SCIPS and *specific editing skills* you learned!

_____ **S**pelling: Are all words spelled correctly?

- Look for words that don't look "right" or have green or red lines (if typed).
- Divide a problematic word into syllables and rewrite it. Think of the root of the word or words that relate to that word (e.g., *imaginative, imagine, image* to help you spell *imagination*).
- Think of other readings where you saw that word. If you cannot self-correct the word, try the dictionary or ask for help. BUT FIRST try your BEST!
- If you are typing, you may use the spelling correction option if it is available.

_____ **C**apital letters: Are all words correctly capitalized? Are capitals for names and places used after a punctuation mark?

_____ **I**ndentation: Are paragraphs indented? Can the reader tell?

- Mark the indentation. When you write, place your finger at the start of the line and start writing after that covered space. Do the same for all your paragraphs. If you type, press Tab.

_____ **P**unctuation: Are all periods, question marks, exclamation marks, and quotation marks used correctly?

_____ **S**entences: Are my sentences clear? Do I have a variation of sentence structures (e.g., simple, complex)?

Be Strategic!

Be Strategic!

Goal Setting

- What am I supposed to do?
- How shall I work on this?
- What do I know to help me do it?

Progress Detector

- Where am I in the process?
- What have I done so far?
- What is next?

Motivation and Self-Reinforcement

- I know this is hard, but I can do it if I use _____.
- Once I get this part done, I can then do the next part, which is _____.
- I did a great job using _____.

Reflection

- How did I do in this task?
- Did the strategy help me reach my writing goals? How did the strategy help me reach my goals? If I didn't reach my goals, why not? What should be my next goals?
- What did I learn that I could use in another task?

Editing Goals for Improvement

Topic: _____

Date: _____

MY EDITING GOALS for improvement:

_____

_____

_____

_____

_____

_____

_____

How much did I improve in editing from my previous paper? What errors have I corrected?

_____

_____

_____

_____

_____

_____

_____

_____

_____

_____

_____

_____

Self-Talk Recording Sheet

Name: _____   **Date:** _____

When I have trouble starting my writing, I might say:

_____

_____

_____

_____

_____

When I have completed something and I can't think about what to do next, I might say:

_____

_____

_____

_____

_____

When I think that something is so hard that I cannot go on, I could say:

_____

_____

_____

_____

_____

Self-Talk Recording Shee

Chapter 3

Making It Work

THE INSTRUCTIONAL SEQUENCE AND ORGANIZATION
OF THE LESSONS

I feel supported by this approach and my students feel empowered and they get
it! . . . Everything was written for me. I copied each lesson, I put all the materials
in a binder, and I felt I was organized and ready to go teach writing. For me it
was such a time saver that all materials were there and I had a choice of good and
not-so-good papers. And it helped to explain how those papers could be better
by applying a rubric that students could independently use. My third graders
are thinkers. They think carefully about what they write and who will read their
papers. Their ideas are more specific and developed and their papers are organized.

— MR. TRAGAS, third-grade teacher

We met Mr. Tragas at the beginning of Chapter 1 and learned about his instructional
challenges. The above quote reflects his experience teaching the genre-based strategy
instruction lessons. Our goal in writing this book is to provide teachers with as much
support as possible in learning a new approach to teaching writing. In Chapter 2 we
explained the principles and overall strategies used in the instructional approach. In this
chapter we explain the instructional sequence that is followed in the lessons; we think of
this sequence as a *strategy for teaching strategies.* Then we offer suggestions and advice
drawn from questions that other teachers have raised. Finally, we explain the organization of the instructional units and teaching materials in Chapters 4–6.

SEQUENCE OF INSTRUCTION: A STRATEGY FOR TEACHING STRATEGIES

Teaching students to use writing strategies requires planning. The SRSD model has
shown the value of giving teachers a flexible sequence of instructional steps (Harris &
Graham, 2009). The advantage to having a single instructional sequence is that it provides consistency for both teachers and students. Once teachers learn to use it, they can
modify it to teach new genres fairly easily. The instructional sequence, or strategy for
teaching strategies, in Figure 3.1 is an elaboration of the six steps included in SRSD. In
Chapters 4–6, we apply the instructional sequence for different genres. There are a number of components to this instructional sequence, which are described below.

Read-Aloud Lesson(s): Introduction to the Genre

- Discuss the purpose.
- Explain the genre elements.
- Apply the genre elements as you read.

Preassessment

Evaluation of Good and Weak Examples and Initial Self-Evaluation

- Teacher evaluation of a good example.
- Teacher evaluation of a weak example.
- Collaborative evaluation of a weak example.
- Small-group evaluation of a weak example.
- Self-evaluation and goal setting.

Memorization

- Practice learning the genre elements and strategies.

Think-Aloud Modeling

- Explain the Writing Strategy Ladder.
- Model the complete process of writing a paper.
- Model self-regulation as part of the process.

Self-Regulation

Collaborative Writing

- Apply the writing strategy as a group.

Guided Practice

- Students apply the strategy to plan and draft their work.

Preparation for Peer Review and Self-Evaluation

- Discuss the purpose of evaluation for revision and how revision differs from editing.
- Teacher evaluation of a weak example.
- Small-group evaluation of a weak example.
- Self-evaluation and goal setting.

Peer Review and Revision

Editing

Publishing

Continuous Guided Practice to Mastery

- Continuous assessment.
- Mini-lessons.
- Differentiation.

Postassessment

FIGURE 3.1. Strategy for teaching strategies.

Read-Aloud Lesson(s): Introduction to the Genre

- **Discuss the purpose.** As you prepare to read the book, briefly discuss the genre of the book (or other text) and its purpose. Ask students if they have ever read or written papers in this genre.

- **Explain the genre elements.** Display the genre elements for students and explain them. Discuss the importance of each in supporting the genre's purpose. Discuss what comes at the Beginning, Middle, and End in this genre. (Note: As you introduce new genres, discuss with students the ways that the content of each section changes depending on the author's purpose.)

- **Apply the genre elements as you read.** Stop regularly during the read-aloud to comment on the genre elements in the text. For example, when reading a story, stop and comment on the characters, setting, and problem. In some cases, you may take notes. After reading, use the elements to retell or summarize what you read. (Note: Repeat the read-aloud task many times before the teaching of the writing lessons; read-alouds can also continue during the writing lessons. The read-alouds can strengthen students' understanding of the elements of the genre and their reading comprehension.)

Preassessment

- Ask students to write in response to a genre-specific prompt after reviewing the elements of that genre. To analyze your students' needs, you can evaluate the papers using the rubric that students will receive. Use this information to group students during small-group instruction, differentiation sessions, and peer review. You could also use this information to select mini-lessons that your students will find useful when writing in that genre.

Evaluation of Good and Weak Examples and Initial Self-Evaluation

- **Teacher evaluation of a good example.** Read a paper that represents a very good *student* example and discuss your general impression of the paper with students. Review the genre elements and introduce the evaluation rubric. As you do this, point out the connection between the elements and the evaluation criteria. Also explain the information in the section called *Other Considerations* and discuss with students how it can affect the quality of a paper. Then identify the elements, underline them, and score them using the genre-based evaluation rubric. Proceed with the *Other Considerations* section of the rubric. Students may participate, but you should lead the process. This activity introduces the evaluation criteria and gives students a model of what they are trying to achieve.

- **Teacher evaluation of a weak example.** Read a weak example, discuss your general impression of the paper, identify the elements, and score the paper using the genre-based evaluation rubric. Students may participate in the identification of the elements, but you should model how to make comments and write suggestions for revisions.

- **Collaborative evaluation of a weak example.** Work with students in an interactive, collaborative way to evaluate a weak example. Ask students to identify the genre elements and offer their evaluations, as you record their ideas. Your goal is to scaffold the application of the evaluation process, to help students make suggestions for revisions, and to suggest revision goals for the writer of the weak example.

- **Small-group evaluation of a weak example.** Students apply the evaluation process to a weak paper in small groups and write suggestions to the writer.
- **Self-evaluation and goal setting.** Students read their own preassessment papers, evaluate them using the genre elements, and set goals for improvement on later papers. They do not actually revise this paper.

Memorization

- **Practice learning the genre elements and strategies**. From this lesson forward, you will provide opportunities for students to review the elements and the writing strategy verbally and in writing. Memorization is a low-level task, but students will not be able to use the strategies independently if they cannot remember the genre elements and strategy steps.

Think-Aloud Modeling

- Explain the Writing Strategy Ladder and the materials that are used for planning, drafting, evaluating, and revising.
- Model the complete process of writing a paper from planning through evaluating and revising. Write your plans and the paper itself on chart paper (or the board) so students can see your work. Think out loud throughout the process so students can see your thinking as you apply the steps of the strategy. Be sure to refer specifically to each step in the strategy as you do it. You will model the process *at your students' level*, producing a paper that would be good for them. You can plan some of your ideas in advance, but it is important that your think-aloud modeling seems live.
- Model self-regulation as part of the process. You should deliberately model having some difficulties and overcoming them. Use self-talk to show students how you set goals, monitor your progress, handle challenges, and congratulate yourself. At the end of the lesson, discuss the process you followed and ask students to tell you some of the things they heard you say. Take notes on their comments.

Self-Regulation

- Review the statements you had noted at the end of the modeling session and discuss the meaning of self-talk with students. Introduce the self-regulation strategy Be Strategic! (see Handout 2.3) and explain and discuss each section. Discuss what students could say in each section. Students then develop their own self-talk and may revise their previous self-talk in later lessons. (Note: Self-regulation is supported throughout the instructional sequence. It is just emphasized as a separate lesson component here.)

Collaborative Writing

- Apply the writing strategy as a group. In collaborative writing, you act as a guide during the application of the strategy, but students should come up with all the ideas and propose the sentences. You also serve as scribe, writing down the plans and text. Begin by asking students how to get started; refer them to the steps of the strategy and the genre elements throughout the process. Adjust your level of support to meet the students' needs. If they get stuck or confused, assume more leadership.

Guided Practice

- Students apply the strategy to plan and draft their work. Teachers monitor students' work and provide support as needed. Teachers can conference briefly with students. It is important to give two types of feedback: feedback on how well they are using the strategy and feedback on their actual writing. The goal is for students to use the strategy and to see that it improves their writing.

Preparation for Peer Review and Self-Evaluation

- **Discuss the purpose of evaluation for revision and how revision differs from editing.** Explain the importance of critical reading and its benefits in self-evaluation and peer review.
- **Teacher evaluation of a weak example.** Review the rubric and point out the connection between the elements, the GO, and the rubric. Think out loud as you identify the elements, score them, write suggestions to the writer, and develop goals for revision.
- **Small-group evaluation of a weak example.** Students apply the evaluation process to a weak paper in small groups.
- **Self-evaluation and goal setting.** Students read their papers, evaluate them using the genre elements, and set goals for revisions.

Peer Review and Revision

- Review the importance of evaluation and revision. Explain the peer review procedures.
- Students meet with a partner or in small groups to review papers written by other students.
- Students revise their papers.

Editing

- Identify an editing issue for students. Model how to correct it in a sample paper and provide collaborative and/or independent practice with that issue. Students then apply the SCIPS editing procedure and the new editing skill to their own papers.

Publishing

- Students complete their revisions and publish their papers.

Continuous Guided Practice to Mastery

- Students work on one or more new papers in the genre and apply the writing process. Teachers provide guidance as needed by individual students. The whole class may need additional modeling or mini-lessons on particular topics, or small groups may need more modeling and support.

- **Continuous assessment.** It is important to monitor and evaluate students' progress as they write more than one paper. Evaluation of students' writing will be done using the genre-specific rubric that was applied to the preassessment writing sample. The rubric may include additional goals that you add after the mini-lessons. These additions will appear in the section of the rubric called *Other Considerations.* The evaluation of the continuous assessments can guide additional instruction in the genre. Teachers can use the assessment results to decide which extra mini-lessons to teach and if any instruction should be repeated for specific students. For example, a teacher might decide that all students need a mini-lesson on how to introduce effectively the topic of their persuasive essays. Alternatively, a teacher might decide that a small group of students needs more work on including reasons in their persuasive essays. The teacher can then meet with them and provide a mini-lesson tailored to the needs of this group.

Mini-Lessons

- At appropriate times during the sequence of lessons, conduct mini-lessons on writing features common to the specific genre. For example, for narratives you might teach lessons on vivid description or on the use of dialogue. Some mini-lessons are included in the lessons in this book, and teachers can develop others. Mini-lessons at the *continuous guided practice to mastery* stage could be more differentiated.

- After you teach a mini-lesson, make sure to add the new writing expectations/objectives to the rubric in the section called "Other Considerations." Students can then evaluate their work and set new goals for improvement.

Differentiation

- During small-group activities, meet and conference with individuals or small groups of students (higher or lower performing).

Postassessment

- We encourage teachers to give students a postassessment after completing all lessons and before they begin a new genre. Teachers can also compare performance on the postassessment with performance on the preassessment to document how much progress was made during the instructional unit. This process can help teachers identify the instructional approaches that were the most (and least) effective for their students. The postassessment results can also help teachers reflect on the effectiveness of their instruction.

SOME SUGGESTIONS AND ADVICE ON INSTRUCTION

During our professional development sessions and our pilot work for the development of the instructional lessons, we had interesting discussions with teachers about the components and principles of this approach. Their feedback, comments, and questions helped us be explicit in our explanations and in the presentation and content of the lessons. We think it is important to share the content of those conversations with you, too. As you try out the lessons in the book, you may want to return to this section to enhance your understanding of some of the fine points of teaching strategies or to resolve problems that occur. If you meet with colleagues in a professional learning community, you may find these suggestions worth discussing.

First, we offer advice related directly to the steps in the instructional sequence. Then we offer a few more general suggestions.

Advice on Instructional Steps

Think-Aloud Modeling

As we discussed, modeling is more than a presentation of information. The point of think-aloud modeling is to show students how you think as you come up with ideas, organize them, and draft sentences. Many students think that writing is easy for good writers, so it is helpful for them to see that you sometimes *get stuck* and struggle. It is important that your modeling seems to be "live" rather than all worked out in advance. In Chapters 4 and 5 on story and persuasive writing we provide sample think-alouds and in all instructional chapters we provide completed materials that you can read in preparation for teaching. We suggest that you read these samples as illustrations and do a little bit of planning about the topic you will model. But during the modeling, we encourage you to refrain from using your notes. This makes it much more authentic for students.

Here are some important points about modeling. First, you should work at the level of your students; that is, you are modeling the use of the strategy to produce a paper that would be a good paper for your students. Second, you should refer to each step of the strategy before you do it, so that students clearly see how you use the Writing Strategy Ladder. Third, you should include self-regulation statements in your modeling; for example, after brainstorming, you might say, "Great, I came up with plenty of ideas. But it's hard to figure out what to say first. I can use my GO to help me organize them."

Think-aloud modeling can be challenging at first. Just remember that if you *get stuck* or it doesn't go entirely smoothly, that's good. Pause and reflect on the problem and how to solve it. This is an important aspect of self-regulation. Students learn more from a model who struggles a bit and copes with that difficulty than from one who writes effortlessly.

Collaborative Writing

In collaborative writing, you are guiding students to use the strategy, and they are coming up with all the ideas and the language. Remember to ask students to explain each strategy step before doing it. One common challenge is that you may not always be able to use all students' ideas, and students may get disappointed. This may be especially true when writing stories. You should acknowledge students' ideas and help them select specific ideas for the GO, using the perspective of the reader. You can also suggest that students could use their ideas later in their own stories.

Another challenge in collaborative writing is the drafting step. This step provides an opportunity for you to model good sentence writing. Ask students to suggest sentences and then adjust the sentences, as needed, as you write them. You may get two or three suggested sentences from students and discuss which one works best. However, this process can be difficult to manage with a whole class. One option is to work with the whole class to draft the Beginning of the paper and then have small groups or individuals work on drafting the Middle and End sections of the paper. Then return to the whole-class setting and have groups share their work while you write the sentences on the board and make adjustments as needed.

Self-Regulation

Self-regulation is important for students' success both in academics and in later life. You should include self-regulation statements in your think-alouds. Each of our instructional chapters includes a discussion of the Be Strategic! components.

In addition, we suggest that after students complete a paper and go through self-evaluation and peer evaluation, they set goals for their next piece. They can record their goals in a journal to use for reflection later. This process may help them appreciate how they accomplished their goals or how they need to work to meet a challenging goal. You could also respond to these journals to support students as they attempt to apply self-regulation strategies. You could clarify a goal, assist students in developing a goal, and/or congratulate them for their honesty and ability to set a specific goal.

It is a good idea to model self-regulation strategies across your curriculum, showing how much you value them by using them yourself. For example, before the start of a lesson (e.g., in math), you could explain to students that in order to keep track of time, you will create an agenda (i.e., set goals). That way you will not forget something important, and you will be able to monitor the completion of your plan (i.e., detect progress). During your work, you can ask questions about your progress, cross out completed items on the agenda, and model for the students how you use a specific strategy to stay on track (motivate and self-reinforce). When you complete the task, you can think about what worked for you (reflect).

Evaluation and Peer Review

One common issue in self-evaluation is that some students may tend to assign high scores to themselves. This tendency may seem to indicate that students just want to give themselves high grades, but it is more likely to indicate difficulty in self-evaluation. Objectively judging one's own performance is very challenging. Students will need to see you model this process in order to understand its value and how to apply the evaluation criteria. Also, they may benefit even more from practice evaluating papers written by others, with your guidance.

Students may also find it challenging to apply evaluation criteria honestly during peer review and may assign only high scores to their partners. Your encouragement, honesty, and leadership when you practice reviewing can help develop a community of learners who are willing to learn from one another. You could also use technology for students' peer evaluations if you are able to use computers for writing. There are a number of software programs that support anonymous peer reviews and allow students to work from their computers to give and receive feedback.

Revision

Students need opportunities to practice making revisions after evaluation. As you will notice in the lessons, we encourage you to work with students to make at least one revision during your modeling. This guidance is necessary because revision is a difficult task. Even though students may be able to identify a specific element that needs to be revised, it is often challenging to make that change.

Editing

This book does not include instructional methods for teaching skills and conventions. You could develop your own editing lessons based on the CCSS's guidelines and your students' needs or use other resources with which you are familiar. Our instructional approach does, however, include a way to integrate skills instruction with composing. During the editing stage, select a skill that your students need to develop, display papers with problems in that skill, model how to make corrections using a think-aloud, and collaboratively practice the process before students make corrections on their own papers.

Integrating Reading and Writing

The lessons' success is based on the practice of reading books out loud during the reading time to discuss the purpose, elements of the genre, and the writers' craft. Those read-alouds work as mentor texts. In addition to introducing the main genre elements, they can be used to introduce a mini-lesson. For example, you might discuss how an author used dialogue to show characters' personalities before teaching a mini-lesson on dialogue.

For the read-alouds we recommend the use of high-quality texts. Suggestions of such texts are given in Chapters 4, 5, and 6. It is important that you read and identify the genre elements before you meet with students. Identifying the elements may be challenging, and you should devote some time to prepare the material. As you prepare, you could use "sticky notes" to mark the genre elements in the text. Then during the read-aloud it will be easy to pause and discuss the elements that you have marked. This will help scaffold students' understanding and use time efficiently.

Continuous Guided Practice to Mastery

Because the transition from guided writing to independent practice is based on mastery and not time, students should be asked to write more than one paper in each genre. One challenge in teaching strategies is deciding when all of your students have achieved sufficient mastery of a strategy to move on to a new strategy or genre. Our recommendation is to use a minimum standard in which all students can explain the main elements of the genre and the steps in the strategy and are able to create a plan and write a paper that includes all the critical genre elements. Fortunately, strategy instruction is flexible enough to permit differentiated instruction. While some students are mastering the basics, others can be developing techniques to improve their writing according to the evaluation criteria.

Differentiation and Mini-Lessons

Differentiation of lessons is based on your evaluation of students' progress. The rubrics facilitate evaluation of students' written products, and your observations and conferences will provide information about how well students are using the strategies. You can differentiate instruction for small groups in two basic ways. First, you can model parts of the writing strategy for groups that need more practice with the basic strategy and genre elements. Second, you can provide additional mini-lessons for groups that are ready to expand their understanding of good writing in the genre. For example, in the instructional chapter on story writing, you could develop a mini-lesson on figurative language. In developing mini-lessons, consider introducing the lesson using a read-aloud that illustrates the feature or technique you will teach (e.g., a storybook with rich, figurative language). Also, plan to show students good and weak examples of papers using the feature, model how you would incorporate the feature by making changes, and give students opportunities to practice.

Advice on General Principles for Using the Lessons

Explicitness

The lessons are explicit and detailed in order to to support your teaching, not to inhibit your creativity or suppress your personality. The more you use your own ideas and writing for modeling, rather than examples from the lesson, the better. You should make the lessons your own, while also following all components within each lesson. You could write your own brief plan before teaching a lesson to assure that you address all sections.

Time

You should make a plan to teach writing every day. For students to become successful writers, they need daily practice. Some of the lessons may take more than one class session. We advise you to consider ahead of time where to divide a lesson. For example, when modeling, it is important to complete the full planning stage so students can see how you transfer ideas to a GO. However, you might save the drafting process for the next day. We encourage you to divide lessons thoughtfully according to your own schedule. It is equally important to provide time for writing instruction and also adequate time for students' writing practice.

Authentic Writing Purposes

In each chapter, we provide sample writing prompts, but you will probably want to develop additional ones. You can also be creative in the presentation of the topics and make the tasks authentic for your students in order to motivate them. In one of our professional development sessions, a teacher collaboratively wrote with students a letter to the principal asking for more recess time. The reasons were not convincing to the principal, who declined their request. It was difficult for students to understand why their reasons were not convincing because they did not understand the principal's perspective. The principal visited the classroom and explained which reasons were not convincing and clear, and why he, as the reader, rejected the request. The students were disappointed but also motivated to convince him! They worked with their teacher on a different letter requesting that Friday be designated a "dress-down" day when uniforms would not be required. This time, students carefully examined their reasons, and they even asked other students if they would be convinced after reading the specific reasons and evidence. They were truly motivated because the task was authentic. And, yes, their request convinced the principal (even if it was only for a month)!

The Teacher as a Writer

It is important for students to see you as a writer and not only as their evaluator. They will value far more the materials and strategies you are teaching if they see you using them. Your participation can help strengthen the sense of community in your classroom.

ORGANIZATION OF THE INSTRUCTIONAL CHAPTERS

This book includes three instructional chapters that address three writing purposes: to narrate, to persuade, and to inform (CCSSI, 2010). Students are taught how to write stories, opinion papers, and compare–contrast essays. Each chapter consists of eight writing lessons, materials for each lesson, completed activities for your reference, and extension activities for teaching related subgenres.

- All instructional chapters follow the same sequence of instruction and are based on the strategy for teaching strategies.
- All instructional chapters begin with an introduction about the genre and about the CCSS for grades 3–5, followed by an outline of the eight writing lessons.
- Each of the writing lessons begins with a short description of the lesson, a list of objectives, assessment information, notes providing suggestions or advice, and a list of materials needed for the lesson.
- Following the eight lessons, we include sections on Publishing Guidelines and Guidelines for Continuous Guided Practice to Mastery, along with additional mini-lessons and extension activities for teaching subgenres. Finally, we present a sample think-aloud appropriate to the genre.
- All reproducible materials (forms and handouts) for the lessons are found at the end of each chapter.

CLOSING THOUGHTS

My students loved this, they loved writing stories, they loved writing their opinions, and it was fun to see what they said about their growth in their journals. The fact that they were actually engaged in the whole writing process, they were able to work together in groups and, you know, be writers and not depend on me was great. The lessons were enjoyable for them. They were enjoyable for me!

—MRS. STEMS, a fourth-grade teacher

Writing is challenging but also rewarding. We are certain that you and your students will find the lessons helpful and engaging. As you teach the three instructional units, you will have a lot of reasons to celebrate writing success with your community of writers! Let's begin!

Chapter 4

Story Writing

Everyone loves a good story. Stories—read around the fire or told in books, television, movies, videogames, or theater—are a primary form of entertainment. They are also fundamental to the ways in which individuals, families, and cultures give meaning to their lives and learn about the world (Bruner, 1986). News stories provide both entertainment and information. People share personal stories with friends to understand each other. In fact, our identity is represented in the stories we tell about ourselves. Parents read stories to their children to entertain them but also to convey values and teach them something about human nature. Similarly, literature and film combine entertainment with meaningful themes. Politicians and businesses use stories to persuade. Histories and biographies inform us about the past, represent our nations and cultures, and guide decisions in the present. Children enter school with a basic understanding of stories, although that understanding may vary depending on cultural background (Heath, 1983). In schools, teachers draw on the entertainment value of stories to help students learn to read and write. Stories serve a multitude of purposes and come in a multitude of genres.

Elementary schools almost universally teach students to read and write fictional stories and personal narratives. Fiction comes in many genres (e.g., realistic fiction, fairytales, fables), but almost always includes common elements: characters, setting, goals and problems, a sequence of actions to solve the problems, and resolution. Substantial research with elementary students and students with literacy problems has demonstrated that reading comprehension and the writing of stories can be enhanced by teaching strategies based on these structural elements (Baumann & Bergeron, 1993; National Institute of Child Health and Human Development, 2000). Personal narratives may have the same elements or may be chronological recountings of experiences without clear problems or resolutions, although a good personal narrative will have some central meaning.

According to the CCSS, students from as early as kindergarten should engage in writing stories and recounting events. In third through fifth grades, they should "Write narratives to develop real or imagined experiences or events using effective technique, descriptive details, and clear event sequences." Table 4.1 presents the specific CCSS criteria by grade level (CCSSI, 2010).

To help students achieve the CCSS expectations and to expand their narrative skills, we developed these detailed lessons that focus on writing fictional stories.

Students learn that the beginning of their story should include clearly described character(s), setting (time and place), and problem. The middle of their story should include logical and clear events and complications that initiate new events or problems, and the end of their story should provide the solution to the problem and convey the character's emotions about the experience.

Teachers introduce the common story elements and key features of fictional narratives during read-alouds. At the most basic level, students learn the story elements and how to use them to understand and retell stories. The writing strategy is also based on using the story elements to plan and evaluate students' own stories. Research shows that such story element strategies can improve both reading comprehension (Fitzgerald & Spiegel, 1983) and writing (Fitzgerald & Teasley, 1986). In addition, knowledge of the story elements prepares students to learn about other features of a narrative, such as rich descriptions of characters and settings and the use of dialogue to show characters' feelings and personalities. Read-alouds function as mentor texts to introduce students to such features of the writers' craft; these features are then taught in writing mini-lessons. This

TABLE 4.1. Narrative Writing Standards for Grades 3–5

Grade 3	Grade 4	Grade 5
Write narratives to develop real or imagined experiences or events using effective technique, descriptive details, and clear event sequences.		
1. Establish a situation and introduce a narrator and/or characters; organize an event sequence that unfolds naturally.	1. Orient the reader by establishing a situation and introducing a narrator and/or characters; organize an event sequence that unfolds naturally.	1. Orient the reader by establishing a situation and introducing a narrator and/or characters; organize an event sequence that unfolds naturally.
2. Use dialogue and descriptions of actions, thoughts, and feelings to develop experiences and events or show the response of characters to situations.	2. Use dialogue and description to develop experiences and events or show the responses of characters to situations.	2. Use narrative techniques, such as dialogue, description, and pacing, to develop experiences and events or show the responses of characters to situations.
3. Use temporal words and phrases to signal event order.	3. Use a variety of transitional words and phrases to manage the sequence of events.	3. Use a variety of transitional words, phrases, and clauses to manage the sequence of events.
4. Provide a sense of closure.	4. Use concrete words and phrases and sensory details to convey experiences and events precisely.	4. Use concrete words and phrases and sensory details to convey experiences and events precisely.
	5. Provide a conclusion that follows from the narrated experiences or events.	5. Provide a conclusion that follows from the narrated experiences or events.

book includes mini-lessons on descriptions of settings and the use of dialogue. Teachers can add other mini-lessons based on their students' needs.

The writing lessons begin with basic fictional narratives. Students learn strategies for using knowledge of story elements and features to plan, draft, evaluate, and revise their own stories. They learn evaluation criteria based on story elements and features and apply them in peer review and self-evaluation activities. Mini-lessons include how to enhance specific narrative features (provide descriptions and dialogue). Specific suggestions are provided for generalizing this instruction to writing other narrative genres in the extension activities at the end of the chapter.

The rest of this chapter includes (1) a lesson outline that provides information about the read-aloud tasks and a synopsis for each writing lesson, (2) sample writing prompts that you could use for assessment and instruction, (3) detailed writing lessons on stories with ready-to-use materials, (4) extension activities for additional genres, and (5) forms that are used in more than one lesson and that you could display in your classroom. Depending on the time you have to teach writing, some lessons may last for more than a day; just think ahead about how you will divide them based on your schedule. The lessons are based on the strategy for teaching strategies (see Figure 3.1). You may want to review the instructional procedures in Chapter 3. Also, you may want to review the Writing Strategy Ladder and the Be Strategic! strategy in Chapter 2.

LESSON OUTLINE

Read-Aloud Lesson(s)

Introduction to the Genre

Students are introduced to the purpose and the elements of stories during read-alouds. These read-alouds are conducted several times prior to the writing lessons to support students' learning of the genre elements and promote discussion about the ways in which authors present the information. The books also function as mentor texts for mini-lessons.

Preassessment

Students write in response to a story-writing prompt (see Sample Topics for Writing Assessment/Instruction on pp. 43–44).

Story-Writing Lessons

Lesson 1: Introduction—Evaluation of Good and Weak Examples and Self-Evaluation

Students review the purpose and elements of stories. They evaluate good and weak papers by applying evaluation criteria. They evaluate their own papers and set personal goals for improvement.

Lesson 2: Modeling How to Write a Story

Students review the elements of stories and observe the teacher during think-aloud modeling of planning, drafting, evaluating to revise, and editing of a story.

Lesson 3: Self-Regulation—Mini-Lesson on Clear Descriptions

Students learn a strategy that helps them monitor their work and reflect on the application of the strategies. Students develop "self-talk." In the second part of the lesson, students are taught a mini-lesson and practice how to improve the descriptions of characters and setting in sample stories by appealing to the five senses.

Lesson 4: Collaborative Writing of a Story

Teacher and students collaboratively use the Writing Strategy Ladder to plan, draft, evaluate to revise, and edit a story. During collaborative writing, the teacher scaffolds students' application of the strategy and does the writing as students provide the ideas and sentences.

Lesson 5: Students Plan and Draft Their Own Stories

Students begin working on their own papers, using the planning and drafting steps of the strategy. The teacher monitors the use of the strategy and provides support as needed.

Lesson 6: Preparation for Peer Review and Self-Evaluation

Students practice evaluating stories, writing suggestions, and making revisions. Students self-evaluate their papers and set goals for revision.

Lesson 7: Peer Review and Revision

Students peer-review in pairs or small groups, applying the evaluation criteria. Students compare their self-evaluation with the comments of their peers, set goals for revision, and make revisions.

Lesson 8: Editing

Students examine their papers for editing errors. By using the editing strategy (SCIPS), students identify surface-level errors and correct them. Teachers can choose to teach a specific grammatical/editing skill, practice the skill with students, and ask students to make changes to their essays. Additionally, students set editing goals and reflect on their performance and progress.

Publishing Guidelines

It is important for students to share some of their work with a larger audience. We have provided guidelines and suggestions for ways to share students' work. These guidelines do not comprise a specific lesson, but rather present ideas for discussing publishing with your students. The specifics will depend on what sort of publishing you have chosen. See Chapter 3 for a discussion of ideas about opportunities for publishing.

Guidelines for Continuous Guided Practice to Mastery

It is important for students to write more than one paper in a genre to develop mastery of it. We encourage teachers to provide multiple opportunities for students to write in the target genre. As students write additional papers, they are likely to work more quickly and feel much more competent. At this point teachers can focus their attention on students who need more support.

Read–Aloud Lesson(s)

INTRODUCTION TO THE GENRE

Students are introduced to the purpose and the elements of stories during read-alouds. These read-alouds are conducted several times prior to the writing lessons to support students' learning of the genre elements and promote discussion of the ways in which authors present the information. The books also function as mentor texts for mini-lessons.

Lesson Objectives

By the end of this lesson, students will be able to:

- Explain the purposes of stories and discuss why, when, and where people may read or write stories.
- Identify the elements of stories.

Materials for the Read-Aloud Lesson

- Form 4.1. Planning Materials (FTAP, Ideas, and GO); use only the GO section.
- Handout 4.1. Chart with Story Elements
- Book: *Babushka's Doll* by Patricia Polacco

Notes

- You can use a different book for your read-aloud. This book is only an example. You may use another book or even texts from other curricula.

- The procedures described in this first lesson focus on the basic objective of introducing story elements and how to use them to understand and retell a story. You can repeat this lesson with different stories as many times as needed to ensure that students know the story elements. You could examine their knowledge of the elements by asking them to complete a quiz and record them. You can consult the list of sample books we provide (see Figure 4.1) or you may choose to use books from your library.

- Later, you can extend the read-alouds to talk about other features of stories and how authors develop specific elements for varying purposes. In this way, you could use those books as mentor texts to introduce mini-lessons. For example, you could discuss with students how an author uses dialogue before teaching the mini-lesson on dialogue. Students could also refer to these books when they make their revisions and use authors' work as a model.

Procedures

Discussion of Stories

- Explain that you will read a story. Ask students why authors write stories and why people tell stories. Have a discussion about the purposes of stories. Explain that stories can be entertaining, can describe an experience, or can teach us something. Explain

---

Sample Wordless Books
- *Time Flies* by Eric Rohmann
- *The Red Book* by Barbara Lehman
- *June 29, 1999* by David Wiesner
- *Free Fall* by David Wiesner
- *Flotsam* by David Wiesner
- *Robot Dreams* by Sara Varon
- *You Can't Take a Balloon into the Metropolitan Museum* by Jacqueline Preiss Weitzman

Sample Fiction Books
- *Honey, Honey—Lion!* by Jan Bret
- *Jumanji* by Chris Van Allsburg
- *Brava Strega Nona* by Tomie de Paola
- *Yeh-Shen: A Cinderella Story from China,* by Ai-Lung Louie
- *Babushka's Doll* by Patricia Polacco
- *Thank You, Mr. Falker* by Patricia Polacco
- *The Crow Boy* by Taro Yashima
- *The Relatives Came* by Cynthia Rylant
- *Ben and Me: A New and Astonishing Life of Benjamin Franklin as Written by His Good Mouse Amos* by Robert Lawson
- *Baseball Saved Us* by Ken Mochizuki

FIGURE 4.1. Sample list of books for read-alouds on story genre.

that there can be many types of stories, such as mysteries (fiction that attempts to solve a crime or resolve an issue by following clues), fairytales (fiction that includes fantastical creatures and may involve magic), and fables (fiction that includes talking animals and teaches a moral).

- Discuss the parts of stories with students. Explain that stories have a Beginning, Middle, and End. The Beginning typically includes the characters, the description of the place and time, and the problem that the characters face. The Middle of the story includes all the events that the characters experience as they attempt to resolve the problem and sometimes other problems that are created in an effort to resolve the initial one. Finally, the End reveals the solution to the problem and the characters' emotions and reflections on the experience.

Introduction of Story Elements

- Display the Chart with Story Elements (Handout 4.1) and explain each element briefly. Explain that good readers pay attention to these elements so that they can understand the story better and remember it so they can retell the story to others. Tell the students that good writers also use the elements when they write their stories, and that later they will learn a strategy for writing stories.

Read-Aloud

- Introduce the book *Babushka's Doll* by Patricia Polacco and show students the cover.
- Explain that you will read the book and take notes on the story elements (use the GO in Form 4.1). You can consult Figure 4.2, which is completed for your reference.
- Begin reading the book. Stop often and ask yourself whether you have learned anything about the story elements. Write notes on the GO.
- When you complete the reading, tell the students that the information on the story elements in the GO will help you to retell the story. Refer to the notes in the GO as you give a simple retelling.
- Explain how the elements helped you understand the story and retell it.

End of Lesson

- Explain that in the next weeks, students will learn how to write stories using the story elements.

Beginning	**Characters:** *Natasha and Babushka*
	Time: *During the day (not specified)*
	Place: *In Babushka's house (not specified)*
	Problem: *Natasha never waits for things and wants Babushka to do things for her promptly.*

Middle	**Event 1:** *Babushka goes to the store for groceries and gives Natasha a doll.*
	     Complication 1: *The doll comes to life and begins to ask for things!*
	 Event 2: *Natasha runs with the doll.*
	     Complication 2: *Natasha is out of breath, but the doll wants to play.*
	 Event 3: *She pushes the doll on the swing.*
	     Complication 3: *The doll wants to go higher and higher, but Natasha is tired.*
	 Event/Action 4: *Natasha pulls the goat cart to entertain the doll.*
	     Complication 4: *Natasha gets tired.*
	 Event 5: *Natasha feeds the doll.*
	     Complication 5: *The doll dirties her dress and cries.*
	 Event 6: *Natasha washes the dress and irons it.*
	     Complication 6: *The doll says that the ironing was not done well, and Natasha cries.*

End	**Solution:** *Babushka comes back and takes the doll. Natasha does not want to play with her again.* *Natasha is not demanding ever again.*

FIGURE 4.2. Example of a completed GO for read-aloud on *Babushka's Doll* by Patricia Polacco (for your reference).

SAMPLE TOPICS FOR WRITING ASSESSMENT/INSTRUCTION

Note: A list of sample writing topics is provided that you could use for preassessment, instruction, guided practice, and postassessment. The topics included in this list should not limit your creativity. You should consider your students and their interests as well as their knowledge base. In these samples we cite topics that include parts of the plot and others that are more general. You could also use picture prompts—and you should feel free to expand on these suggestions.

Sample Writing Topics with Part of the Plot Provided

1. Imagine this! You wake up one morning and you cannot make a sound. You open and close your mouth and move your lips, but no sound can be heard. Write a story, saying what could have happened and what could happen next.

2. Imagine this! Your parents have bought a new car. When you try to get into the car, you hear the car talking to you! Write a story saying what the car says and what could happen next.

3. Imagine this! A boy wakes up in the middle of the night and hears a creaking sound coming from his ceiling. What could that be? Write a story about what will happen next.

4. Imagine this! One Saturday you go to the library and check out a book. At home later, you discover a $100 bill in the book. Write a story about what you do with the money.

Sample General Writing Topics

1. Write a story about a girl who found a magic glass.

2. Write a story about two friends who landed on a strange island.

3. Write a story about a day full of surprises.

4. Write a story about an apple that didn't want to grow.

Story-Writing Lessons

LESSON 1: INTRODUCTION—EVALUATION OF GOOD AND WEAK EXAMPLES AND SELF-EVALUATION

Students review the purpose and elements of stories. They evaluate good and weak papers by applying evaluation criteria. They evaluate their own papers and set personal goals for improvement.

Lesson Objectives

By the end of this lesson, students will be able to:

- Identify the elements of a story.
- Evaluate a story by identifying its elements and evaluating the quality of those elements.
- Set specific goals for improving their own stories.

Assessment Information

The teacher assesses whether students can (1) recall the story elements, (2) apply the evaluation criteria to score papers, and (3) set personal goals for improvement. The teacher may give quizzes to assess students' knowledge of elements, may take notes during informal observations, and may read students' journals to review their goals.

Notes

- Students will self-evaluate their preassessment paper. You can also score students' papers using the rubric in Form 4.2 to analyze your class's needs, but do not share your scores with students. After students self-evaluate, they will develop their learning goals. Therefore, it is better not to impose your scores on students but allow them to develop—and later perhaps revise—their own goals.

- We provide you with sample papers for this lesson; however, depending on your students' grade, level, and needs, you may decide to use different samples.

- During practice applying the evaluation criteria, students also work in small groups. You may want to assign students to groups ahead of time.

- During students' self-evaluation, you may also evaluate a paper you have written. It is important for students to see *you* as a writer.

Materials for Lesson 1

- Form 4.2. Rubric for Self-Evaluation and Peer Review of Story Writing
- Form 4.2 (copies for students' self-evaluation and small-group evaluation)
- Handout 4.1. Chart with Story Elements
- Handout 4.2. A Well-Written Paper for Evaluation, "Chickcherry and a Stormy Adventure"
- Handout 4.3. A Weak Paper for Evaluation, "The Donkey in the Field"
- Handout 4.4. "Castles and Ghosts and a Lost Ball"
- Handout 4.5. "Spinning Away: A Lesson on Friendship"
- Students' preassessment (see sample topics for writing assessment/instruction, pp. 43–45)

Procedures

Review

- Discuss and review the purpose of stories. Encourage student responses. The level of discussion will depend on how much your students know. A main purpose of stories is entertainment, and they can also help us to understand other people. Specific kinds of stories have special purposes. For example, a fable teaches a specific lesson; historical fiction helps us understand past times.

- Review the story elements using the chart in Handout 4.1. Refer to the completed form from your read-aloud, too.

Identification and Evaluation of Story-Writing Elements in a Well-Written Paper and a Weak Paper

- Explain to students that it is important to know the elements of stories in order to tell if a story is well written. Explain that if they know the elements, they can also understand and retell the story better.

- Explain that you will read well-written and poorly written papers to develop your and your students' "critical reading skills." You will read the stories, identify the elements, score each element using a rubric (Form 4.2), and make suggestions for revision goals.

- Display or draw the rubric on the board.

- Explain that the rubric contains the same elements as the elements' chart (Handout 4.1) and the GO you completed during the read-aloud. Explain the scoring system (*0* means that the element is absent, *1* means that the element is present but is not clear or well developed, and *2* means that the element is well developed for the reader). Point out the similarities in the information between the story elements and the evaluation criteria of the rubric.

- Point to the section of the rubric called *Other Considerations*. Explain that in a story, writers need more than the story elements when evaluating a paper. Transition words and other features can also affect the quality of the paper. Read each of the *Other Considerations* from the rubric and briefly discuss how each one could affect a story's quality.

Evaluation of a Well-Written Paper

- Explain that you will first read and examine the elements of a well-written paper.

- Display for students and read out loud a well-written paper (see Handout 4.2). Share with students your general thoughts about the story.

- Explain that in order to tell whether this is a well-written story, you will look for the elements and score them. You can display or draw the rubric for this task. Underline each element, explain your reasoning for scoring, and assign a score. Students can participate, but you should lead the task.

- Complete the rubric and then respond to the questions at the end with the students' input. Discuss students' general comments about the paper.

Evaluation of a Weak Paper

- Briefly review the elements of story writing. Explain that you will read a second paper and evaluate it using the story elements (see completed Figures 4.3 and 4.4 for your reference).

- Display for students and read out loud the paper "The Donkey in the Field" (see Handout 4.3). If there are editing issues, point them out, but do not shift the focus of the

---

The Donkey in the Field

There was <u>a donkey</u> [CHARACTER—NO NAME] that always <u>wanted to sing in the field</u> [PROBLEM] when the other animals were resting. The fox had recently given birth to her babies and she was trying to put them to sleep when donkey began his singing:

"I am the most grey donkey in the Great, Green field. I am grazing in green grass and I am glad that I have a gorgeous voice and a glamorous mane!"

<u>The fox approached the donkey and begged him to be quiet</u> [EVENT 1], <u>but the donkey rudely told her to put cotton buds in her ears and her babies' ears and let him enjoy the day</u> [COMPLICATION 1]. <u>The fox left the field</u> fuming!

The next day she went to the forest council and asked for all the animals to find a solution [EVENT 2]. No one had any idea, but they were all tired of the donkey's singing [COMPLICATION 2].

<u>They didn't know what to do so they all began singing</u> [EVENT 3]. <u>As they sang they felt happy and they understood that the donkey was singing because he was happy. Their solution would be to make the donkey sad!</u> [COMPLICATION 3]

They tried it, but the donkey did not get sad. They <u>decided to leave the forest.</u> [SOLUTION] [NO EMOTION]

FIGURE 4.3. Example of a weak paper, "The Donkey in the Field," with elements identified (for your reference).

lesson to them. Ask students to share their general impressions about the paper. Then explain that you will evaluate the paper using the evaluation rubric.

- Think out loud as you look for each element, underline it, and score it. Also, take some notes about things the writer could do to improve elements that have scores of 0 or 1. You can invite students to help you identify each element, but you should model the process of making suggestions. Try to be specific in your comments; students will follow your lead when they work independently. When you provide comments and take notes for making suggestions, use the phrase "Perhaps the writer could say. . . ." This will help students develop a model about how to make constructive suggestions when they peer-review.

- Discuss the goals that the writer should set and explain that setting goals helps writers focus their attention and effort.

Discussion

- Ask students why and how you evaluated the story. Stress the importance of learning the elements and explain how they can be helpful to a writer.

Collaborative Evaluation of a Weak Paper

- Explain to students that you will read additional papers and use the evaluation rubric to score them and to set goals for the writers.

- Display for students and read out loud a weak paper (use Handout 4.4 or 4.5). Evaluate the paper with students and set goals for the writer. (Note: Your role during this activity

		0 Not there	1 Could be better	2 Great!
Beginning	**Characters**: Is the main character named and described clearly? Are other characters described?		✓	
	Time: Can you tell when the story happens?	✓		
	Place: Is the place described clearly?		✓	
	Problem: Is there a clearly described problem that sets the story in motion?		✓	
Middle	**Events**: Is there a clear, logical sequence of events to try to solve the problem? Are the events interesting?		✓	
	Complications: Are there clear, logical complications that initiate new events or problems? Are they interesting?		✓	
End	**Solution**: Is the ending a logical solution to the problem?			✓
	Emotion: Can you tell how the characters feel?	✓		
Other Considerations	Is there a title that clearly connects to the information in the story?		✓	
	Were the characters' personalities and emotions shown throughout the paper? Did the writer **show,** not tell?		✓	
	Were things described vividly? Could the reader see what the characters saw?		✓	
	Were transition words used appropriately throughout the story?	✓		

Reviewer/Writer as a Reader

• Overall, was the story interesting to you as a reader? Why? *Yes, it had an interesting plot.*

• What revisions should be made? *The story could be improved in many ways! The writer could give a time, mention the name of the main character and the names of the other characters, and also explain the problem more. The solution is very sudden as well. Perhaps the writer could give additional details. Finally, the author does not let the reader know how the donkey feels when the story ends. The words are not bad, but are not elaborated enough to help the reader see what the writer means.*

Goals

• What could be the writer's goals for the current and future papers? *The writer should consider working on improving the descriptions of the characters and the problem. The writer could also work more on the solution. In future papers the writer should try to be more descriptive, follow the elements, and work in more than one draft!*

FIGURE 4.4. Example of a completed rubric for a weak paper, "The Donkey in the Field" (for your reference).

is to scaffold students' application of evaluation criteria. Ask them process questions [e.g., "What should we do next?"], ask them to find the elements for you to underline, and ask them to give you their scores and explanations so you can complete the rubric. Finally, ask them to make suggestions to the writer. If students have difficulties or if their responses are not accurate, reassume control of the activity.)

Small-Group Evaluation of a Weak Paper

- Ask students to work in groups to read a story (use Handout 4.4 or 4.5), identify its elements, and complete the rubric (copies of Form 4.2). Ask students to underline the elements and label them at the side of the paper. Make sure they assign a score and provide suggestions to the writer.
- Discuss students' scoring and suggestions as a group.

Self-Evaluation of Students' Papers and Goal Setting

- Discuss and explain the importance of setting goals with students.
- Ask students to read their own preassessment, evaluate the story using the story elements (copies of Form 4.2), and set goals for their own writing. Ask them to be specific about their goals, following your earlier examples.

Differentiation

- You may want to conference with individuals or small groups of students to assist them with the application of the rubric. However, do not impose your scoring on the students. They should develop their own goals, but you could guide them to set realistic ones. Students will have the opportunity to revise their goals based on their performance later.

Reflection Activity

- **Journal writing.** You can ask students to write a journal entry in response to the following questions:
    1. What did I learn about *my* story writing?
    2. What should be my goals for improvement? What could I do to reach those goals?

End of Lesson

- Review the elements of stories and explain to students that it is important to learn them. Explain how this learning can be helpful to them as readers and writers.

LESSON 2: MODELING HOW TO WRITE A STORY

Students review the elements of stories and observe the teacher during think-aloud modeling of planning, drafting, evaluating to revise, and editing of a story.

Lesson Objectives

By the end of this lesson, students will be able to:

* Recall the elements of narratives.
* Recall the steps of the Writing Strategy Ladder and explain their components.

Assessment Information

The teacher (1) informally assesses whether students understand and can use the steps of the Writing Strategy Ladder and (2) uses students' written responses during review to identify those who may need assistance learning the story elements.

Notes

* During the review stage of this lesson (see beginning section of procedures) you can ask students to complete the provided memorization sheet (see Form 4.3) or you can ask them to write the elements on a blank sheet. Students should perform this task for multiple days to practice learning the elements.
* A Sample Think-Aloud for Story Writing, with materials, is included on pages 75–81 as an example of a good think-aloud in this genre. You should not refer to it during teaching, but you may consult it to understand the process before you give this lesson. You can use parts of the sample or prepare by planning on a new topic. The think-aloud should sound "live" when you do it, and the planning and writing should be your own.

Materials for Lesson 2

* Form 4.1. Planning Materials (FTAP, Ideas, and GO)
* Form 4.2. Rubric for Self-Evaluation and Peer Review of Story Writing
* Form 4.3. Support in Memorization of Story Elements (optional)
* Handout 2.1. Writing Strategy Ladder (from Chapter 2)
* Handout 2.2. SCIPS for Editing (from Chapter 2)
* Handout 4.6. Transition Words

Procedures

Review

- Ask students to write the story elements, then to self-evaluate and set goals for learning any elements they may have missed.

- Discuss the importance of each element.

- Depending on your students' grade and age, you may encourage them to develop their own memorizing technique (e.g., a song or a chant).

Introduction to the Writing Strategy Ladder

- Explain to students that you will teach them a strategy for writing narrative papers and that this strategy follows the process of writing. Each step tells what to do and how to do it. Explain that it is a useful strategy because it helps students stay on track and not skip a step. In other words, it helps them be successful writers.

- Display the Writing Strategy Ladder, point, read, and explain each of the steps (see Handout 2.1).

Plan

- Point to the first step and ask students why writers always need to start by planning. Encourage student responses (you may want to record their responses and make a plan to address misconceptions).

- Explain that planning is something that good writers do because it helps them figure out their ideas and organize them before writing. You may want to ask students if they would make a plan about what to buy from the grocery store before going there, or not. Explain that if they did not make a plan, they might buy things they did not really need, or forget things that were important, or get completely distracted and go to a different store instead of the grocery store!

- Explain that in the planning section, students, as good writers, will follow specific steps: FTAP, Ideas/Brainstorm, and Organize their ideas with a GO. You can display Form 4.1 and write each component on the board.

FTAP

- Write each letter, say what it stands for, and discuss why it is important.
  - **F** stands for *Form.*
  - **T** stands for *Topic.*
  - **A** stands for *Audience.* Discuss the importance of thinking about your audience when trying to tell a story. Discuss what might engage the audience in a story (language, descriptions, etc.).
  - **P** stands for *Purpose.* Explain that stories can have many purposes: They can entertain, they can help us learn about people, and/or they can give us a message about

life. You can refer to the purposes of some of the stories that you have used in read-alouds.

IDEAS/BRAINSTORM

- Point to "Ideas" and explain that the next step is to come up with as many ideas as possible about the topic. Explain that writers will Brainstorm. They will think of many ideas about their story, their characters, the setting (time and place), the plot, and the ending of the story. Explain that while writers develop these ideas, they should think of their audience and what would be entertaining or important to those readers.

GRAPHIC ORGANIZER

- Display the GO (see Form 4.1) and point out that it has the elements of stories exactly as students have seen them in previous lessons. Explain that the goal is to select the best ideas, organize them, and add more during drafting. Add that when writers plan, they write the elements of a story using a paper and a pen/pencil, and they do not need to use a copy of this GO. Explain that knowledge of the elements can empower students because they will not need to have a GO. If they know the elements, they will be able to replicate the GO any time they need to write a story.

Draft

- Point to the second step of the strategy ladder and explain that good writers make sure to use their plan to write a first draft. Discuss the reasons for this. Also, explain that good writers use transition words and display Handout 4.6.

Evaluate to Revise

- Point to the Evaluate to Revise step of the ladder and say that good writers always go back to their paper to check for its meaning and organization and to make any changes that might improve it. Explain that for this step they will use the rubric that contains the evaluation elements (if you have it on display, point to Form 4.2). Explain that you could write the elements and assign a score next to them instead of using the rubric. Remind students about the connections between the elements, the evaluation criteria, and the information in the GO.

Edit

- Point to Edit (you can point to Handout 2.2 if you have it on display) and explain that good writers also check for errors that could affect the quality of the paper (e.g., spelling, indentation, grammar).

Publish

- Finally, point to Publish and explain that writers should celebrate their work and share it with others!

Modeling Story Writing

- Explain that you will write a paper and show students how to write their own stories by thinking out loud as a student, so they can hear how you think and how you handle the challenges that come with writing (see Sample Think-Aloud on pp. 75–81).

- Explain that you are a student for the moment and were asked to write a story on the following topic: **"Write a story about a bee and a bear. Your story will be read at a school celebration, where it will be shared with students and parents."**

- Think aloud and ask yourself what are the steps of the strategy you need to follow. Explain that the steps are Plan, Draft, Evaluate to Revise, Edit, and Share, and that you need to start with planning. Write the steps of the ladder at the side of the board. Underline *Plan*.

Plan

FTAP

- Ask yourself what is the first part of planning. Write *FTAP* on the board and complete each section. Clearly explain what is the Form, what is the Topic, who is the Audience, and what is the writing Purpose. Briefly comment on how use of the FTAP helps you better understand what you need to do as a writer.

IDEAS/BRAINSTORM

- Ask what you should do next. Refer to the elements' chart to determine your next step. Generate ideas about the topic.

GRAPHIC ORGANIZER

- Ask what your next step should be. Explain that you should organize your ideas and select the best ideas for your story. Draw the GO and transfer ideas from the Brainstorm step. When you write an idea on the GO, cross it out on the Brainstorm list to make the process clearer to students.

- Make sure to use self-talk to ask what you have done and where you are in the process, and to encourage yourself to continue even though the task is challenging.

Draft

- Ask what you should do next. Respond by pointing to the strategy ladder and explain that you need to begin drafting. Explain how to use transition words. Place a checkmark next to the word *Plan* that you had underlined earlier. Point to the steps you wrote earlier and underline *Draft*. Explain that you will draft your paper.

- Use self-talk to guide your work (e.g., "What have I done so far?"), support your next step ("What should I do next?"), and handle challenges (e.g., "This is really difficult for me. I can't remember what I'm supposed to do, but I can find out if I use my strategy ladder to see what I should do next").

- Compose the story. Refer to the notes on the GO as you develop sentences. Consult the transition words document and practice developing orally the sentences before writing them down. (Note: In case you run out of time, stop after you have developed the ideas and have completed the GO. During the next lesson, review the steps of the strategy, the elements of BME, and your planning before you proceed with drafting.)

Evaluate to Revise

- Ask what would be your next step. Point to the Writing Strategy Ladder and explain that now you will need to evaluate and revise your paper. In order to do that, you will use the evaluation rubric (see Form 4.2). Point out the similarities between the evaluation criteria, the story-writing elements, and the GO.

- Apply the rubric to the story and score each element. Think aloud as you make decisions. Identify the areas that need to be improved and set goals for the next paper.

- Make at least one revision.

Edit

- Explain that for editing you have a helpful technique (SCIPS, Handout 2.2), but for now you will reread and look for spelling errors only.

Publish

- Explain that this could be a great story and after you revise and edit it, you could share it with the students and teacher of another class.

Discussion of the Modeling and Self-Regulation

- Ask students to tell you if they remember some of the things you said to yourself as you wrote. They will mention parts of the strategy and ideas that you talked about. Lead them to talk about some of the self-regulation statements you made and the moments you were frustrated but continued working. Record students' responses and some of the statements you made. Explain that these statements helped you complete your writing without experiencing stress and that you will discuss the statements with the students in the next class.

Optional Commitment

- Explain that students need to make a commitment to learn the strategy and the elements. For this, they can promise as a group to learn the strategies or they can sign a learning contract. The contract contains a mutual agreement to learn the story-writing elements, to learn the steps of the Writing Strategy Ladder, and to apply them when they work independently.

Additional Activities

- After you complete at least one revision, students can work in groups to make a different revision. They can share their thoughts about how to improve a specific element and then work on completing that revision.

Reflection Activities

- **Journal writing.** You can ask students to write a journal entry about the Writing Strategy Ladder and how it can help them with their own writing. Students could revisit the goals they had set in the previous class and explain how the strategy can assist them in improving as writers.
- **Class discussion.** You can discuss as a class how the writing strategy helps students as writers.

End of Lesson

- Review the genre elements, the steps of the Writing Strategy Ladder, and its components.

LESSON 3: SELF-REGULATION—MINI-LESSON ON CLEAR DESCRIPTIONS

Students learn a strategy that helps them monitor their work and reflect on the application of the strategies. Students develop "self-talk." In the second part of the lesson, students are taught a mini-lesson and practice how to improve the descriptions of characters and setting in sample stories by appealing to the five senses.

Lesson Objectives

By the end of this lesson, students will be able to:

- Develop their own self-talk.
- Provide clear and detailed descriptions in their stories.

Assessment information

- The teacher informally assesses whether students can (1) develop self-talk and (2) make revisions to their paper using information from the mini-lesson.

Notes

- This lesson has two parts that could easily be taught separately. You could teach the self-regulation strategies one day and the mini-lesson on another.

- In preparation for this mini-lesson, you could do a read-aloud of a book (e.g., *Yeh-Shen: A Cinderella Story from China* by Ai-Ling Louie) that provides detailed descriptions of characters, events, and setting (time and place) and discuss the importance of the use of descriptions. You could use this information as a starting point for the mini-lesson.

- This is a sample mini-lesson. You may choose to replace it with a different lesson that you think would be more supportive to your students' story writing.

Materials for Lesson 3

- Form 2.2. Self-Talk Recording Sheet (from Chapter 2)
- Form 4.4. Chart of Senses
- Handout 2.3. Be Strategic! (from Chapter 2)
- Handout 4.7. "Eggy the Hen"

Procedures

Review

- Review the parts of the writing strategy and the elements of stories. Keep in mind that the purpose of learning the strategies is for students to be able to apply them across subject areas (e.g., in social studies where they may be asked to write a story from the perspective of a historical figure). Therefore, it is important for students to learn the information and also discuss where else they might use it.

Self-Regulation and Self-Statements

- Remind students that when you modeled how to write a story, you thought out loud. Explain that in addition to following the Writing Strategy Ladder, you also showed them how you dealt with writing challenges. You can refer to the notes you took at the end of Lesson 2.

- Explain that the self-talk you used helped you stay on task and complete the assignment. Tell students that this type of self-talk and self-regulation (self-checking) is something that they can use across academic and nonacademic tasks. For example, if they know that they have soccer practice at 5:00 P.M. and have to meet their friend to take the 15-minute walk together, they should not leave their home at 4:50 or start looking for their gear at 5:00. If they do, they will be late. Instead, they will make sure to have their gear in place, so as not to have to look for it at the last minute, and they will leave at least 20 minutes earlier to be there on time. What they do, in reality, is self-regulate. Give other examples (e.g., play in the afternoon after they complete their homework).

- Display Form 2.4, Be Strategic!, and explain each part. Tell students that these questions should become part of their internal writing voice that keeps them focused. Explain each section of the poster and how you applied it when you thought aloud.

- Explain that all writers can be successful if they use their strategies and do not let themselves get discouraged.

- Show students the self-talk sheet (Form 2.2) and discuss as a group some statements they could include in each section. Discuss statements they could use to stay on task, to use their strategies, and to stay engaged. Ask them to write those statements on a blank sheet or on the self-talk sheet (see Form 2.2). Then ask students to place those sheets where they can be easily accessed and will not be lost (e.g., taped to their writing folder or to their desk). Tell students to refer to them as they work.

Clear Descriptions: Mini-Lesson

Discussion of the Use of Descriptions

- Explain that clear descriptions of time, place (setting), and events help the reader create a visual image and "see" the story. If a story does not have any descriptions, the reader may not like it or may not understand it.

Evaluation of a Paper

- Display for students and read out loud a weak paper (see Handout 4.7, "Eggy the Hen," or any story with weak descriptions). Use the evaluation rubric (see Form 4.2) to evaluate it, assign a score to each element, and determine the writer's goals. Point out that there were very few descriptions.

- Ask students if they could picture where Eggy lived and what she was like as a character. The descriptions of the barn, the place, and the character and her actions are very limited; as a result, readers cannot picture the place or understand Eggy's character, using their mind's eye.

Use of Senses to Describe

- Ask students to name their senses (sight, hearing, taste, smell, and touch). Explain that they could use their knowledge about senses to give details that would bring the setting to life and allow the reader to "live" the story.

Use of Senses to Describe: Teacher Practice

- Explain that you will use words to describe your home so that people who have not seen it would be able to recognize it in the neighborhood. Display the senses chart (see Form 4.4). Then write the senses on the board and describe your home. (Note: You could instead describe shells or tangrams or other images.)

- When you have completed the task, write a paragraph and show a picture of two or three houses. Ask students to determine which is the house you described based on the information. Discuss the value of clear, detailed descriptions.

Use of Senses to Describe: Group Practice

- Ask students to work with you to describe their classroom or any other place. Ask them for descriptive words for each one of the senses. Record the information as a group. Then collaboratively construct complete sentences and write a paragraph.

- Refer back to the story. Ask the students to work with partners to develop clear descriptions about the place or the events and the scenery using their senses. Ask each student to complete his or her own sheet and rewrite the sections of the story. Have students share their work in a group.

Differentiation

- While students are working in small groups, you could work with a small group of students who need more support.

Reflection Activities

- **Journal entry.** You can ask students to develop a journal entry that explains how using their own senses can help them with their writing. Another entry should describe how the use of self-talk can help them stay on task and motivated.

- **Class discussion.** Discuss as a group what parts of the writing strategy seem challenging to students and what they could do to be successful.

End of Lesson

- Explain the importance of self-monitoring the writing task. Review the importance of detailed descriptions that allow the reader to "see" the information.

LESSON 4: COLLABORATIVE WRITING OF A STORY

The teacher and students collaboratively use the Writing Strategy Ladder to Plan, Draft, Evaluate to Revise, and Edit a story. During collaborative writing, the teacher scaffolds students' application of the strategy and does the writing as the students provide the ideas and sentences.

Lesson Objectives

By the end of this lesson, students will be able to:

- Demonstrate that they know the meaning of the strategy steps and can contribute appropriately to planning, drafting, and revising.

Assessment Information

The teacher informally assesses whether students (1) know the meaning of the strategy steps and (2) can apply them as a group to Plan, Draft, Evaluate to Revise, and Edit.

Notes

- You can complete FTAP and Ideas/Brainstorm for two topics, and select the topic for which you have the most ideas, or you could present students with one topic.
- You should complete the planning step as a whole class. For drafting, there are several options that you can try. You can draft together with the whole class or you can ask students to compose independently or in small groups. During small-group work, you might work with a group of students that needs support.

Materials for Lesson 4

- Form 4.1. Planning Materials (FTAP, Ideas, and GO)
- Form 4.2. Rubric for Self-Evaluation and Peer Review of Story Writing
- Handout 2.1. Writing Strategy Ladder (from Chapter 2)
- Handout 4.6. Transition Words
- Students' completed self-talk sheets (Form 2.2) from Lesson 3
- Sample Topics for Writing Assessment/Instruction (see pp. 43–44)

Procedures

Review

- Review the steps of the Writing Strategy Ladder and the elements of stories. Ask students to record them on a sheet independently. Then ask them to check with a partner and self-correct and set study goals.

Introduction to Collaborative Writing

- Explain to students that you will work together as a group to write a story. You can present a topic or decide between the two after doing FTAP and Ideas. Explain that you will work together and go through each step of the strategy to write a story.

Plan

- Ask students what is the first thing they need to do when they are asked to write. Students should respond that it is planning with FTAP and generating Ideas/Brainstorming. You can give students copies of the planning materials or ask them to write FTAP/Brainstorm and draw the GO on their notebooks instead.

FTAP AND IDEAS

- Write *FTAP* and *Ideas/Brainstorm* on the board. Underline or circle *Brainstorm*.
- Ask students what *FTAP* means and why it is important. Record their answers on the board. If students are not able to answer, provide explanations. Continue the same process for the completion of the Ideas/Brainstorm step.
- At the end of Ideas/Brainstorm, stop and examine the ideas as a group.

GRAPHIC ORGANIZER

- Ask students what the next step is. Refer to the Writing Strategy Ladder to determine the next step. Complete the GO as a group.
- Refer repeatedly to the writing strategy and remind students to use their self-statements when they do not know what they should do.

Draft

- Ask what the next step is and refer students to the Writing Strategy Ladder.
- Write the paper using the ideas from the GO and transition words.

Evaluate to Revise

- Discuss what the next step would be after drafting. Remind students to use the Writing Strategy Ladder.
- Complete with students the evaluation rubric, identify areas for improvement, and make one revision.

Edit

- Ask what the next step is and explain that you will be learning a general approach for editing. At this point you can reread for spelling errors and make corrections.

Differentiation

- Rotate around the classroom and assist students as they write. You can also work with a small group of students that needs additional support. You could use your preassessment data to identify students with common misunderstandings and form groups.

End of Lesson

- Review the steps of the Writing Strategy Ladder and stress the importance of using all of its components when writing.

LESSON 5: STUDENTS PLAN AND DRAFT THEIR OWN STORIES

Students begin working on their own papers, using the planning and drafting steps of the strategy. The teacher monitors the use of the strategy and provides support as needed.

Lesson Objectives

By the end of this lesson, students will be able to:

- Apply the planning and drafting steps of the strategy to generate and organize ideas appropriately.
- Write a story that includes the story elements.

Assessment Information

The teacher informally assesses whether (1) students are using the strategy appropriately and (2) their writing includes the elements and is well written, in general.

Notes

- This is the beginning of guided practice. Students should write more than one paper.
- This lesson may take more than one session, depending on the time available. However, two sessions should be enough. Set expectations for when students should finish.
- We encourage you to plan and write your own paper. It is important for your students to see that you write, too. You could use your paper to self-evaluate in Lesson 7.

Materials for Lesson 5

- Students' completed self-talk sheets (Form 2.2) from Lesson 3
- Handout 2.1. Writing Strategy Ladder (from Chapter 2)
- Handout 4.6. Transition Words
- Form 4.1. Planning Materials (FTAP, Ideas, and GO)
- Form 4.3. Support in Memorization of Story Elements (optional)
- Sample Topics for Writing Assessment/Instruction (see pp. 43–44)

Procedures

Review

- Review the steps of the Writing Strategy Ladder and the elements of stories. Students can write the elements on a blank sheet or in Form 4.3.

Students Begin Their Writing

- Explain to students that they will start working on their stories and that they should make sure to use the Writing Strategy Ladder's steps, the elements of stories, and their self-statements to write great stories.

Choosing Topics

- You can choose how to assign topics. One option is to display the list of topics (see Sample Topics for Writing Assessment/Instruction, pp. 43–44) and let students select a topic. Another option is to assign the same topic to all students. This might be easier for some students; it can support collaboration among students at the planning stage, and it can lead to more class discussion during revision. A third option is to let students choose their own topics, instead of limiting them to the ones on the list. If you ask students to select among a list of topics or develop their own topic, ask them to do the FTAP and Ideas/Brainstorm before they make a final topic selection. By analyzing the task and developing ideas, they can strategically evaluate whether they have sufficient information to write a full paper on a topic or not.

Guiding Practice

- As students work, you can monitor their progress and conduct very brief conferences. In conferencing, you should talk to students about how they planned their piece and look at the planning sheets as well as the developing paper. Such feedback encourages students to understand that using the strategy is important to improving their writing. Remember that assessment focuses on both strategy use and writing performance.

- Remind students to use self-talk as they work independently.

Differentiation

- Plan to work with small groups of students that need additional help. Informally assess whether students use the planning strategy and whether they include all the elements in their drafts. In addition, if you notice during your observations that there are students who do not use the planning materials, you should stress the importance of their use and work with them. You could also use your preassessment data to identify individuals who struggle with specific elements. For example, if your preassessment data have indicated that five students struggled to create a clearly described problem, you may work with those students during this time.

Reflection Activity

- **Class discussion.** Discuss with students how the Writing Strategy Ladder helped them complete their writing.

End of Lesson

- Review the steps of the Writing Strategy Ladder and explain the importance of dialogue in "bringing characters to life" and allowing the reader to make inferences about the characters and their intentions.

LESSON 6: PREPARATION FOR PEER REVIEW AND SELF-EVALUATION

Students practice evaluating stories, writing suggestions, and making revisions. Students self-evaluate their papers and set goals for revision.

Lesson Objectives

By the end of this lesson, students will be able to:

- Apply the evaluation rubric to evaluate papers written by others.
- Use their evaluations to make revisions and offer suggestions for revision.
- Self-evaluate their papers and set revision goals.

Assessment Information

The teacher informally assesses whether students can (1) apply the evaluation criteria, (2) make revisions using the evaluation results, and (3) self-evaluate their papers and set revision goals.

Notes

- You could also plan to self-evaluate the paper you wrote. That way your students will also see you as a writer in class.

Materials for Lesson 6

- Form 4.2. Rubric for Self-Evaluation and Peer Review of Story Writing
- Form 4.2 (copies for students' evaluation in small groups and for their self-evaluations)
- Handout 2.1. Writing Strategy Ladder (from Chapter 2)
- Handout 4.8. "Say Food No More"
- Handout 4.9. "More Than What Your Eyes Could See"
- Handout 4.10. "Watch What You Wish For!"
- Students' completed self-talk sheets (Form 2.2) from Lesson 3

Procedures

Review

- Review the writing strategy steps and the elements of stories.

Discussion of the Importance of Evaluation and Revision and the Role of Peer Review

- Ask students what would be the next step in the writing process. Point to Evaluate to Revise on the Writing Strategy Ladder (see Handout 2.1). Ask students what they think revision is and discuss how it differs from editing.

- Explain that revising means to review the written paper and make any needed changes. These changes can involve adding, deleting, and/or clarifying ideas and reorganizing the information to be clearer to the reader.

- Ask students how they will know what type of changes they need to make. Explain the meaning of *evaluation* and remind them about the evaluation rubric that they used in the first lesson. Display the rubric and discuss how the evaluation criteria are connected to the story elements and the GO.

- Explain that they will participate in peer review. Each student will work with a partner to evaluate each other's papers and make suggestions for revision. To prepare for this step, the class will work together to practice evaluating papers written by students they do not know.

- Explain that giving feedback is an important aspect of reviewing and that it can help students better understand the evaluation criteria and use them during self-evaluation. Emphasize the importance of being honest and giving detailed suggestions to the writer.

Modeling Evaluation for Peer Review

- Display a paper for students (any story from Handouts 4.8–4.10).

- Read the paper out loud and explain that reading the story out loud helps you find any initial problems with the paper.

- Then underline the elements. You can use different colors for different elements; however, your students should do whatever you do. You want the process to be simple but explicit.

- Use the rubric to assign a score. Explain why you assigned that score and be very specific in your reasoning. Write notes at the side of each element for what you should do to improve it (for a score of 1 or 0). Begin your suggestions by writing and/or saying, "Perhaps the writer could say. . . ."

- Identify what revisions need to be made in this paper and what goals the writer would set for a future paper.

- Make at least one revision.

- Explain to the students that when they are reading their work or the work of their peers, they need to be honest, identify the elements, assign a score, and write suggestions to help the writer improve.

Optional Variation

- After you read the paper out loud, you can identify the elements and use them to complete the GO. Then score the paper using the rubric and discuss how an incomplete GO could explain the text's poor score. This would be a nice way to review that also stresses the importance of careful planning.

Collaborative Practice of Evaluation

- Display a different paper (see Handouts 4.8–4.10) and with students' feedback identify the elements, assign a score, and record specific suggestions for revisions.

- With students' feedback, make at least one revision. You can also ask students to work in small groups.

Small-Group Practice on Evaluation

- Display a different paper (from Handouts 4.8–4.10) and give copies of the paper to students. Also, give them copies of the rubric (Form 4.2). Ask them to follow the same procedure you used when modeling and then as a group, make specific suggestions to the writer and at least one revision. (Note: Students may work in small groups or pairs.)

Students Work on Their Own Papers to Self-Evaluate

- Explain that knowledge of elements and practice evaluating papers written by others can help writers be better at self-evaluation.
- Tell students to underline the elements in their papers, score them, and set goals for revisions.

Differentiation

- Evaluation and self-evaluation can be challenging for some students. You may want to work with students in small groups to complete this task.

End of Lesson

- Explain that evaluation is a critical component of writing and can support students in making revisions. Explain that evaluation could also help students be helpful reviewers.

LESSON 7: PEER REVIEW AND REVISION

Students peer-review in pairs or small groups, applying the evaluation criteria to compare their self-evaluation with the comments of their peers, set goals for revision, and make revisions.

Lesson Objectives

By the end of this lesson, students will be able to:

- Apply the evaluation criteria to give specific feedback to peers.
- Make revisions to their essays.

Assessment Information

The teacher informally assesses if students can (1) apply the evaluation criteria and give feedback to peers and (2) make revisions to their essays.

Notes

- When students work on revisions, you may want to meet with them to discuss their work. In general, give them feedback on their use of the strategy, not only on the end product. Ask them how they used the planning materials, then ask them to review their GO and see how it matches their paper. Discuss their evaluation and revision goals.

- For students who raise concerns about their ability to constructively complete the peer review, you may want to provide additional practice on the reviewing process using additional papers.

- Students can work in pairs or in groups of three. If they work in groups of three, trade papers using a clockwise direction.

- You can assign students to groups based on informal observations of students' needs and abilities to apply the evaluation rubric and write suggestions. You could also consult the preassessment data and the needs of specific students and may group students according to their strengths and weaknesses. For example, you may ask a student who had an excellent description of the setting and characters (score of 2) to work with a student who received a lower score.

- Support students with the revision task, but do not complete the revisions for them. If they have challenges with handwriting, they can dictate to you.

Materials for Lesson 7

- Form 4.2. Rubric for Self-Evaluation and Peer Review of Story Writing
- Form 4.2 (copies for peer review)
- Handout 2.1. Writing Strategy Ladder (from Chapter 2)
- Students' completed self-talk sheets (Form 2.2) from Lesson 3

Procedures

Review

- Discuss the elements of stories and the steps of the Writing Strategy Ladder. Review the meaning of evaluation and revision.

Peer Review

- Explain that peer review is a process whereby partners meet to evaluate each other's papers and give suggestions so that the partners can make revisions and improve their grades.

Peer Review Procedures

- Write the steps of the peer review sequence on the board and explain each one:

  1. Meet with your partner and read your paper to each other.

     a. Explain that in the process of reviewing, the writer will read his or her paper out loud.

  2. Switch papers.

  3. Reread your partner's paper, evaluate it using the rubric, and write specific suggestions.

     a. Explain that the reader/reviewer will read the paper again and evaluate it using the rubric. The goal of the reader/reviewer is not only to identify the presence or absence of the elements, but also to give specific suggestions to the writer to help improve his or her grade.

  4. Meet with your partner and discuss your scoring, comments, and suggestions.

  5. Explain that in the meeting, the writer will say something that was interesting or that he or she liked, explain his or her scoring, and give suggestions to the writer. Then the reviewer will listen to the partner's comments.

- Explain that the writer should not be upset with the reviewer/reader but should appreciate the efforts that the reviewer made to give specific suggestions for improvement.

- Explain that you have been practicing peer review all this time by using papers written by unknown students. This is a practice that has prepared you to meet with a "live" partner to complete this task.

Completing Peer Review

- Students meet with their partners to complete the peer review process.

Revisions

- Students compare their self-evaluation sheets with their partner's comments and determine what revisions to make. Students work on revising their own papers.

Optional Variation

- You can ask reviewers to complete the evaluation rubric and the GO using the information from the writers' papers. Then, when they meet with their writers, they can compare the GOs they developed and the ones the writers used to write their papers. This comparison will help reviewers make more specific suggestions for improvement so that writers can better understand what areas are confusing and how to improve their GOs.

Differentiation

- You can plan to work with a small group of students that is having difficulty making revisions. You might take notes or work as an external monitor reminding them to use their self-statements when they get frustrated.

- As students work, you can also meet with them to conference, asking them about their strategy use and their revision goals and prompting them to explain their reasoning. You should provide feedback on students' use of the planning materials, on their application of the writing process, and on their goals. Because this feedback helps students understand the importance of using the strategies to improve their writing, it should not concern only the final product.

Reflection Activity

- **Class discussion.** Ask students to compare their self-evaluation rubrics with the reviewers' feedback and comments. If the reviewers have also completed GOs, ask writers to compare their GOs with the reviewers' GOs. What did they learn about planning? What revisions could they make to their GOs? What are their future goals?

- **Journal writing.** Ask students to examine their preassessment and the goals they had set previously. You can ask them to compare their performances with their preassessments. Then ask students to record their new goals in their journals. You can also ask them to respond to the question, "What strategies have been helpful to you and what strategies will you use in the future and why?"

End of Lesson

- Explain that collaboration among writers is helpful and that the process of peer review is clearer if students use the elements to provide specific suggestions.

LESSON 8: EDITING

Students examine their papers for editing errors. By using the editing strategy (SCIPS), students identify surface-level errors and correct them. Teachers can choose to teach a specific grammatical/editing skill, practice the skill with students, and ask students to make changes to their essays. Additionally, students set editing goals and reflect on their performance and progress.

Lesson Objectives

By the end of this lesson, students will be able to:

- Set goals for improving their editing.
- Apply editing procedures to make changes.

Assessment Information

The teacher informally assesses whether students (1) apply previous editing goals to make editing changes and (2) use the skills they were taught to edit their work.

Notes

- Based on your observations and readings of students' work, you may identify common grammatical problems (e.g., use of run-on sentences). Develop an editing mini-lesson or plan to meet with different groups of students to address specific editing issues. Ask students to record the editing areas that they should pay attention to when working on the editing goals sheet (Form 2.1).

- SCIPS (Handout 2.2) is a general editing checklist. The goal is to identify specific editing needs of students and to provide a targeted mini-lesson. In this way students can practice improving that specific skill (see Lesson 3).

Materials for Lesson 8

- Form 2.1. Editing Goals for Improvement (from Chapter 2)
- Handout 2.1. Writing Strategy Ladder (from Chapter 2)
- Handout 2.2. SCIPS for Editing (from Chapter 2)
- Your choice of materials for a specific editing and grammatical goal

Guidelines

Introduction to Editing

- Point to the Writing Strategy Ladder and ask students to identify the next step of the strategy. Ask why editing is important and what is the difference between editing and revising.

Editing Mini-Lesson

- Identify a specific editing issue of your students. Explain the issue, model how to correct it on a sample paper, and collaboratively practice its correction as a group. Then review the SCIPS editing process and ask students to practice reviewing their papers for the specific editing skill they practiced and for the rest of the editing goals they have included in their editing goals sheets. You can also ask students to meet with a partner for peer editing. When students finish, ask them to add this editing skill to their editing goals sheets. You can also add this new editing goal to a class wall chart for future reference.

Reflection Activity

- **Journal writing**. Ask students to complete Form 2.1, Editing Goals for Improvement, and examine how they have progressed across time.

PUBLISHING GUIDELINES

It is important for students to share some of their work with a larger audience. We have provided guidelines and suggestions for ways to share students' work. These guidelines do not comprise a specific lesson, but rather present ideas for discussing publishing with your students. The specifics will depend on what sort of publishing you have chosen. See Chapter 3 for a discussion of ideas about opportunities for publishing.

Review

- Review the elements of stories and the steps of the Writing Strategy Ladder.

Publishing

- Point to the Writing Strategy Ladder and ask students to identify the next step of the strategy. Discuss why publishing and sharing are important aspects of the writing process.

- Students prepare their papers for publishing. In addition to general approaches for publishing (see Chapter 3), we provide some specific approaches for sharing stories below:

  1. Students from your class can become mentors of students from lower grades. Your students can visit their partners and read their stories to them. In addition to the benefits of collaboration, students can be motivated by the position of a "storyteller" and "mentor."

  2. You can create a book of stories, display it at the school's main office or outside your classroom, and ask readers to write their comments on a poster or a notebook next to the book. It is possible that students may provide inappropriate comments, especially if their comments are anonymous. To avoid this, you should model the process of giving feedback. Teachers provide a model of giving feedback when they evaluate papers and when they prepare students for peer review. However, for students who did not have instruction on giving feedback and on peer review, you could develop a template that structures students' responses. In this template you may ask readers to respond to two main questions: 1. What did they like about the story, and why? and 2. What did they find confusing, and why?

  3. You can make use of Voicethread (*www.voicethread.com*); ask your students to digitally save their work and record their voices as they read their stories. Then you

can share the Voicethread with other classrooms and ask viewers to respond (using voice, video, or typing). Teacher modeling or the use of a template (see previous explanation) to support students' comments can be used to assist students in giving appropriate comments.

GUIDELINES FOR CONTINUOUS GUIDED PRACTICE TO MASTERY

It is important for students to write more than one paper in a genre to develop mastery of it. As students write a second paper, they typically work more quickly and feel much more competent. Teachers can then focus their attention on students who need more support.

Mastery Objectives

By the end of all lessons on story writing, students will be able to:

- Apply the planning and drafting steps of the writing strategy to generate and organize ideas appropriately.
- Write a story that includes the story elements.
- Write a story that has clear descriptions of characters, setting, and events.

Assessment Information

The teacher informally assesses whether students (1) can apply the writing strategy to plan, draft, and evaluate to revise; (2) write clear descriptions of characters, setting, and events; and (3) accurately apply the evaluation criteria to give suggestions and make revisions.

Notes

- You might teach another mini-lesson before students work on a new paper (see the end of this section). Dialogue is an important feature of this genre and can help students enhance their characters and "show" their personalities to the reader. You should discuss the use and function of dialogue in a read-aloud prior to this mini-lesson (e.g., *Chicken Sunday* by Patricia Polacco).
- Students work on a new paper. For this task, complete the following:
  - Give students a choice of topics (see Sample Topics on pp. 43–44).
  - Remind students to use the Writing Strategy Ladder and the genre elements and materials.
  - Keep the planning materials on display (FTAP, Ideas, GO), but ask students to draw them instead of using printed copies.
  - As students work, conference with them about how they use the strategy and how their writing is progressing.

   ○ Conduct self-evaluations and peer reviews. You can collaboratively review a paper prior to students' self-evaluations and peer reviews to remind students of the importance of giving honest feedback and detailed suggestions. Monitor students' suggestions at the self-evaluation and peer review stage to ensure that their comments are productive.

   ○ Remind students to edit using SCIPS and to remember their editing goals (do not teach a new editing skill).

   ○ Plan for sharing by helping students prepare their papers for publishing.

   ○ Have students write a journal entry in which they reflect on their growth. They can respond to the questions, "How did my writing improve? What worked for me as a writer? What are my goals for my next paper?"

- If students need additional support during guided practice, you could plan to conduct additional mini-lessons or to model with groups of students. You should also continue conferencing with small groups during all steps of the writing process. Remember that the goal is *mastery*.

- Once students have completed the second paper, you can ask them to work on another one, or you can proceed with an extension activity (e.g., personal narratives). An explanation about how to develop additional lessons can be found in Chapter 7.

ADDITIONAL MINI-LESSON: USE OF DIALOGUE

Students discuss and practice adding dialogue to stories, then revise stories written by other students to include dialogue.

Lesson Objectives

By the end of this lesson, students will be able to:

- Revise stories to include dialogue.
- Correctly use quotation marks.

Assessment Information

The teacher informally assesses whether students (1) revise stories to include dialogue and (2) correctly use quotation marks.

Procedures

Introduction to Dialogue

Explain to students that they can bring their stories to life by using dialogue. Dialogue helps their characters explain how they think and what they feel, thereby helping the reader to better understand them and their actions. To better illustrate the use of dialogue, you can use an example from a published story.

Use of Dialogue: Teacher Practice

- Display Handout 4.11, "Baseball People and a Game to Remember." With students' feedback, evaluate the paper using the evaluation criteria and point out that even though the elements are present, the quality of the paper could be greatly improved. Identify revision goals for the writer. Model the addition of inner talk and dialogue. Explicitly show how to use quotation marks. Make a revision.

Use of Dialogue: Collaborative Practice

- Ask students to work in groups to add dialogue and share with other groups. You could use a new paper or ask students to work in a different section of the paper used for teacher practice.
- Discuss how the use of descriptions and dialogue add to the quality of a story. Discuss how the reader can now better understand the character and his or her personality.

EXTENSION ACTIVITIES

Personal Narrative

Working on a personal narrative is a natural extension to this set of lessons. All of us are storytellers, and when we describe something that happened in our day, we are creating a *narrative*. There are some specific differences between the genre of personal narratives and the genre of fictional stories. One difference is that the main character in a personal narrative is the author of the paper; thus, the story is written in first person. In addition, a personal narrative is about a specific moment or an event in the writer's life that had some meaning. It might be an experience that taught the writer something or that was funny or moving. The narrative should convey that meaning. Finally, many personal narratives include problems and their solutions, like fictional stories, but some do not. It is all right not to include a problem and its solution as long as the story shares what was meaningful about the experience being described.

Mystery Writing

Mysteries are another genre of fictional writing that students are drawn to and enjoy reading. A number of mystery books are aimed at young readers (e.g., *Nate the Great* by Marjorie Weinman Sharmat, *Cam Jansen* by David Adler). The main difference between mysteries and the fictional stories in this chapter would be the inclusion of clues that the character will need to use in order to resolve the problem/mystery. The mystery story will include a main problem and then the actions and events will provide clues that will lead the character to finally solve the mystery. Another feature of most mysteries is the "red herring," a false clue deliberately included to lead the reader astray and sustain the suspense.

Historical Fiction

This genre is one that connects nicely with social studies. The setting in a historical fiction story connects to a specific time in the past that has some historical significance. Usually the main character is fictional, but other characters may be real historical figures. The problems of the main character must make sense in the context of the historical time. Writing historical fiction can be an excellent way to engage students in learning about the past and understanding the problems faced by people at that time. This sort of historical understanding is critical to learning history. For example, in learning about the Oregon Trail, students might write a fictional piece about young people who traveled to Oregon with their families for free farmland. Writing such a story would require understanding the problems and perspectives of the people who made the trip as well as the Native Americans they met along the way.

Fables

Fables are another type of writing that would be a fairly simple extension to fictional stories. Your students may have read Aesop's Fables, and you could also use those for read-alouds during your instruction. Fables include all the basic elements of other fictional genres. In addition, they conclude with a moral, or a lesson for the readers. In addition, because the characters in a fable are often animals, personification is a characteristic of such stories.

Sample Think-Aloud for Story Writing

Say something like this: "I am a student and my teacher has asked me to write a story. The topic I was given is: **'Write a story about a bee and a bear. Your story will be read at a school celebration, where it will be shared with students and parents.'** I like to write, but writing is hard! However, I know I can write a great story if I try my best and use my strategy. What do I need to do first? Okay, my strategy ladder says that I need to plan. I know that I need to do three things when I plan: I need to FTAP, brainstorm ideas, and complete my GO. What shall I do first? I know, I'll start with FTAP!"

Write FTAP on the board vertically, with one letter underneath the other.

Say, "F stands for *Form*."

Write *Form* next to F.

Say, "I should decide what I am writing. Well, I am writing a story. T stands for *Topic*."

Write *Topic* next to T.

Say, "So, what is my topic? My topic is 'Write a story about a bee and a bear.' Okay, I will write this next to the word *Topic*."

Write *a story about a bee and a bear* next to *Topic*.

Say, "What do I need to do next? I need to say who my audience is, because *A* is for *Audience*."

Write *Audience* next to *A*.

Say, "Well, my teacher said that it will be the entire school and parents. I will write that next to *Audience*."

Write *teachers, parents, school* next to *Audience*.

Ask, "What is my next step? *P* is for *Purpose*, so I need to tell why I am writing this. Well, it will surely help me with my writing, but I am also writing it to entertain my friends, parents, and teachers. I want them to see how good my story is, and I want them to like it. I will write *entertain my parents, teachers, school* next to *Purpose*."

Write *entertain my parents, teachers, school* next to *Purpose*.

Ask, "What have I done so far? I finished the Form, Topic, Audience, and Purpose part of my planning. What do I need to do next? I need to Brainstorm Ideas. Since I'm writing a story, I need to think of ideas about my characters, the place, time, the problem, and the solution. I could use the planning GO for this, but I already know the parts, so I will just jot down ideas next to the elements I need to write in a story."

Write the word *Ideas* on the board. Next write the BME and the elements next to them.

Say, "Let me think! I will write *buzzing* for the bee and I will write that her name is *Beezy*, and I will write *sleeping* for the bear because I think that bears sleep a lot. I will call the bear *Snorry* because the bear may be snoring. I will say that they live in a field, maybe?"

Write some ideas.

Say, "This is hard now! I need to think of something for the problem. They can fight for the honey, or the bee gets annoyed and cannot get her honey because the bear snores, or the bear wants to steal the honey. I will write all these ideas down."

Write *fight for the honey, the bee gets annoyed and cannot get her honey because the bear snores, the bear wants to steal the honey*.

Say, "I have so many problems so far. I cannot go on to say how to find a solution because I cannot choose only one, so I need to think about which one would be best to entertain my audience. I know, though, that in the end I want them to be friends and visit each other and play together. So I will write that."

The completed FTAP and Ideas/Brainstorm look like this:

Plan

Form: *a story*

Topic: *write a story about a bee and a bear*

Audience: *teachers, parents, students*

Purpose: *entertain my parents, teachers, students*

Ideas

Brainstorm

B—*bear/Snorry, bee/Beezy*

long time ago, in a field?

buzzing, sleeping/the bear steals the honey/the bear snores—the bee gets annoyed and cannot get her pollen because the bear snores

M—*fight for the honey/the bear wants to steal the honey. The bear goes to the cave, the bee tricks the bear*

E—*fight/friends visit each other and play, the bear leaves*

Ask, "What have I done so far? I came up with ideas and I think I did a pretty good job! What do I need to do next? My strategy step on my ladder says that I need to organize my ideas. How do I do that? Oh, yes! I need to use my GO."

Draw the GO on the board or on a transparency.

Say, "I will draw the GO because the goal is for me to know the elements and structure of a story and be able to organize my ideas even when I do not have a printed GO with me. I know I need to learn it, so I will try my best!"

Complete the GO using the information from the Ideas/Brainstorm step. The completed GO is shown in Figure 4.5.

Say, "I think I did a great job! I like the information in my GO. Now I need to start my story. Let me think how I could start. I could start by mentioning the general time and say, 'Once upon a time' exactly as I said in my GO."

Write *Once upon a time* on the board.

Beginning	**Characters:** *Buzzing bee and snoring bear, bee is little, bear is big and loud.*
	Time: *Once upon a time.*
	Place: *In a forest in Yellowstone Park.*
	Problem: *The bear snores loudly and the bee cannot get pollen.* *The bee goes back to the same flower by accident.* *The other bees complain, and she may get in trouble with the queen.* *The bee may lose her position.*
Middle	**Event 1:** *Bee tries to talk nicely to the bear.* **Complication 1:** *The bear is rude.* **Event 2:** *Bee tricks the bear with a lie: salmon on the other side of the forest.*
End	**Solution:** *The bear leaves and finds berries on the other side of the forest. The bee can now make honey.*

FIGURE 4.5. Example of a completed GO form.

Say, "Now I need to say who my characters are, so I will say who they are, their names, and I will also say something about the place they live. I will say, **'Once upon a time there was a little bee named Beezy and a big bear named Snorry. They lived in a small part of the forest of the Yellowstone Park.'**"

"This is so hard! Writing is not as easy, but I know I can do it if I use my strategy! I have finished with the time and the characters. Perhaps I can say something more about my characters? I could say what they looked like. I will say, **'The bee was little, the bear was big.'**"

Continue thinking aloud and write the story. Here is what your story might look like, finished:

Once upon a time there was a little bee named Beezy and a big bear named Snorry. They lived in a small part of the forest in Yellowstone Park. They didn't really know each other, as they had nothing in common. The bee was little, the bear was big. The bee was always working, collecting pollen to make honey, and the bear always slept. The bee was buzzing, and the bear was snoring.

The bee was not happy with the bear. His snoring was so loud and so annoying that there were times the bee would lose track of her work and go back to the same flower instead of visiting a new flower. This kept her behind and she was not making her quota! The other bees had started to complain, and Beezy was afraid that they would report her to the queen. Beezy did not want to have to leave the hive or become a nurse and take care of the queen's larva. She liked being a working bee! Beezy decided to go to the bear and ask her to do something about his snoring. She flew next to the bear and said, "Please, Big Bear, could you please try to breathe like other animals and not snore so loudly when you sleep? I cannot think and do my work. There are times that I even lose my balance when I fly and fall!"

The bear looked at the bee with his eyes half closed and said, "Who do you think you are to tell me how to sleep or what to do! I am bigger than you, I have a bigger head, I am smarter, and I can breathe as I wish!"

The bee realized that the big bear's head was indeed big, but the bear was not that clever, so she decided to trick the bear. "Oh, big, strong bear, I wonder why you are here sleeping when I heard from my travels, from flower to flower and from the whispers of the wind, that salmon has arrived at the river on the other side of the forest. I am not asking you to stop snoring for me really, but I wonder why a strong, smart bear like you is not at the river eating fresh salmon but is staying here in the den instead!"

"Salmon?" said the bear. "Why was I not told about it! Why did my cousins not come to wake me up?"

"I don't know," said the bee. "Perhaps they wanted to keep the salmon for themselves."

The bear stood up immediately and, without saying a word to the bee, ran away.

Finally, the bee had managed to get rid of the bear and could concentrate on her work! She was all excited and began buzzing around as she had not done for a long time! As for the bear, on his way to the other side of the forest he found no salmon but tons of berries. He was so excited to find them because he loved berries! So he decided to make a new den there. It seems that the trick that the bee played on the bear worked for both of them!

When you complete the story, say, "I think I did a very good job! Did I finish, though? No, I did not! I need to complete my rubric and see how I could make my story even better and what goals I could set to improve my writing in general."

Display the rubric or write the elements and the scoring system next to them, but keep the story on the board as well. Read each part of the rubric and highlight or underline the information in the story that corresponds to that element. Then mark your score on the rubric.

Say, "What is the first thing I should look for? My rubric says *Beginning* and in the Beginning I need to talk about my character, the place, the time, and the problem. So, the first thing that my rubric asks is, '*Is the main character named and described clearly? Are other characters described?*' I need to read the beginning of my story to see if I have names for my characters and if I have described them clearly. I said '**Once upon a time there was a little bee named Beezy and a big bear named Snorry. They lived in a small part of the forest in Yellowstone Park. They didn't really know each other, as they had nothing in common. The bee was little, the bear was big.**'"

Highlight or underline the information and say, "Certainly my characters have a name! I think, though, that I could say a bit more about them and describe them a bit more. Perhaps I could say what they liked, what they disliked, and how they acted around other animals and insects. I will put a *1* on my rubric."

Say, "The next thing my rubric asks me is, '*Can you tell when the story happens?*' I said, '**Once upon a time,**' Well, the time is general; perhaps I could have said the season, too. I will give myself a score of *1.*

"Next, my rubric asks, '*Is there a **place** that is described clearly?*' I think I did a good job with this because I said a place and I named it, too! Perhaps I could describe it a bit more, though, so the reader could picture the place! I should give myself a score of *1.*

"Next my rubric asks, '*Is there a clearly described problem that sets the story in motion?*' I said in my story, '**The bee was not happy with the bear. His snoring was so loud and so annoying that there were times the bee would lose track of her work and go back to the same flower instead of visiting a new flower. This kept her behind and she was not making her quota! The other bees had started to complain, and Beezy was afraid that they would report her to the queen. Beezy did not want to have to leave the hive or become a nurse and take care of the queen's larva. She liked being a working bee!**'"

Underline the information.

Say, "I think that I described clearly the problem and how annoying the bear's snoring was to Beezy! I will give a score of *2* to myself.

"*The next part of the rubric is about the Middle part of the rubric and asks, 'Is there a clear, logical sequence of events to try to solve the problem? Are the events interesting?' and 'Complications: Are there clear, logical complications that initiate new events or problems? Are they interesting?*' I said, '**Beezy decided to go to the bear and ask him to do something about his snoring. She flew next to the bear and said, "Please, Big Bear, could you please try to breathe like other animals and not snore so loudly when** you sleep? I cannot think and do my work. There are times that I even lose my balance when I fly and fall'"! This was the first event. The complication was that the bear was rude. The next event was that the bee decided to trick the bear. For that I wrote, '**The bee realized that the big bear's head was indeed big, but the bear was not that clever, so she decided to trick the bear. "Oh, big, strong bear, I wonder why you are here sleeping when I heard from my travels, from flower to flower and from the whispers of the wind, that salmon has arrived at the river on the other side of the forest. I am not asking you to stop snoring for me really, but I wonder why a strong, smart bear like you is not at the river eating fresh salmon but staying here in the den instead!'**

"I think that both events and complications are clear, so I will give a score of *2.*

"Next I need to look at the End part of the rubric. The rubric asks, '*Solution: Is the ending a logical solution to the problem?'* In my story I said, '**The bear stood up immediately and without saying a word to the bee, ran away. Finally, the bee had managed to get rid of the bear and could concentrate on her work!'**

"The next question asks, '*Emotion: Can you tell how the characters feel?'* In the story I said, '**She was all excited and began buzzing around as she had not done for a long time! As for the bear, on his way to the other side of the forest, he found no salmon but tons of berries. He was so excited to find them because he loved berries! So he decided to make a new den there. It seems that the trick that the bee played on the bear worked for both of them!'** I think I did a great job! Not only did I describe the ending, but I also described the characters and their feelings. I should get a score of *2* for both.

"Finally, I need to check for other things that can affect my paper. This is the *Other Considerations* part of my rubric. The question is: "*Is there a title that clearly connects to the information in the story?"* Well, I forgot to add a title, so I should give a score of *0* for my title. The next question asks, '*Were the characters' personalities and emotions shown throughout the paper? Did the writer show, not tell?'* I think I could have done better maybe by adding a bit more dialogue. I will give myself a score of *1.* The next question asks, '*Were things described vividly?'* Well, I think I could have done a better job with the descriptions of the characters and maybe of the place or the way the bear ran away. I should get a score of *1.* The final question on the rubric says, '*Were transition words used appropriately throughout the story?'* I only used *finally* at the end. Maybe I could use some transitions for the events."

Underline or circle the transition words.

Say, "I think I should get a *1* for my transitions."

Complete the rubric and then read and respond to its ending questions. The completed rubric is shown in Figure 4.6.

Then make one revision. The revision could look like this:

Once upon a time, <u>a few spring seasons ago,</u> there was a little bee named Beezy and a big bear named Snorry. They lived in a small part of the forest in Yellowstone Park. <u>The bee was in a hive beneath a tree that belonged to the colony for many seasons.</u> <u>A lot of larvae had grown here to be dedicated working bees.</u> The bear was living in a

			0 Not there	1 Could be better	2 Great!
Beginning	**Characters:** Is the main character named and described clearly? Are other characters described?			✓	
	Time: Can you tell when the story happens?			✓	
	Place: Is the place described clearly?			✓	
	Problem: Is there a clearly described problem that sets the story in motion?				✓
Middle	**Events:** Is there a clear, logical sequence of events to try to solve the problem? Are the events interesting?				✓
	Complications: Are there clear, logical complications that initiate new events or problems? Are they interesting?				✓
End	**Solution:** Is the ending a logical solution to the problem?				✓
	Emotion: Can you tell how the characters feel?				✓
Other Considerations	Is there a title that clearly connects to the information in the story?				✓
	Were the characters' personalities and emotions shown throughout the paper? Did the writer **show,** not tell?			✓	
	Were things described vividly? Could the reader see what the characters saw?			✓	
	Were transition words used appropriately throughout the story?			✓	

Reviewer/Writer as Reader

- Overall, was the story interesting to you as a reader? Why? *Yes, it was funny and had a realistic plot. Great problem.*

- What revisions should be made? *I did not have a title. Also, the place was not well described. I could have also done a better job with my transition words.*

Goals

- What could be the writer's goals for the current and future papers? *I should try to complete all the parts of stories. Titles are important, too.*

FIGURE 4.6. Example of a completed rubric.

<u>cave that was well hidden by three bushes. Inside that cave there were tree roots and</u> <u>rocks but the bear did not mind them. The bee and the bear</u> didn't really know each other, <u>and</u> they had nothing in common. The bee was little, the bear was big. The bee was always working, collecting pollen to make honey, and the bear always slept. The bee was buzzing, and the bear was snoring.

Make a few editing changes and complete the think-aloud.

Chart with Story Elements

Beginning	**Characters**: Is the main character named and described clearly? Are other characters described?	
	Time: Can you tell when the story happens?	
	Place: Is the place described clearly?	
	Problem: Is there a clearly described problem that sets the story in motion?	
Middle	**Events**: Is there a clear, logical sequence of events to try to solve the problem? Are the events interesting?	
	Complications: Are there clear, logical complications that initiate new events or problems? Are they interesting?	
End	**Solution**: Is the ending a logical solution to the problem?	
	Emotion: Can you tell how the characters feel?	

Chickcherry and a Stormy Adventure

Once upon a time there was a little hen whose name was Chickcherry. Chickcherry was always cheerful and had a great number of animal and insect friends. Her name was unique. It was given to her by her mother, the great hen, who was so proud of Chickcherry's cherry-colored feathers. How much Chickcherry loved her beautiful, bright feathers! She always looked for opportunities to stand in front of puddles and admire her reflection on the water. Chickcherry had plenty of opportunities to do that. She lived on a farm, and there were always little puddles of water either from the clumsy pigs that were dropping the water pail or from the clean rain that was falling from the sky.

One day, Chickcherry heard thunder and saw lightning in the sky. She knew that the Big Rooster of the Sky was about to let the rain drop. Chickcherry always managed to be close to the barn, but that day it happened that she was far away. She was trying to find juicy worms and was far up on the hill when the rain began. Chickcherry did not like the rain, but she was not afraid of it. After all, it always made beautiful puddles where she could admire her image. She walked as fast as her feet could take her toward the barn. She was soaking wet when she reached the barn. By chance, the rain stopped the moment she stepped her foot in the barn. Chickcherry decided to stay in the warm and dry barn rather than go back out in the muddy field and farmyard! She disliked mud so much. Instead, Chickcherry decided to sleep. She lay in her nest and closed her eyes. Chickcherry woke up from a strong shake of her nest and a loud moo. She opened her eyes and saw her friends, the animals of the barn, looking at her with angry faces and yelling at her. She could not make out what they were saying, but when the Big Horse spoke, everyone else stopped.

"Who are you," asked the Big Horse, "and what did you do to our Chickcherry?"

"I am Chickcherry," Chickcherry said. "What kind of a mean joke is this?"

"You took away our Chickcherry," said Mr. Pig.

"No, I did not," replied Chickcherry. "I am Chickcherry."

"Oh Big Rooster," said Miss Duck, "she sounds like Chickcherry! She is a witch!"

"What are you all talking about?" asked Chickcherry. "I am Chickcherry! Can't you all see my bright, cherry feathers?"

The moment she said that she opened her wings, but they felt heavier and when she turned her head to look at them she thought she was having a nightmare. Her cherry-bright, lovely, beautiful feathers were BROWN, DARK, and DISGUSTING!

Chickcherry was so astonished by the view that she could not say a clack for a second, but then she jumped up and began screaming, "Kooooooooo, Ko, Ko, Ko, Kooooooooooooo" and running in circles. The rest of the animals began to agree with Miss Duck and, terrified, moved away, thinking that she was a witch!

Chickcherry ran out of the barn. She was devastated.

(continued)

Chickcherry and a Stormy Adventure (page 2 of 2)

The house cat that was nearby meowed at her and made her a sign to come closer. Chickcherry was not friendly with that cat. She was always mean to other animals and she would chase them or steal their food! At this moment, though, Chickcherry was desperate. She ran close to the cat who meowed and told her that she knew what had happened to her.

"You know," said the cat, "I should not be helping you, but I am so kind and I am so nice and I am such a charitable soul that I will tell you."

"What, what, what?" asked Chickcherry three times in a row!

"The Big Rooster of the Sky has cursed you for always saying that you are the most beautiful hen in the barn and in the world."

"But, but . . . I said nice things to the other animals as well," said Chickcherry.

"Stop resisting the truth," said the cat, "or else you may turn black like a crow."

Chickcherry sniffed away her tears and bit her tongue.

"What shall I do?" she asked.

"If you bring me milk from the cow, fish from the duck that swims at the pond, then I will take care of this problem for you."

"How?" Asked Chickcherry.

"You do not need to know," said the cat and walked away.

Chickcherry walked reluctantly into the barn and carefully approached the cow. She tried to explain to her what she wanted, but the cow almost stepped on her. Chickcherry left the barn terrified and walked to the pond, hoping that the duck would be kinder.

When she approached the duck and tried to reason with her, the duck dove into the pond and went far away.

Chickcherry was determined to get at least one fish, so she decided to dive into the water. She put one claw in, then a toe, then one foot, and tried not to put her second foot in, but balance herself, as she didn't really like diving in the water. However, as she tried to balance herself, she lost her balance and fell. . . . Oh how much she disliked water! She held her breath and then quickly jumped out. It was then that the duck approached her screaming, "Chickcherry, Chickcherry you are back!"

Chickcherry looked at her reflection and she could see herself again. She had her cherry-bright feathers back! How, though, she wondered, and then she realized what had happened. It was not that the Big Rooster was disappointed in her. It was not that she had done something wrong. It was that she had gotten muddy in the rain, and her feathers looked brown! So what about the cat and what she had said? When Chickcherry shared her experience with the duck, Miss Duck told her that the mean cat was trying to take advantage of her.

Chickcherry decided not to ever speak to the cat again. She returned to the barn where all her friends ran to hug her and kiss her! Chickcherry was the happiest chick in the whole world. She had her friends and her bright cherry feathers back! The next time the cat offered her help, Chickcherry decided that she would check with her friends before doing anything.

The Donkey in the Field

There was a donkey that always wanted to sing in the field when the other animals were resting. The fox had recently given birth to her babies, and she was trying to put them to sleep when donkey began his singing:

"I am the most grey donkey in the Great, Green field. I am grazing in green grass and I am glad that I have a gorgeous voice and a glamorous mane!"

The fox approached the donkey and begged him to be quiet, but the donkey rudely told her to put cotton buds in her ears and her babies' ears and let him enjoy the day. The fox left the field fuming!

The next day she went to the forest council and asked for all the animals to find a solution. No one had any idea, but they were all tired of the donkey's singing.

They didn't know what to do, so they all began singing. As they sang they felt happy and they understood that the donkey was singing because he was happy. Their solution would be to make the donkey sad!

They tried it, but the donkey did not get sad. They decided to leave the forest.

Castles and Ghosts and a Lost Ball

Writing Prompt: *One morning a child looks out the window and discovers that a huge castle has appeared overnight. The child rushes outside to the castle and hears strange sounds coming from it. Someone is living in the castle! The castle door creaks open. The child goes in.*

The moment Josh stepped his foot in the castle, the door shut closed behind him. He could not open it. Josh took a few more steps trying to find the origin of the strange sounds, but he could not tell where they came from. He saw a door on his right, and then he saw a princess. But this was not an ordinary princess. She was a ghost princess, and Josh could tell right away because she flew across the room.

"Boo," said the princess!

"Aaaaa!" said Josh and immediately ran backward, but the moment he turned, the princess appeared in front of him again laughing.

"I am sorry, I am sorry!" said the princess. "Do not run away, I would like some company. I am princess Batia and I live here with my brother Mitt. We are good ghosts like Casper, I promise. Here take this present!"

The moment she said that she handed Josh a baseball. He looked at it and saw his name and some other names, too, but the light was too dim to read them all.

Josh looked at the princess. He asked her when the castle was built and how it appeared in one night. Batia explained that the castle was built many years ago, and it only appeared on Halloween. She also explained that it appeared like this because of a spell that could be broken only when the Red Socks won the series. The moment she said that, Josh felt the fear creeping up his back. "Gosh!" thought Josh. "I am a Red Socks fan. How likely is it that I may get the spell too, and be visible only on Halloween?" That thought got him running within seconds to the next room that had a window and more light. He glanced at the ball but did not stop running. He kept on running and went to a bedroom that had a window, and he saw another ghost. This was a prince ghost, and he held a mitt. He must have been Prince Mitt. Josh turned to the left and went in a small closet. "That is the end of me," he thought. He closed his eyes and that moment he heard, "Wake up! Wake up! It's Halloween morning." Josh opened his eyes and saw his brother laughing and jumping up and down on his bed. "It was just a dream," whispered Josh! He looked at his hand and there was no baseball there anymore. "Too bad in a way!" he thought. All the Red Socks players had signed that ball!

Spinning Away: A Lesson on Friendship

Once upon a time there was a spider named Spinny.

One day Spinny was at work spinning his web when he saw another spider with beautiful colors approaching.

"Good morning, grey spider," said the colorful spider.

"Good morning to you, too," responded Spinny. "What brings you to my webland?"

"Oh," said the new spider. "I decided to move from the other side of the house to this one as the sun is brighter and warmer. Do you mind if I do?"

"I certainly do!" said Spinny with an angry voice. "This is my side of the house, and I like it to stay this way!"

"But we can share the sun, and you will have some company, too!" responded the beautiful spider.

"I don't want company!" Spinny said angrily. "I just want my peace and quiet!"

The beautiful spider looked at Spinny with surprise.

"Wow, you are rude!" she said. "I just wanted to be your friend, and I thought you would like to be my friend too."

"I don't need friends!" said Spinny and turned his back.

"Well, my name is Swirly, in case you wondered. I will leave you alone and go back to the other side of the house. I will be as far away as you need me to be."

After saying that Swirly turned and walked to the other side of the house. There, she began crafting her web. It was such a strong web, and there were no holes or errors in her design. It was surely the strongest web Spinny had ever seen! He was not going to admit it though. He turned to his work and tried to patch up his web that had more holes than a spaghetti strainer.

The days went by and Spinny could see that Swirly always had a great catch. Her web was full of silk-covered flies and mosquitoes, but Spinny's was as empty as a dried-up well. Spinny was hungry and his stomach was growling with persistence. The growling was so loud that sometimes the wind would carry it to the other side of the house and Swirly would hear it. She felt so bad for Spinny, but she could do nothing, as his stubbornness was bigger than his brain.

Transition Words

Beginning—for time and place

- Once upon a time, . . .
- Once, . . .
- Long ago, . . . OR In a time not long ago, . . .
- In the . . .

Beginning—for description of events or characters

- Also, . . .
- In addition, . . .
- Further, . . .
- Furthermore, . . .

Middle—for sequence of actions

- First, . . .
- Second, . . .
- Then, . . .
- Next, . . .
- In addition, . . .

End

- Finally, . . .
- In the end, . . .

Eggy the Hen

Once upon a time there was a hen whose name was Eggy. Eggy lived with her friends, the farm animals, in a barn.

Eggy was happy with her friends, but she was always so sad to be a hen. Eggy wanted to be a cow. So, one day she went to the house, bathed herself in white flour and drew black spots with a marker and walked in the field.

The rooster who saw her asked her why she was covered in flour, but the hen told him that she was a cow. The rooster told her that she was not a cow but a hen, but Eggy ignored him.

The cow nearby saw Eggy and asked her why she was covered in flour, but Eggy told her that she was now a cow. The cow laughed and asked her to moo. Eggy tried to moo, but the only thing she could do was cluck.

She felt embarrassed, and as she ran back to the barn she ruffled her feathers for the flour to go away. Then she took a bath and went to see her friends, the hens. She decided that it was so much funnier to be able to cluck than moo and from then on, she was happy to be a hen.

Say Food No More

Writing Prompt: *Imagine this! You open your eyes and you are in an alien spacecraft. What will happen next?*

I closed my eyes. I opened them again. I closed them again and forced my brain to think that I was sleeping and I was waking up in my room to see my annoying brother. I opened one eyelid. I closed it again. I was not in a dream. I was in a real nightmare. I was in a spacecraft. I opened my eyes and walked across the room. "Hold on, George," I thought. "How can I possibly breathe in this environment? Do aliens also breathe oxygen like humans? Well, I guess they do," I thought, and took another breath.

I walked across the space. Everything was so shiny and metallic. I was scared to touch anything. And then my stomach growled once, and then twice and three times. I was hungry and needed to eat. I decided to explore the spacecraft. I could tell we were moving because I was getting dizzy exactly as if I was onboard a ship. I looked around for a door, but there was no door. I figured that the residents of this ship would be more advanced and did not need any doors, but how did they move from one room to the other? I went around the room and touched the metallic surface of the wall. I kept on going around hoping that I would feel the opening to another room. There was nothing. "This is ridiculous," I yelled and hit the wall. That moment a metallic sheet moved inward and up and a new room appeared in front of my eyes. I walked in, and my nose was immediately captivated by what my eyes saw laying on top of a metallic table. There was FOOD, and the salvation to my hunger. I started eating nonstop until I felt something grabbing my shoulder and shaking me. "Stop drooling and kicking!" It was my annoying brother, and I had a nightmare.

More Than What Your Eyes Could See

Nancy stared out her window to the house across the street. It was an abandoned house. Two of its windows were broken and the siding was falling off. When it was windy, you could hear an eerie sound as the wind passed through the broken windows. "I wonder what is inside the house," thought Nancy.

"Five hundred," said Marcus as he approached Nancy. Marcus was her neighbor and they have been friends since they were in first grade.

"What did you say?" asked Nancy.

"Half of 1,000 is 500," said Marcus.

"Stop with your silly jokes," said Nancy. "I want to see what is inside that house."

"I am not going in there," replied Marcus. "My father says that it is a haunted house."

"Haunted-smaunted," said Nancy. "Don't be a child!"

"Well, I am sorry I am not interested in breaking into someone else's house!" said Marcus.

"We are not breaking into the house! We can just take a peek," suggested Nancy.

"Okay," said Marcus, "I am okay with that."

Marcus and Nancy got across the street and dared each other to step into the yard. Then they both walked toward the house. From the porch they peeked through a broken window, and to their astonishment they saw a fire in the fireplace, food on the table, and a room full of toys and books. How was this possible? The house was abandoned, and there was no smoke coming out of the chimney. There was not supposed to be any of these things happening. Before Marcus and Nancy had a chance to share their thoughts, a trap door in the floor opened, and they both fell underneath the house. They landed on top of a pile of cushions. It was then that they saw a green humanoid across the room. This was Charlie who was an alien and loved Earth. He loved Earth so much that he had begged his parents to let him stay. To protect him, his parents had turned the exterior of the house to an unattractive and scary-looking place, so no one would bother Charlie. But Charlie was lonely. Marcus, Nancy, and Charlie became the best friends ever.

Watch What You Wish For!

Jack put the book on Greek myths on his lap and yawned. It was still raining, and he did not have anything else to do but read that book he borrowed from his aunt. His aunt was a traveler and an explorer, and every time she saw him would ask him if he had read that book and when could she have it back. So, this rainy Friday afternoon was the best day to finish the book and tell his aunt that he had read it. He had just finished one chapter and was half way through another one about King Midas. The first chapter described how Midas had his ears turned into a donkey's ears as a punishment by the god Apollo, and in this chapter Midas had been given the gift of the gold touch. It would be fun to have donkey ears, thought Jack, or be able to have whatever he touched turn into gold. With donkey ears he would probably be able to hear better; also, if he could turn everything into gold, he would be rich. He hadn't even finished that thought when one of the book pages turned and out of the book jumped the gods Apollo and Dionysus. Jack jumped up and the book fell on the floor. Jack wanted to be like King Midas, so the gods granted him Midas's "gift."

But Jack did not tell them what gift he wanted. Did he get the ears or the golden touch? Hesitantly, he brought his hands to his head and touched his ears. Indeed he had donkey ears. Jack could not believe his touch. He ran to a mirror and he could indeed see his "gift." He did have donkey ears. This was so cool!

He could hear everything. Jack went to meet his parents. His mother's screams were too loud for his ears. The same second, his father jumped up and his laptop almost broke as it hit the ground. His parents' questions were hurting his ears. His mother was calling their family doctor while his father put on his glasses, and was demanding that Jack hold still so he could look at his ears and find his real ones. Why did he even wish to have donkey ears? Didn't he learn from Midas's story? If his parents reacted that way, imagine how the world would react. Jack managed to escape his father and run to his room.

His father ran behind him while his mother called their doctor. Jack was upset with the book and his aunt who got it for him. He kicked it away and the book ended up underneath his bed.

"I wish I had the other gift," said Jack.

The moment he said that his ears turned back into regular, little human ears. As he stepped back and touched his door to let his father in, the door turned yellow and heavy. It was gold! He pushed the door but the door was too heavy to open. Jack got panicked. Is that what happened to that chapter he never finished? Where was that book? He remembered kicking it, and as he tried to reach it from underneath the bed, the bed turned into gold. He touched another book, which turned into gold and with that one he touched his nightstand. The nightstand did not turn into gold. Using that book, Jack pulled out the book of myths, turned the pages, and read the rest of the chapter. He needed to wash in the river Pactolus and had to go to Turkey. What if he washed himself in the rain, he thought. Jack opened his window and held his hand out. That moment he saw little pieces of gold fall off his hands. He did the same with his other hand and then within minutes he was free of gold. It was at that moment that he heard a loud voice, "Will you for once close the window? Look, it is raining and water is coming in," his mother said rushing to close the window by his bed. All this was a dream? What if . . .

Baseball People and a Game to Remember

It was a Saturday afternoon when John walked with his father to baseball practice. John did not like baseball, but he did not want to disappoint his father who was a baseball fan and always was willing to practice with him. John would much rather play soccer, but when he tried to discuss it with his older brother, Peter, he scolded him and told him that baseball was far better than soccer. Well, John did not think so, but sometimes silence is golden. John looked at the field and sighed.

During practice, the most unexpected thing happened. John had finished his practice and was sitting on the bench when the ball hit him on the head. John held his head, screamed with pain and felt tears developing in his eyes. His father ran toward him and so did the other players, but what did John see. They were all tiny baseballs and were rolling on the floor. John began to laugh, but then he looked at himself and saw that he was also a baseball. He tried to walk, but the only thing he could do was roll. It was then that he fainted.

"Are you okay, son?" John heard his father's voice and felt water running on his face.

He opened his eyes and saw his father's worried face.

"You surely gave us a scare!" said the coach.

"Where am I?" asked John.

"You fainted, John, that is all," said his dad. "I think it is time to go back home. What do you think?"

"I can give you a lift," said the coach.

On the way home, John was struggling with the thought of telling his father that he did not want to play any more baseball. Once they reached home and before they walked in, he turned to his dad and told him that he did not want to play baseball, but he preferred to play soccer. His father told him that if he had been hit with a soccer ball, he would have been seeing stars. In the end though, he told him that he would still support him no matter what he chose to do. The next day, John and his dad enrolled John in a soccer team. This was the last time that John saw little baseball people in his life!

Planning Materials

PLAN

Form: What am I writing?   Essay/Paper   Paragraph   Letter   Other _____

T

A

P

IDEAS

Brainstorm

(continued)

Story Graphic Organizer (GO)

Beginning	**Characters:**
	Place:
	Time:
	Problem:
Middle	**Events/Complications:** 1. 2. 3. 4.
End	**Solution:**
	Emotion:

Rubric for Self-Evaluation and Peer Review of Story Writing

Date: _____

Writer's Name: _____ Reviewer's Name: _____

		0 Not there	1 Could be better	2 Great!
Beginning	**Characters**: Is the main character named and described clearly? Are other characters described?			
	Time: Can you tell when the story happens?			
	Place: Is the place described clearly?			
	Problem: Is there a clearly described problem that sets the story in motion?			
Middle	**Events**: Is there a clear, logical sequence of events to try to solve the problem? Are the events interesting?			
	Complications: Are there clear, logical complications that initiate new events or problems? Are they interesting?			
End	**Solution**: Is the ending a logical solution to the problem?			
	Emotion: Can you tell how the characters feel?			
Other Considerations	Is there a title that clearly connects to the information in the story?			
	Were the characters' personalities and emotions shown throughout the paper? Did the writer **show,** not tell?			
	Were things described vividly? Could the reader see what the characters saw?			
	Were transition words used appropriately throughout the story?			

Reviewer/Writer as Reader

• Overall, was the story interesting to you as a reader? Why?

• What revisions should be made?

Goals

• What could be the writer's goals for the current and future papers?

Support in Memorization of Story Elements

Date: _____   Writer's Name: _____

Beginning	• _____
	• _____
	• _____
	• _____
Middle	• _____
	• _____
End	• _____
	• _____
Other Considerations!	_____
	_____
	_____
	_____

What did I miss? _____

_____

_____

What should be my study goals? _____

_____

_____

Chart of Senses

Topic: _____ Date: _____ Name: _____

	Sight	
	Hearing	
	Smell	
	Touch	
	Taste	

From *Developing Strategic Writers through Genre Instruction: Resources for Grades 3–5* by Zoi A. Philippakos, Charles A. MacArthur, and David L. Coker Jr. Copyright 2015 by The Guilford Press. Permission to photocopy this material is granted to purchasers of this book for personal use only (see copyright page for details). Purchasers can download additional copies of this material from *www.guilford.com/philippakos-forms*.

Chapter 5

Persuasive Writing

Persuasive writing is all around us, including everything from the emotional appeals of advertisements, to everyday conversations about the latest news, to reviews of books and movies, to editorials on public issues, to the evidence-based reasoning of scientific papers. In school, persuasive writing usually means argumentative writing. However, it can also include critical evaluations, such as book or movie reviews, and other responses to texts. In argumentative writing, writers take a position on an issue and offer reasons supported by evidence, examples, or explanations. As students get older, it is also expected that they will offer counterarguments or discuss both sides and propose a compromise. In critical evaluations, writers offer an evaluation—another kind of opinion—and support it with reasons and evidence. At the elementary school level, the CCSS (CCSSI, 2010) expect students to write opinion pieces about topics and about books they have read.

Persuasive, or argumentative, writing can be challenging for students (Coirier & Golder, 1993; Golder & Coirier, 1994; Carter, Patterson, Donovan, Ewing. & Roberts, 2011; Ferretti, MacArthur, & Dowdy, 2000). One reason that persuasive writing is challenging is because it requires writers to consider the perspectives of other people. In an oral argument, each side can listen to the positions and thoughts of others because they are presented in dialogue. However, in persuasive writing, the writer must anticipate the reaction of readers and plan to convince people who have different perspectives. Generating convincing reasons requires attention to an audience as well as topic. Writers need to think about their audience and whether the reasons and evidence they use will be convincing to their readers.

As students get older, they face the additional challenge of considering opposing positions explicitly and either rebutting them or suggesting compromise solutions. Addressing opposing positions creates new challenges. People have a natural tendency to pay attention to reasons that confirm their opinions and ignore conflicting evidence. But critical thinking requires careful consideration of multiple perspectives, and one of the main reasons for teaching persuasive writing is to develop critical thinking.

Another reason that persuasive writing is difficult is that students have little experience reading persuasive texts (Duke, 2000). Most of their reading is narrative and informative, which means they have less understanding of the content and organization of persuasive texts. However, teachers can provide read-alouds of children's literature selections that include persuasion. They can also consider raising critical questions while teaching literature, science, and social studies. For example, to prepare students to write book reviews, teachers can engage students in evaluating the qualities of the literature used in read-alouds and supporting their evaluations with specific evidence from the texts.

The CCSS provide guidelines for students' persuasive writing (see Table 5.1). From as early as kindergarten, young students are expected to respond persuasively via drawing and to express an opinion about a book. By the end of second grade they are expected to include reasons on their papers and a clear conclusion. In grade 3, they are expected to provide an introduction to their topic, a clear opinion, reasons that support their stated opinion, and a conclusion. In grades 4 and 5, students are expected to provide a clear organization of a persuasive essay; introduce their topic; support it with reasons, including facts and details; and finally provide closure. In addition, students should be able to use transition words to link ideas and show the relationship between them. Also, they are expected to clearly organize their work in a way that supports the flow of ideas and to use resources appropriately to support their analysis (e.g., use sources as evidence in text).

TABLE 5.1. Persuasive Writing and Reading Standards for Grades 3–5

Grade 3	Grade 4	Grade 5
Writing		
Write opinion pieces on topics or texts, supporting a point of view with reasons.	*Write opinion pieces on topics or texts, supporting a point of view with reasons and information.*	1. Introduce a topic or text clearly, state an opinion, and create an organizational structure in which ideas are logically grouped to support the writer's purpose.
1. Introduce the topic or text they are writing about, state an opinion, and create an organizational structure that lists reasons.	1. Introduce a topic or text clearly, state an opinion, and create an organizational structure in which related ideas are grouped to support the writer's purpose.	2. Provide logically ordered reasons that are supported by facts and details.
2. Provide reasons that support the opinion.	2. Provide reasons that are supported by facts and details.	3. Link opinion and reasons using words, phrases, and clauses (e.g., *consequently, specifically*).
3. Use linking words and phrases (e.g., *because, therefore, since, for example*) to connect opinion and reasons.	3. Link opinion and reasons using words and phrases (e.g., *for instance, in order to, in addition*).	4. Provide a concluding statement or section related to the opinion presented.
4. Provide a concluding statement or section.	4. Provide a concluding statement or section related to the opinion presented.	
	Reading informational texts	
	Draw evidence from literary or informational texts to support analysis, reflection, and research.	
	Apply grade 4 reading standards to informational texts (e.g., "Explain how an author uses reasons and evidence to support particular points in a text").	Apply grade 5 reading standards to informational texts (e.g., "Explain how an author uses reasons and evidence to support particular points in a text, identifying which reasons and evidence support which point[s]").

The detailed lessons in this chapter focus on the genre of opinion essays. Students write about controversial topics that involve a decision or action (e.g., Should students go on field trips or not?). Topics draw on students' common everyday knowledge. Students learn to introduce the issue and state their opinion in the introduction, provide reasons supported by evidence, and conclude by restating their opinion and leaving the reader with something to think about.

In addition to the detailed lessons, several extensions are discussed briefly. The first extension is an alternative genre of persuasive writing: book reviews. Like general opinion essays, book reviews include an opinion—an evaluation of the book—supported by reasons, evidence, and a conclusion. The genre elements differ slightly; reviews begin with information about the book and use different types of evidence. This genre requires students to use evidence from texts and meet the expectation of the CCSS that students will write persuasively about "texts" as well as topics.

The second extension is to write short argumentative responses to texts, especially literature. Students are asked to write a short response that gives their position related to specific questions about the text. Students must then use specific evidence from the text to support their position. Such short responses give students practice using information from texts as part of persuasive writing, but without having to integrate too much information or write a full essay. At the same time, they are gaining practice with a genre that will be important later in school.

The third extension involves using sources to write opinion essays, and the fourth extension adds explicit consideration of opposing positions. Although the CCSS do not call for students to use opposing positions until middle school, recent research findings suggest that students in grades 4 and 5 are able to develop this element (Philippakos, 2012). Teachers can decide whether to include these more advanced lessons after considering the experience of their students with persuasive writing.

The lessons follow the general outline described in Chapter 3. In preparation for writing instruction, teachers introduce the elements and features of persuasive writing through read-alouds and discussion. Because there are not many persuasive texts in elementary school, we have used fiction to introduce the genre. Students learn to identify opinions and the reasons and evidence used to support them. They consider whether the reasons make sense and whether the points that the character makes are valid or not. This instruction is intended to improve reading comprehension and prepare students for writing. It can also serve as the introduction to a mini-lesson on an element; a mini-lesson on convincing reasons is provided.

The writing lessons begin with a general discussion of persuasion and an analysis of good and weak examples of opinion essays. As in other instructional chapters, instruction focuses on the elements and features of the genre. The genre elements are reflected in the planning strategy and in the evaluation criteria used during revision. Students learn planning strategies to develop their ideas and organize them in a clear manner. In addition, instruction in evaluation is critical. Finally, the lessons include writing tasks that do not involve explicit consideration of opposing positions.

The lessons are based on the Strategy for Teaching Strategies (see Figure 3.1). You may want to review the instructional procedures in Chapter 3. Also, you may want to review the Writing Strategy Ladder and the Be Strategic! strategy in Chapter 2.

The rest of this chapter includes (1) a lesson outline that provides information about the read-aloud tasks and a synopsis for each writing lesson, (2) sample writing prompts that you could use for assessment and instruction, (3) detailed writing lessons on opinion essays with ready-to-use materials, (4) extension activities for additional genres, (5) resources for the teaching of additional genres, and (6) forms that are used in more than one lesson and that you could display in your classroom.

LESSON OUTLINE

Read-Aloud Lesson(s)

Introduction to the Genre

Students are introduced to the purpose of persuasive writing and the elements of the genre during read-alouds that are conducted several times prior to the writing lessons and serve three functions: They support students' learning of the genre elements and promote discussion of the ways that authors present the information. The books also function as mentor texts for mini-lessons.

Preassessment

Students write in response to a persuasive writing prompt (see Sample Topics for Writing Assessment/Instruction).

Persuasive Writing Lessons

Lesson 1: Introduction—Evaluation of Good and Weak Examples and Self-Evaluation

Students review the purpose and elements of persuasion. They evaluate good and weak papers, applying evaluation criteria. They evaluate their own papers and set personal goals for improvement.

Lesson 2: Modeling How to Write a Persuasive Paper

Students review the persuasive elements and observe the teacher during think-aloud modeling of planning, drafting, evaluating to revise, and editing of a persuasive paper.

Lesson 3: Self-Regulation—Mini-Lesson on Convincing Reasons

Students learn a strategy that helps them monitor their work and reflect on the application of the writing strategies. As a part of this lesson, students develop "self-talk." In the second part of the lesson, students discuss and practice the development of convincing reasons.

Lesson 4: Collaborative Writing of a Persuasive Paper

Teacher and students collaboratively use the Writing Strategy Ladder to Plan, Draft, Evaluate to Revise, and Edit a persuasive paper. During collaborative writing, the teacher scaffolds students' application of the strategy and does the writing as students provide the ideas and sentences.

Lesson 5: Students Plan and Draft Their Own Persuasive Papers

Students begin working on their own papers, using the planning and drafting steps of the strategy ladder. The teacher monitors the use of the strategy and provides support as needed.

Lesson 6: Preparation for Peer Review and Self-Evaluation

Students practice evaluating persuasive papers, writing suggestions, and making revisions. Students also self-evaluate their papers and set goals for revision.

Lesson 7: Peer Review and Revision

Students peer-review in pairs or small groups, applying the evaluation criteria. Students compare their self-evaluations with the comments of their peers, set goals for revision, and make revisions.

Lesson 8: Editing

Students examine their paper for editing errors. By using the editing strategy (SCIPS), students identify surface-level errors and correct them. Teachers can choose to teach a specific grammatical/editing skill, practice it with students, and ask students to make changes to their essays. Additionally, students set editing goals and reflect on their performance and progress.

Publishing Guidelines

It is important for students to share some of their work with a larger audience. See Chapter 3 for a discussion of ideas about opportunities for publishing. These guidelines do not comprise a specific lesson, but rather present ideas for discussing publishing options with your students. The specifics will depend on what sort of publishing you have chosen.

Guidelines for Continuous Guided Practice to Mastery

It is important for students to write more than one paper in a genre to develop mastery of that genre. As students write additional papers, they typically work more quickly and feel much more competent. Teachers can then focus their attention on students who need more support.

Read–Aloud Lesson(s)

INTRODUCTION TO THE GENRE

Students are introduced to the purpose of persuasive writing and the elements of the genre during read-alouds that are conducted several times prior to the writing lessons and serve three functions: They support students' learning of the genre elements and promote discussion of the ways that authors present the information. The books also function as mentor texts for mini-lessons.

Lesson Objectives

By the end of this lesson, students will be able to:

- Explain the meaning of persuasion and discuss why, when, and where people speak, read, and write persuasively.
- Identify the opinion, reasons with evidence, and conclusion in persuasive texts.
- Discuss some things that make reasons convincing.

Materials for Read-Aloud Lesson

- Form 5.1. Planning Materials (FTAP, Ideas, GO)—only use the GO section
- Handout 5.1. Chart with Persuasive Elements
- Book: *Dear Mrs. LaRue: Letters from Obedience School* by Mark Teague

Notes

- You can use a different book than the sample book used in this lesson for your read-aloud. For this task, you may consider the list of books we provide in Figure 5.1. Remember

---

- *I Wanna Iguana* by Karen Kauffman Orloff
- *I Wanna New Room* by Karen Kauffman Orloff
- *Click, Clack, Moo* by Doreen Cronin
- *Earrings* by Judith Viorst
- *Dear Mrs. LaRue* by Mark Teague
- *Hey, Little Ant* by Philip M. Hoose
- *The Perfect Pet* by Margie Palatini
- *My Brother Dan's Delicious* by Steven L. Layne
- *Duck for President* by Doreen Cronin
- *Old Henry* by Joan W. Blos
- *Oil Spill* by Melvin Berger
- *George vs. George* by Rosalyn Schanzer
- *Can I Have a Stegosaurus, Mom? Can I? Please!* by Lois G. Grambling

FIGURE 5.1. Sample list of books for read-alouds on persuasive genre.

that you can conduct more than one read-aloud before you begin the writing lessons, and you can also continue using them after you begin your writing instruction.

Procedures

Discussion of Persuasion

- Explain to students that often authors attempt to persuade readers on a topic through their characters and plot. Ask students if they have heard the word *persuasion* and if they have ever used persuasion. Support them in making connections to personal experiences (e.g., have a sleepover, eat ice cream, not do homework). Explain that persuasion is used when a person tries *to convince* others to agree with his or her opinion.

- Explain that people of all ages write persuasively, too. Discuss when people might write persuasively. Some examples that students might mention or that you could suggest include letters to the principal or a teacher, political campaigns, advertisements, book and movie reviews.

Introduction of Persuasive Elements

- Explain that for a persuasive paper to be effective, there are specific parts that need to be present. Using the chart with persuasive elements (see Handout 5.1), explain that persuasive papers have a Beginning, Middle, and an End. Explain that the Beginning has information about the topic and the writer's opinion. The Middle has the reasons for the writer's opinion and evidence to support the reasons. (Note: if you decided to include an opposing position, you should use Handout 5.17 and explain that the Middle has the "ME" section that provides reasons and evidence to support the writer's opinion and the "OTHERS" section that states the opposing position, the reasons, and the rebuttal.) Finally, the End has a restatement of the writer's opinion and a message to the reader. If you have taught story writing, point out to students that this type of writing also has a Beginning, Middle, and End.

Read-Aloud

- Explain that you will read a book in which the character is attempting to persuade another character to agree to do something. The character is writing letters, and together you and the students will try to identify the persuasive elements and record them. Students should think about the content and how convincing the character is.

- Read the book *Dear Mrs. LaRue: Letters from Obedience School* by Mark Teague. As you read, stop after each letter and ask yourself about the persuasive elements. Ike's opinion is that he should not be at the obedience school, and each letter gives reasons and evidence (e.g., he is a much better behaved dog compared to the other residents of the site—they are bad dogs, and he is not). Discuss whether the reasons and evidence are convincing. Using the genre elements, complete the graphic organizer (GO) in Form 5.1 (see Figure 5.2 for a completed example).

Beginning	**Topic:**
	Opinion: *Ike should not be in the obedience school.*
Middle	**Reason** 1: *He does not belong there.*
	Evidence: *The other dogs are very bad.*
	Reason 2: *The school is not good.*
	Evidence: *He is mistreated. He is asked to perform "meaningless tasks." He is refused the right to use a typewriter because it "disturbs other dogs."*
	Reason 3: *She needs him and should be with her.*
	Evidence: *He has saved her multiple times. She needs him to cross the street. They had joyful times together.*
End	**Restate Opinion:**
	Think:

FIGURE 5.2. Example of a completed GO for read-aloud on *Dear Mrs. LaRue: Letters from Obedience School* by Mark Teague (for your reference).

- Once you have completed the task, review the information and the purpose of persuasive writing. Discuss whether Ike's reasons were convincing and whether Mrs. LaRue should listen to his plea.

End of Lesson

- Explain that in the next weeks students will learn how to write opinion essays that are convincing to their readers.

SAMPLE TOPICS FOR WRITING ASSESSMENT/INSTRUCTION

Note: A list of sample writing topics is provided that you could use for preassessment, guided practice, and postassessment. The topics included in this list should not limit your choices. Consider developing topics that will engage your students and that will be authentic in your setting.

1. Your school is considering canceling all field trips because they cost a lot of money and some families cannot afford to pay for them. Some people say that this is a good idea and that the school is thinking about the families' needs. Others say that field trips are important for students' learning and should not be cancelled. Write a paper explaining whether you think that students should go on field trips or not. Use specific reasons and examples to support your response.

2. Technology is a big thing today! Some people say that students should learn how to use all kinds of technology from as early as first grade. Other people say that students in the early grades are too young for some kinds of technology. Choose one technology tool (e.g., word processing, videogames) and write a paper explaining whether you think that students should learn how to use that tool early in their school life or not. Use specific reasons and examples to support your response.

3. Many schools ask their students to wear uniforms. Some people say that this is good because it helps students be kinder and nicer to each other. Other people disagree and say that wearing uniforms constrains students' creativity. Write a paper explaining whether you think that students should wear uniforms or not. Use specific reasons and examples to support your response.

4. Some people are worried about what students learn at school and think that students should spend more time learning from teachers. Therefore, they suggest reducing recess time only to 5 minutes so that more time can be used for reading and math instruction. Other people say that students should have time to play and stretch their muscles. Write a paper explaining whether you think that recess time should be reduced or not. Use specific reasons and examples to support your response.

5. Students often have small pets at school such as hamsters or lizards. Some people say that larger pets such as cats, dogs, and rabbits should not be in the classroom because they can be disruptive. Other people say that all pets help children learn how to care for others. Write a paper explaining whether you think that students should be allowed to have larger pets in the classroom or not. Use specific reasons and examples to support your response.

6. Recently, a lot of schools have added instruction in a language other than English. Some people say that this is a nice addition because the students are learning about a culture other than their own. Other people say that learning a new language can confuse students in their own language, and schools should not teach a language other than English. Write a paper advocating whether you think that schools should teach a second language or not. Use specific reasons and examples to support your response.

7. A lot of parents ask their children to do chores at home. Some people say that doing chores can help children become responsible adults. Other people disagree and say that children should not do chores and should enjoy their life as they grow up. Write a paper explaining whether you think that children should be asked to do chores at home or not. Use specific reasons and examples to support your response.

Persuasive Writing Lessons

LESSON 1: INTRODUCTION—EVALUATION OF GOOD AND WEAK EXAMPLES AND SELF-EVALUATION

Students review the purpose and elements of persuasion and evaluate good and weak papers, applying evaluation criteria. They evaluate their own papers as well and set personal goals for improvement.

Lesson Objectives

By the end of this lesson students will be able to:

- Recall the elements of persuasion.
- Apply the evaluation criteria to score and comment on a paper.
- Evaluate their own papers and set specific goals for personal improvement.

Assessment Information

The teacher assesses whether students can (1) recall the persuasive elements, (2) apply the evaluation criteria to score papers, and (3) set personal goals for improvement.

Notes

- Students will self-evaluate their preassessment paper. You can also score students' papers using the rubric in Form 5.2.

- We provide you with sample papers for this lesson; however, depending on your students' grade, level, and needs, you may decide to use different samples.

- During practice applying the evaluation criteria, students also work in small groups. You may want to assign students to groups ahead of time. For this you may use preassessment data (see Chapter 3) and consult the study guide on pages 244–245.

- During students' self-evaluation, you can also evaluate a paper you have written. It is important for students to also see you as a writer.

Materials for Lesson 1

- Form 5.2. Rubric for Self-Evaluation and Peer Review of Persuasive Writing
- Form 5.2 (copies for students' self-evaluations and for small-group evaluations)
- Handout 5.1. Chart with Persuasive Elements
- Handout 5.2. Well-Written Paper for Evaluation, "Saturday: This is Our Day!"

- Handout 5.3. Weak Paper for Evaluation, "Vending Machines in Cafeterias: Not for the Best but for the Worst"

- Handout 5.4. "Vending Machines: Why Not?"

- Handout 5.5. "Vending Machines: Necessary"

- Students' preassessment (see sample topics for writing assessment/instruction, pp. 106–107)

- Completed chart of elements from read-aloud

Procedures

Review

- Ask students what persuasion is and why people write persuasively. Refer to the chart you completed during one of the read-alouds and to the elements of persuasion. Review the elements. You may also give a quiz and ask students to record the elements of persuasive writing.

Identification and Evaluation of Persuasive Elements in a Well-Written Paper and a Weak Paper

- Explain that in order to tell whether a paper is well written, it is important to know the genre elements and their organization. In persuasion, readers would first expect to read the writer's position, then read the reasons and evidence, and finally the conclusion.

- Explain that writers can develop their "readers' sense" by reading well-written papers and weak papers. They can then look for the elements and use a rubric to evaluate the presence and quality of those elements and record suggestions for improvement. Explain that this process will help students better learn the elements.

- Present and explain the elements of the rubric for evaluation and its scoring system (0 means that the element is absent, 1 that the element is not clear or well-developed, and 2 means that the element is clearly developed) (Form 5.2). Point out that it contains the elements of persuasion. Also point to the section of the rubric called *Other Considerations*. Explain that in a persuasive paper, writers need more than the elements when they evaluate it. Transition words and other features can also affect the quality of the paper. Read each of the *Other Considerations* from the rubric and briefly discuss how its presence or absence could affect the quality of a persuasive paper. Explain that students will use this rubric when working with their peers and when they evaluate their own work.

Evaluation of a Well-Written Paper

- Explain that you will first read and examine the elements of a well-written paper with the students.

- Display for students and read out loud a well-written paper (Handout 5.2). After you have completed the read-aloud, discuss with students their general impressions of the paper. Explain what your first reaction to this paper is (e.g., liked it, was convinced, appreciated the language used). Explain that this is a well-written paper, but in order to be certain, you will look for the elements and score them using the rubric in Form 5.2.

- Display or draw the rubric on the board.

- Read each evaluation question from the rubric and invite students to locate that element in the paper. Underline each element, turn to the rubric, assign a score, and explain your thinking. When you provide comments and take notes for making suggestions, use the phrase "Perhaps the writer could say. . . ." This will help students develop a model about how to make constructive suggestions when they peer-review. Students can participate, but you should lead the process. Refer to the elements when you decide the next step to take. Complete the rubric and then respond to its questions at the end with your students' input.

Evaluation of a Weak Paper

- Briefly review the elements of persuasion. Explain that you will read a second paper with the students and evaluate it using the persuasive elements.

- Display the paper (Handout 5.3) for students and read it out loud. If there are editing issues, point them out, but do not shift the focus of the lesson to them. Ask students to share their general impressions of the paper. Then explain that you will evaluate the paper using the evaluation rubric.

- Think out loud as you look for each element, underline it, and score it (see Figures 5.3 and 5.4). In instances where you think that a score of 1 is too generous but a score of zero is too strict, you may assign half a point (i.e., evidence for Reason 2 in Figure 5.4).

Vending Machines in Cafeterias

In our school we have cafeteria food and it is the best. We have salads and fruits, and we get pizza every Friday. In general, we have healthy options and everyone supports a healthy lifestyle [TOPIC]. Say no to vending machines! [OPINION]

One reason [TRANSITION] is that if vending machines are in schools, students will be tempted to buy unhealthy snacks [REASON 1]. Most snacks contain saturated fats that can increase the levels of cholesterol in the blood, and then increase the risk for a heart attack. In general snacks and unhealthy options do not contain the vitamins and nutrients that young bodies need to develop [EVIDENCE].

[? NO TRANSITION] Vending machines contain snacks that cost far more than in a super market. [REASON 2] Have you seen the price of chocolates and potato chips in vending machines? [EVIDENCE]

In conclusion, [TRANSITION] vending machines should not be allowed in schools because they can cause more harm than good [RESTATE OPINION]. If people want to eat vending-machine snacks, they could bring their own unhealthy food [THINK].

FIGURE 5.3. Example of a weak paper, "Vending Machines in Cafeterias: Not for the Best but for the Worst," with elements identified (for your reference).

		0 Not there	1 Could be better	2 Great!
Beginning	**Topic:** What is the topic and why should the reader care about it?			✓
	Opinion: Is the writer's opinion clear?		✓	
Middle	**Reason 1:** Is the first reason connected to the opinion and is it clear and convincing to the reader?			✓
	Evidence: Is there enough evidence to support the reason? Is the evidence explained?			✓
	Reason 2: Is the second reason connected to the opinion and is it clear and convincing to the reader?			✓
	Evidence: Is there enough evidence to support the reason? Is the evidence explained?		✓	
	Reason 3: Is the third reason connected to the opinion and is it clear and convincing to the reader?	✓		
	Evidence: Is there enough evidence to support the reason? Is the evidence explained?	✓		
End	**Restate Opinion:** Did the writer restate his or her opinion?			✓
	Think: Did the writer leave the reader with a message to think about the topic?	✓		
Other Considerations!	Is there a title that clearly refers to the information in the paper?		✓	
	Is the paper's tone appropriate for the audience? Was the writer respectful to the reader?			✓
	Are there clear and appropriate transition words used throughout the paper?		✓	

Reviewer/Writer as Reader

- Was the paper overall convincing? Why? *Not that much. The paper could have had better-developed reasons and clearer explanations. The paper would have been stronger if the writer had more evidence to support the second reason. For example, he could have said how much a chocolate costs at the super market compared to a vending machine.*

- What revisions should be made? *The writer needs to add a transition word for reason 2, add a reason and evidence and add something to think about in the conclusion. Also he needs to add evidence to reason 2 and improve the title.*

Goals

- What should be the writer's current and future goals? *For now the writer needs to work on the transition word, the reasons, and the ending of the paper. In the future the writer should set a goal to use the elements to write his paper and think carefully about how to use the transition words.*

FIGURE 5.4. Example of a completed rubric for a poorly written persuasive paper, "Vending Machines in Cafeterias: Not for the Best but for the Worst" (for your reference).

- Explain your reasoning for your scoring. Also, take some notes about things the writer could do to improve a specific element. Remember to use the phrase "Perhaps you could say . . ." to record or state your suggestions for improvements and revision. You can invite students to help you identify each element, but you should model the process of making suggestions. Try to be specific in your comments; students will follow your lead when they work independently.

- Finally, discuss the goals that the writer should set and explain that setting goals helps writers know where to focus their attention across all subjects (e.g., social studies).

Discussion

- Ask students why and how you evaluated the paper. Stress the importance of learning the elements and explain how they can be helpful to a writer.

Collaborative Evaluation of a Weak Paper

- Explain to students that you will read papers and use the evaluation rubric to score them and set goals for the writers. Discuss how setting clear revision goals can help the writer.

- Display a weak paper (see Handout 5.4), and with students' input identify the elements and evaluate it. (Note: Your role during this activity is to scaffold students' application of evaluation criteria. Ask them process questions [e.g., "What should we do next?"], ask them to (1) find the elements for you to underline, (2) tell you the score they assign with explanations for you to complete the rubric, and (3) make suggestions for you to take notes. If students have difficulties or if their responses are not accurate, reassume control of the activity.) Begin your suggestions by writing or saying "Perhaps the writer could say. . . ."

Small-Group Evaluation of a Weak Paper

- Ask students to work in groups on a different paper (see Handout 5.5) to identify the elements of persuasion, complete the rubric, and identify goals for the writer.

- Ask students to underline the elements and label them at the side of the paper. Make sure they give a score and suggestions to the writer.

- Discuss students' scoring and suggestions as a group.

Self-Evaluation of Students' Papers and Goal Setting

- Discuss and explain the importance of goal setting.

- Ask students to read their own preassessment papers, evaluate them using the elements of persuasion (copies of Form 5.2), and set goals for their own writing. Ask them to be specific about the goals they set and congratulate honest evaluations.

Differentiation

- You may want to meet with individuals or small groups of students to assist them with the application of the rubric. Try not to impose your scoring on the students. They should develop their own goals, but you could guide them to set realistic goals.

Reflection Activity

Journal writing. You can ask students to write a journal entry in response to the following questions:

1. What did I learn about *my* persuasive writing?
2. What should be my goals for improvement?

End of Class

- Review the elements of persuasion and discuss why a writer should always make sure to include all of them. Discuss how the use of the elements and the use of the evaluation rubric can help a writer set appropriate, realistic goals.

LESSON 2: MODELING HOW TO WRITE A PERSUASIVE PAPER

Students review the persuasive elements and observe the teacher during think-aloud modeling of planning, drafting, evaluating to revise, and editing of a persuasive paper.

Lesson Objectives

By the end of this lesson, students will be able to:

- Recall the elements of persuasion.
- Recall the steps of the Writing Strategy Ladder and explain their components.

Assessment Information

The teacher (1) informally assesses whether students understand the steps of the Writing Strategy Ladder and its components and (2) uses students' written responses to identify those who may need assistance learning the elements of persuasive writing.

Notes

- During the review stage of this lesson (see procedures), you can ask students to complete Form 5.3, Memorization Sheet for Persuasion, or you can ask them to write the elements on a blank sheet. You can also ask them to complete this task across several lessons to see how they improve.

- A sample think-aloud with materials (see pp. 139–145) is included as an example of a good think-aloud in this lesson. You should not refer to it during teaching, but you could consult it to understand the process. It is important that your think-aloud sounds "live" when you do it. You can use parts of the sample or you can prepare by planning on a new topic. In either case, the planning and writing process should be your own. The provided think-aloud is a model you could use across different lessons.

Materials for Lesson 2

- Form 5.1. Planning Materials (FTAP, Ideas, GO)
- Form 5.2. Rubric for Self-Evaluation and Peer Review of Persuasive Writing
- Form 5.3. Memorization Sheet for Persuasion
- Handout 2.1. Writing Strategy Ladder (from Chapter 2)
- Handout 2.2. SCIPS for Editing (from Chapter 2)
- Handout 5.6. Transition Words

Procedures

Review

- Ask students to write the elements of persuasion. Hold a class discussion about the importance of each element. You can spend some time working on memorization or play memory games to support students' learning the elements.

Introduction to the Writing Strategy Ladder

- Explain to students that you will teach them a strategy for writing persuasive papers and that this strategy follows the process of writing. On each step it tells what to do and how to do it. Explain that it is a useful strategy because it helps students stay on track and not skip a step.
- Display Handout 2.1, point to, read, and explain each step of the ladder. (Note: If you have already used the strategy for story writing, you can emphasize the few differences for persuasion.)

Plan

- Ask students why writers always need to start by planning. Encourage student responses (you may want to record students' responses and make a plan to address misconceptions).
- Explain that in the planning section they will follow specific steps: FTAP, generate

Ideas/Brainstorm, and organize ideas with a GO. You can display Form 5.1, and then write each component on the board.

FTAP

Write each letter, tell what it stands for, and discuss why it is important.

- **F** stands for *Form*.
- **T** stands for *Topic*.
- **A** stands for *Audience*. Discuss the importance of thinking about your audience when trying to convince them.
- **P** stands for *Purpose*. Explain that in persuasive writing, the purpose is to convince.

IDEAS/BRAINSTORM

- Point to *Ideas* and explain that the next step is to come up with as many ideas as possible about the topic. To do that, writers *Brainstorm*. It is helpful to think of ideas both *for* and *against* the topic because it helps to think of more ideas and to consider the audience. You can point to the Ideas/Brainstorm chart from Form 5.1 or draw the T-chart on the board.

GRAPHIC ORGANIZER

- Display the GO (see Form 5.1) and point out that it has the elements of persuasion exactly as in previous lessons. Explain that the goal is to select the best ideas, organize them, and add more during drafting. Add that writers can write the elements in a paper when planning, and they do not need to use the printed copy of the GO because they can draw it on their own.

Draft

- Point to *Draft*, the second step of the strategy ladder, and explain that good writers make sure to use their plan to draft the first version of their paper. Discuss the reasons for this step. Also, explain that good writers use transition words; display the chart with the transition words (see Handout 5.6).

Evaluate to Revise

- Point to the Evaluate to Revise step of the ladder and say that good writers always go back to check their papers for meaning and organization and to try to make changes to improve them. Explain that to do this, they will need to use the evaluation rubric that contains the evaluation elements and a section called "Other Considerations" (if you have it on display, point to Form 5.2). Add that they could write the elements and assign a score next to them instead of using the rubric. Point out that the elements of persuasion are the ones used in the GO and on the evaluation rubrics. Stress again the importance of remembering the elements.

Edit

- Point to *Edit* (you can point to Handout 2.2 if you have it on display) and explain that good writers also check for errors that could affect the quality of the paper (e.g., spelling, indentation, grammar).

Publish

- Finally, point to *Publish* and explain that writers should celebrate their work and share it with others!

Modeling Persuasive Writing

- Explain that you will write a paper and show the students how they will work when asked to write an opinion essay. Tell them that first, you will think aloud, so that students can hear how you think and see how you handle the challenges that come with persuasive writing (see the Sample Think-Aloud for Persuasive Writing on pp. 139–145).

Plan

- Tell students that you were asked to write a persuasive paper about playing videogames. Write the topic on the board. The topic asks, "Should children be allowed to play videogames for a long time or not?"
- Think aloud and ask yourself which steps of the strategy you need to follow. Explain that the steps are Plan, Draft, Evaluate to Revise, Edit, and Publish and that you need to start with planning. Write the steps of the ladder at the side of the board. Underline *Plan*.

FTAP

- Ask yourself what is the first part of planning. Write *FTAP* on the board and complete each section. Then ask what would be next. Say, "It would be Ideas/Brainstorm."

IDEAS/BRAINSTORM

- Draw a T-chart and develop the answer to the topic's question on the two sides of the chart (*in favor* and *against*). Then begin generating ideas for each side. When you have enough ideas, choose the side with which you agree. State your opinion clearly.

GRAPHIC ORGANIZER

- Begin to transfer your ideas to the GO. As you work on this task, cross out the ideas from the T-chart to clarify the use of those ideas on the GO.

- Make sure to use self-talk to ask what you have done and where you are in the process and to encourage yourself to continue even though the task is challenging.

Draft

- Ask what you should do next. Place a checkmark next to the word *Plan* that you had underlined earlier. Point to the steps you wrote earlier and underline *Draft*. Explain that you will draft your paper.

- Use your self-talk to guide your work (e.g., "What have I done so far?"), support your next step (e.g., "What should I do next?"), and handle challenges (e.g., "This is really difficult for me. I cannot remember what I am supposed to do, but I can find out if I use my strategy ladder to see what I should do next").

- Begin drafting. In this process, consult the chart with the transition words and think out loud as you use them. (Note: In case you run out of time, make a plan to review the steps of the strategy and the BME elements of persuasion when writing the persuasive essay next time.)

Evaluate to Revise

- Ask what the next step would be. Point to the Writing Strategy Ladder and explain that now you will need to Evaluate to Revise your paper. In order to do that, you will use your rubric with the elements (see Form 5.2). Point out the similarities between the elements, the GO, and the rubric.

- Apply the rubric to the paper. Identify the areas that need to be improved and set goals for the next paper. Make at least one revision.

Edit

- Explain that for editing, you have a helpful technique (SCIPS), but for now you will reread and look for spelling and punctuation errors only.

Publish

- Explain that you could share this paper with another class or with another teacher. Tell students that you could do so after you revised and edited it.

Discussion of the Modeling and Self-Regulation

- Ask students to tell you if they remember some of the things you said to yourself as you wrote. They will mention parts of the strategy and ideas that you talked about. Lead them to talk about some of the self-talk you used. Record students' responses and write some of the statements and comments you made. Explain that these statements and self-talk helped you complete your writing without experiencing stress and that you will discuss those statements with the students in the next class.

Optional Commitment

- At this point, students make a commitment to learn the strategy and the elements. For this, you can have students promise as a group to learn the strategies, or you can have them all sign a learning contract. If your students have already signed a learning contract for story writing, you may identify what would be different in this genre, make additions to the contract, and renew the commitment with students.

Additional Activities

- After you complete at least one revision, students can work in groups to make a different revision. They can also share their thoughts about how to improve a specific element and then work at completing that revision.

Reflection Activities

- **Journal writing.** You can ask students to write a journal entry in which they say how they think the Writing Strategy Ladder can help them with their own writing. Students could revisit the goals they had set in the previous class and explain how the strategy can assist them to improve as writers.
- **Class discussion.** You can discuss as a class how the writing strategy can help students as writers.

End of Lesson

- Review with the students the steps of the Writing Strategy Ladder and the persuasive elements.

LESSON 3: SELF-REGULATION—MINI-LESSON ON CONVINCING REASONS

Students learn a strategy that helps them monitor their work and reflect on the application of the strategies. As a part of this lesson, students develop "self-talk." In the second part of the lesson, students discuss and practice the creation of convincing reasons.

Lesson Objectives

By the end of this lesson, students will be able to:

* Develop their own self-talk.
* Differentiate between convincing and less convincing reasons.
* Use the "If . . . then" statement for evidence and explanations.

Assessment Information

* The teacher informally assesses whether students can (1) identify and justify convincing reasons, (2) develop self-talk, (3) differentiate between convincing and less convincing reasons, and (4) make revisions using information from the mini-lesson.

Notes

* To function as an introduction to the mini-lesson, you can use a book during your read-aloud that includes weak reasons and discuss with students the importance of convincing reasons (e.g., *The Cow Who Wouldn't Come Down* by Paul Brett Johnson).

* This is a sample mini-lesson. You could choose to replace it with a lesson that you find that would be more appropriate for your students.

Materials for Lesson 3

* Form 2.2. Self-Talk Recording Sheet (from Chapter 2) (optional)
* Form 5.3. Memorization Sheet for Persuasion
* Handout 2.3. Be Strategic! (from Chapter 2)
* Handout 5.7. Reasons for Topic on Field Trips

Procedures

Review

* Review the steps of the Writing Strategy Ladder and the elements of persuasive writing (you can use Form 5.3). You should provide multiple opportunities for students to share, record, and repeat this information when working with a partner or with members of their group.

Self-Regulation and Self-Talk

* Remind students that when you modeled how to write a persuasive paper, you thought out loud. In addition to following the Writing Strategy Ladder, you also showed them how you dealt with writing challenges. It may be helpful to refer to the notes you took at the end of Lesson 2.

- Explain that persuasive writing and writing in general can be difficult. As a result, writers may get confused and may forget what they have completed and what they need to do next. Tell students that this is why you stopped and checked where you were in the writing process, what you had completed, and asked yourself questions about what you should do next when you were writing. Also, sometimes you got frustrated, and you wanted to stop. Instead of stopping, however, you used the strategy and reminded yourself that by using it, you could complete the writing task. Further, when you were able to complete a step or a task, you congratulated yourself, and this made you feel good and motivated.

- Display Handout 2.3, Be Strategic!, with the procedures that writers should use when self-monitoring and self-regulating. Tell them that these statements and questions should become part of their internal writing voice to keep them focused. Explain each section of the poster and how you applied it when you thought out loud.

- Explain that all writers can be successful if they use their strategies and do not let themselves get discouraged.

- Discuss self-talk phrases students could use to stay on task, to use their strategies, and to remain engaged. Ask them to write those phrases on a blank sheet or to use the self-talk sheet (see Form 2.2). Then ask students to place those sheets somewhere where they can be easily accessed and will not get lost.

- If you have already done this task for a different genre, ask students to refer to the statements they made previously and to consider which ones were helpful to them or not, and then to make revisions.

Convincing Reasons and Evidence: Mini-Lesson

Discussion

- Explain to students that the core of persuasion is based on developing convincing reasons. Writers often simply develop ideas and choose reasons without thinking that the reasons need to be convincing to the reader.

- Stress that it is important for the writer to take the perspective of the reader and think about what would be convincing. Explain that this is the most challenging aspect of persuasive writing: thinking for readers and the audience when they are not present.

Idea Generation

- Explain that you will examine some reasons and decide whether these reasons would be convincing or not.

- Display the topic "Field Trips or Not?" (see Figure 5.5). Discuss with students their ideas about this topic.

- Explain that a good way to better understand the topic would be to do the FTAP and Ideas/Brainstorm steps. Complete the FTAP and Ideas (T-chart) with students'

Field Trips or Not?

Schools take their students on field trips and teachers spend time planning for them. Some people think that field trips should not take place anymore because they are very expensive. Others disagree and say that field trips are important for students' learning. Do you think that students should go on field trips or not? In your response use specific reasons and examples.

FIGURE 5.5. Topic on field trips.

feedback. Because it is likely that your students will take different positions on the question, develop ideas for both sides (*in favor* and *against*).

Evaluation of Reasons: Teacher Practice

- Explain that students from another school wrote their opinion about this topic and developed reasons. Display these reasons and tell students to think as a group about whether or not they are convincing and why.

- Display the sample reasons shown in Handout 5.7. Discuss what they mean and consider whether the parents and the school board would be convinced by those reasons in favor and against.

- Read the first reason out loud and explain how you would evaluate it. Be sure to show students your thinking. Speculate about what the reader might think.

Evaluation of Reasons: Group Practice

- Give students the opportunity to express their thinking and explain why or why not a reason would be convincing to the audience. This will also give you the opportunity to understand better the challenges your students face in this genre.

Developing Reasons and Evidence: Teacher Practice

- First, select the more convincing reasons, and then discuss as a group what evidence and explanations students could give to develop a convincing paragraph. Draw a T-chart and write a reason on one side and evidence on the other. Show students how to complete the task by thinking out loud.

- Explain that a good way to write evidence is to use an "If this . . . then" statement. Give an example for one of the reasons (see Figure 5.6 for your reference).

Developing Reasons and Evidence: Group Practice

- Work with students to complete the table in Figure 5.6 for another reason.

- You can ask students to write the paragraph independently or in small groups. Share as a group.

Reason	Evidence
Transition + restatement of opinion + a reason *Or* Transition + if . . . then statement	**Evidence and examples**

Sample

Reason	Evidence
An additional reason in favor of field trips is that field trips help students learn information. **Or** **An additional reason is that** *if* we have field trips, *then* we will learn a lot more information about a topic.	Field trips are usually connected with what we learn at school. For example, our field trip to the Museum of National History was connected with our social studies unit. When we visited the museum, everything we learned at school came to life and we were able to make connections. Learning would be so boring without real-life experiences.

FIGURE 5.6. Reason and evidence table and a completed sample.

Differentiation

- While students are working on their paragraphs independently or in small groups, you could work with a small group of students that needs more support.

Reflection Activities

- **Journal entry.** You can ask students to write a journal entry explaining why it is important to use convincing reasons for the reader. Also, ask them what difficulties they experience when developing convincing reasons.
- **Class discussion.** Discuss as a group what steps and components of the writing strategy seem challenging to students and what they could do to be successful in this genre.

End of Lesson

- Review the importance of self-talk with students, as well as the importance of developing and selecting convincing reasons when writing to persuade readers to accept a particular position on a topic.

LESSON 4: COLLABORATIVE WRITING OF A PERSUASIVE PAPER

Teacher and students collaboratively use the Writing Strategy Ladder to Plan, Draft, Evaluate to Revise, and Edit a persuasive paper. During collaborative writing, the teacher scaffolds students' application of the strategy and does the writing as the students provide the ideas and sentences.

Lesson Objectives

By the end of this lesson, students will be able to:

- Demonstrate that they know the strategy steps and can contribute appropriately to planning, drafting, and revising.

Assessment Information

The teacher informally assesses whether students (1) know the meaning of the strategy steps and (2) can apply them as a group to Plan, Draft, Evaluate to Revise, and Edit a persuasive paper.

Notes

- You can complete FTAP and Ideas/Brainstorm for two topics and select the topic for which you have the most ideas, or present students with one topic.
- You should complete the planning step as a whole class. For drafting, you can work with the whole class or ask small groups to work on individual elements (e.g., introduction, first reason). Then reassemble the whole class to combine the elements drafted by the groups. During that time, you can work with a group of students that needs support. You may decide which students to include in small-group meetings by consulting the preassessment results.

Materials for Lesson 4

- Form 5.1. Planning Materials (FTAP, Ideas, GO)
- Form 5.2. Rubric for Self-Evaluation and Peer Review of Persuasive Writing
- Form 5.3. Memorization Sheet for Persuasion (optional)
- Handout 2.1. Writing Strategy Ladder (from Chapter 2)
- Handout 5.6. Transition Words
- Sample Topics for Writing Assessment/Instruction (see pp. 106–107)
- Students' completed self-talk sheets (Form 2.2) from Lesson 3

Procedures

Review

- Review the writing strategy steps and elements of persuasion (you can use Form 5.3). Ask students to independently record them, then to check with a partner, and finally to reexamine their study goals.

Collaborative Writing of a Persuasive Essay

- Explain to students that you will work together to write a persuasive paper. You can present one topic or decide between the two after doing FTAP and Ideas.

Plan

- Ask students what is the first thing they need to do when they are asked to write. Students should respond that it is planning with FTAP and generating Ideas/Brainstorming.

FTAP AND IDEAS

- Write FTAP and Ideas/Brainstorm on the board. Underline or circle *Brainstorm*.
- Ask students what FTAP means and why it is important. Record their answers on the board. Continue the same process for the completion of Ideas/Brainstorm.
- At the end of Ideas/Brainstorm, *stop* and examine the ideas as a group. Ask which side presents more convincing ideas. The goal at this stage is not to disappoint the students whose side is not selected, but to stretch students' thinking. They should consider which side is more likely to appeal to the reader. Select a side and state the position clearly.

GRAPHIC ORGANIZER

- Ask students what the next step is in the process. They should respond that completing the GO comes next. Students may need help selecting the reasons from the Ideas/Brainstorm step and matching them with evidence. The goal is to have a GO with a fully organized plan.
- Refer to the writing strategy and remind students to use their self-talk when they do not know what they should do next.

Draft

- Ask what the next step is and remind students to use the Writing Strategy Ladder.
- Write the paper. Refer frequently to the GO and use the chart (Handout 5.6) with the transition words.

Evaluate to Revise

- Discuss what would be the next step after drafting.
- Complete the evaluation rubric with students, identify areas for improvement, and make one revision.

Edit

- Ask what the next step is and explain that students will be learning a general approach for editing. At this point you can reread the essay for spelling errors and make corrections.

Differentiation

- During the drafting stage, if you have decided to ask students to work in small groups or independently, you can work with a group of students that needs additional support. You could use your preassessment data to identify students with common misunderstandings and form groups.

End of Lesson

- Review the steps of the strategy and the elements of persuasion.

LESSON 5: STUDENTS PLAN AND DRAFT THEIR OWN PERSUASIVE PAPERS

Students begin working on their own papers, using the planning and drafting steps of the strategy. The teacher monitors the use of the strategy and provides support as needed.

Lesson Objectives

By the end of this lesson, students will be able to:

- Apply the planning and drafting steps of the strategy to generate and organize ideas appropriately.
- Write a persuasive paper that includes the persuasive elements.

Assessment Information

The teacher informally assesses whether (1) students are using the strategy appropriately and (2) their writing includes the elements and is well written, in general.

Notes

- This is the beginning of guided practice; students should write more than one paper.
- This lesson may take more than one session, depending on the time available. However, two sessions should be enough. Set expectations for when students should finish.
- We encourage you to plan and write your own paper. It is important for your students to see that you write, too. You could use your paper to self-evaluate in Lesson 7.

Materials for Lesson 5

- Form 5.1. Planning Materials (FTAP, Ideas, GO)
- Form 5.3. Memorization Sheet for Persuasion (optional)
- Handout 2.1. Writing Strategy Ladder (from Chapter 2)
- Handout 5.6. Transition Words
- Sample Topics for Writing Assessment/Instruction (see pp. 106–107)
- Students' completed self-talk sheets (Form 2.2) from Lesson 3

Procedures

Review

- Review the strategy steps and the elements of persuasion (you can use Form 5.3) as well as ways to develop convincing reasons.

Choosing Topics

- You can choose how to assign topics. One option is to display the list of topics and let students select one. Another option is to assign all students to work on the same topic; this might be easier for some students and lead to more class discussion during revision. A third option is to let students choose their own topics instead of limiting them to the ones on the list. If you ask students to select among a list of topics or develop their own topic, ask them to do the FTAP and Ideas/Brainstorm before they make their final topic selection. By analyzing the task and developing ideas, they can strategically evaluate whether or not they have sufficient information to write a full paper on the topic.

Guiding Practice

- As students work, you may monitor their progress and conduct very brief conferences. In conferencing, you should talk to the students about how they planned and check their planning sheets as well as the developing paper. Such feedback encourages students to understand that using the strategy is important to improving their writing. Remember that assessment focuses both on strategy use and writing performance.
- For the Ideas/Brainstorm step, encourage students to think of ideas on both sides of the issue. By doing that, they can be certain that they have a sufficient selection of convincing ideas.
- For the GO confirm that students have organized their ideas logically under each reason. If they did not use all the ideas from the brainstorm step, discuss why.
- Remind students to use self-talk as they work independently.
- **Option.** You might require students to show you their completed FTAP, Ideas/Brainstorm, and GO before they start writing. If the class is large or you have difficulty monitoring all the students, this step might ensure that they do the planning first. If

some students have selected the same topic, you might permit them to meet together to brainstorm their ideas.

Differentiation

● Informally assess whether students use the planning strategy and whether or not they include all the persuasive elements in their drafts. Observe students as they work and reinforce the use of the planning materials. If some students face difficulties managing the materials, plan to work with them. You could also use your preassessment data to identify individuals who need support with specific elements (i.e., reasons and evidence) and work with them in a small-group format. If students seem to be having trouble with a particular component of the strategy, you can plan to address it in a later lesson, or you can plan a mini-lesson.

Reflection Activity

● **Class discussion.** Discuss with students how the Writing Strategy Ladder helped them complete their writing.

End of Lesson

● Review the importance of self-talk. You can also discuss how the use of the strategies helped students write.

LESSON 6: PREPARATION FOR PEER REVIEW AND SELF-EVALUATION

Students practice evaluating persuasive papers, writing suggestions, and making revisions. Students also self-evaluate their papers and set goals for revision.

Lesson Objectives

By the end of this lesson, students will be able to:

● Apply the evaluation rubric to evaluate papers written by others.
● Use their evaluations to make revisions and suggestions for revisions.
● Self-evaluate their papers and set revision goals.

Assessment Information

The teacher informally assesses whether students can (1) apply the evaluation criteria, (2) make revisions using the evaluation results, and (3) self-evaluate their papers and set revision goals.

Notes

- You could also plan to self-evaluate the paper you wrote. In that way, your students will see you as a writer, too.

Materials for Lesson 6

- Form 5.2. Rubric for Self-Evaluation and Peer Review of Persuasive Writing
- Form 5.2 (copies for students' evaluation in small groups and for self-evaluations)
- Handout 2.1. Writing Strategy Ladder (from Chapter 2)
- Handout 5.8. "No School on Saturdays"
- Handout 5.9. "No Uniforms!"
- Handout 5.10. "School in June and July? Why Not?"

Procedures

Review

- Review the strategy steps and the elements of persuasion.

Discussion of the Importance of Evaluation and Revision and the Role of Peer Review

- Refer to the next step of the Writing Strategy Ladder: Evaluate to Revise (see Handout 2.1). Ask students to explain why it is important to revise, what they think revision is, and how it is different from editing.
- Ask students how they will know what type of changes they need to make. Explain the meaning of evaluation. Remind them about the evaluation rubric that they used to evaluate persuasive essays in the first lesson. Display the rubric and discuss how the evaluation criteria are connected to the elements of persuasion.
- Explain that they will participate in peer reviews. They will work with a partner to evaluate each other's papers and make suggestions for revision. To prepare for this step, the class will work together to practice evaluating papers written by students they do not know.
- Explain that giving feedback is an important aspect of reviewing and that practice evaluating papers written by other writers can help students learn the evaluation criteria and be better at self-evaluation. Explain and emphasize the importance of being honest and giving specific suggestions to the writer.

Modeling of Evaluation for Peer Review

- Display a paper for students (any from Handouts 5.8–5.10).
- Read the paper out loud. Tell students that when they self-evaluate or evaluate others' papers, they always need to read the paper out loud.

- Underline the elements. It may help to use different colors for each element. Be sure to ask your students to evaluate their texts the same way you model the process. It's a good idea to be simple but explicit.
- Use the rubric (see Form 5.2) to assign a score. Explain why you assigned that score and be very specific in your reasoning. Write notes at the side of each element for what you should do to improve it (if it has a score of *1* or *0*). Begin your suggestions by writing and/or saying "Perhaps the writer could say. . . ."
- Identify what revisions need to be made now and what goals the writer should set for another paper.
- Make at least one revision.
- Explain to students that when they read their work or the work of their peers, they need to be honest and try to find the elements and make revisions, wherever needed. Explain that their goal is for the reader to understand the paper. Tell them to use their self-talk statements if and when they are uncertain or feel overwhelmed.

Optional Variation

- After you read the paper out loud, you can identify the elements and use them to complete the graphic organizer (GO). Then score the paper using the rubric and discuss how missing information on the GO could explain the text's poor score. This would be a nice way to review and stress the importance of careful planning.

Collaborative Practice of Evaluation

- Display a sample paper and collaboratively work with the students to identify the elements and goals for the writer and to make one revision.

Small-Group Practice of Evaluation

- Display a different paper and give copies to students. Ask them to follow the same procedure you used earlier. Students can work in small groups for this task or in pairs.

Students Work on Their Own Papers to Self-Evaluate

- Explain that knowledge of elements and practice evaluating papers written by others can help writers become more skilled at self-evaluation.
- Tell students to work on their papers by underlining the elements, scoring them, and setting goals for revisions.

Differentiation

- If evaluation and self-evaluation are challenging for some students, you may want to work with them in small groups to complete this task.

End of Lesson

- Review the elements and the reasons for completing evaluations with honesty. Explain that the process of evaluation prepares students to be honest and helpful reviewers during peer review.

LESSON 7: PEER REVIEW AND REVISION

Students peer-review in pairs or in small groups, applying the evaluation criteria. Next, students compare their self-evaluations with the comments of their peers, set goals for revision, and make revisions.

Lesson Objectives

By the end of this lesson, students will be able to:

- Apply the evaluation criteria to give specific feedback to peers.
- Make revisions to their own essays.

Assessment Information

The teacher informally assesses whether students can (1) apply the evaluation criteria and give feedback to peers and (2) make revisions to their essays.

Notes

- When students work on revisions, you may want to meet with them to discuss their work. In this meeting, first ask how they used the planning procedures, how they evaluated their work, and what comments they received from their reviewers. Then discuss their revisions. In general, give them feedback on their use of the strategy, not only on the end product.
- For students who struggle to complete the peer review, you may want to provide more practice on the reviewing process, using additional papers.
- Students can work in pairs or in groups of three. Trade papers in groups of three in a clockwise direction.
- You can assign students to groups based on their needs in applying the evaluation rubric and in making suggestions. You could also consult the preassessment data and

the conclusions you reached regarding the needs of specific students. Based on this information, you may form mixed-ability groups. For example, you may ask a student who clearly states his or her opinion and reasons to work with a student who received a low score on these elements. An additional way to provide extra support is for students to engage in peer evaluation more than once. You may assign the first pairs, but then students may peer-review with a reader of their choice.

- Support students with the revision task, but do not complete the revisions for them. If they have challenges with handwriting, students can dictate to you, but the ideas should come from them.

Materials for Lesson 7

- Form 5.2. Rubric for Self-Evaluation and Peer Review of Persuasive Writing
- Form 5.2 (copies for students to use for peer review)
- Handout 2.1. Writing Strategy Ladder (from Chapter 2)
- Students' completed self-talk sheets (Form 2.2) from Lesson 3

Procedures

Review

- Review the strategy steps, the elements of persuasion, and the purpose and benefits of peer review.

Peer Review

- Explain that during peer review, the partners meet, read each other's paper, and provide comments.

Peer Review Procedures

- Write the steps of the peer review sequence on the board and explain each one:
  1. Meet with your partner and read your paper to each other out loud.
     a. Explain that reading out loud is important to hear whether sentences are well written.
  2. Switch papers.
  3. Reread your partner's paper, evaluate it using the rubric, and write specific suggestions.
     a. Explain that the reader/reviewer will read the paper again and evaluate it using the rubric. The goal of the reviewing process is to identify the presence or absence of the elements, and to give specific suggestions to the writer to help the writer improve her or his grade.

4. Meet with your partner and discuss your scoring, comments, and suggestions.

5. Explain that in the meeting, the reviewer will point out something in the paper that was interesting or that he or she liked, explain the scoring, and give suggestions to the writer. Then the reviewer will listen to the partner's comments.

- Explain that the writer should not be upset with the reviewer/reader, but should appreciate the efforts made to help the writer improve his or her paper.

- Explain that they have been practicing peer review all this time by using papers written by unknown students. This is a practice that has prepared you to work with a "live" partner.

Completing Peer Review

- Students meet with their partners to complete the peer review process.

Revisions

- Students compare their self-evaluation sheets with their partner's comments and determine what revisions to make. Students work on revising their own papers.

Optional Variation

- You can ask reviewers to complete the evaluation rubric and the GO using the information from the writer's paper. Then, when the reviewer meets with the writer, they can compare the GO they developed together and the one the writer used to write his or her paper. This will help the reviewer make specific suggestions for improvement and for the writer to better understand which areas are confusing.

Differentiation

- You can plan to work with a small group of students that is having difficulty making revisions as a scribe or as an external monitor, reminding them to use their self-statements when they get frustrated.

- As students work, you can also meet with them to conference. During conferences, you should ask students about their strategy use and revision goals, and you should prompt them to explain their reasoning. The feedback you provide should concern students' use of the planning materials, their application of the writing process, and their goals. This kind of focused feedback helps students understand the importance of using the strategies to improve their writing. Therefore, your feedback should focus on strategy use, not only on the final product.

Reflection Activities

- **Class discussion.** Ask students to compare their self-evaluation rubrics with reviewers' feedback and comments. If the reviewers have also completed the GO, ask writers to compare their GO with the reviewers' GO. What did writers learn about planning? What revisions could they make to their GO? What are their future goals?

- **Journal writing.** Ask students to examine their preassessment and their goals, comparing their scores from the preassessment with their scores from this paper. Then ask students to record their new goals in their journals. You can also ask them to respond to the question, "What strategies have been helpful to you and what strategies will you use in the future and why?"

End of Lesson

- Review the importance of giving honest feedback and developing clear goals for revisions.

LESSON 8: EDITING

Students examine their papers for editing errors. By using the editing strategy (SCIPS), students identify surface-level errors and correct them. Teachers can choose to teach a specific grammatical/editing skill, practice it with students, and ask students to make changes to their essays. Additionally, students set editing goals and reflect on their performance and progress.

Lesson Objectives

By the end of this lesson, students will be able to:

- Set goals for improving their editing skills.
- Apply editing procedures to make changes in their papers.

Assessment Information

The teacher informally assesses whether students (1) apply previous editing goals to make editing changes and (2) use the skills they were taught to edit their work.

Notes

- SCIPS (see Handout 2.2) is a general editing checklist. The goal is to identify specific editing needs of students and to provide a targeted mini-lesson. Then students can practice improving that specific skill (see Chapter 3).

- It is very likely that some students will be in need of developing different editing skills. This is an opportunity to differentiate your editing lessons and to provide explicit support to specific groups. With your support, students can work on a specific skill, record their editing goals, and make changes to their essays.

- The objectives will be based on your grade's instructional goals and on your students' needs.

Materials for Lesson 8

- Form 2.1. Editing Goals for Improvement (from Chapter 2)
- Handout 2.1. Writing Strategy Ladder (from Chapter 2)
- Handout 2.2. SCIPS for Editing (from Chapter 2)
- Your choice of materials for a specific editing and grammatical goal

Procedures

Review

- Review the Writing Strategy Ladder and ask students to explain each step and the elements of persuasion.

Editing

- Point to the Writing Strategy Ladder and ask students to identify the next step of the strategy. Also ask students why they think that editing is important and to explain how editing is different from revising.

Editing Mini-Lesson

- Identify a specific editing issue of students. Explain it, model how to correct it on a sample paper, and collaboratively practice its correction as a group. Then review the SCIPS editing process and ask students to practice reviewing their papers for the specific editing skill they practiced and for the rest of the editing goals they have included on their editing goals' sheets (Form 2.1). You can also ask students to meet with a partner for peer editing. When students have finished their work, ask them to add this editing skill to their editing goals' sheets. You can also add this new editing goal to a class wall chart for future reference.

Reflection Activity

- **Journal writing.** Ask students to complete Form 2.1, Editing Goals for Improvement, and examine how they progress over time.

PUBLISHING GUIDELINES

It is important for students to share some of their work with a larger audience. See Chapter 3 for a discussion of ideas about opportunities for publishing. These guidelines do not constitute a specific lesson, but rather present ideas for discussing publishing with your students. The specifics will depend on what sort of publishing you have chosen.

Review

• Review the elements of persuasion and the steps of the Writing Strategy Ladder.

Publishing

• Review the importance of publishing and sharing written work with an audience.

• Students prepare their papers for sharing. Besides general approaches for publishing (see Chapter 3), you may want to consider the following suggestions. If you have assigned the same topic to all students, it is very likely that they are divided in their opinions.

   1. It would be engaging for students who disagree about an issue to compile their reasons as a group and, with your support as a moderator, hold a debate for another class to watch.

   2. The students who comprise the audience of the debate can later discuss which side was more convincing to them and explain why.

      a. Alternatively, audience members can record their opinions on note cards. The cards can be counted and then the results, with the reasons for the audience's majority choice, can be presented to the class. This is a way for students to consider their reasons and their effects on an actual audience.

GUIDELINES FOR CONTINUOUS GUIDED PRACTICE TO MASTERY

It is important for students to write more than one paper in a genre to develop mastery of it. When students write a second paper, they are likely to work more quickly and feel much more competent. Teachers can then focus their attention on students who need more support.

Mastery Objectives

By the end of all lessons on persuasion, students will be able to:

• Apply the planning and drafting steps of the writing strategy to generate and organize ideas appropriately.
• Write a persuasive paper that includes elements of persuasion.
• Write a persuasive paper with clear and convincing reasons.

Assessment Information

The teacher informally assesses whether students can (1) apply the writing strategy to plan, draft, evaluate to revise; (2) provide convincing reasons; and (3) accurately apply the evaluation criteria to give suggestions and make revisions. *Mastery instruction* means that instruction should continue until all students can use the strategy to write a paper that includes at least all of the basic elements.

Notes

- Students will work on a new paper. For this task, complete the following:
  - Give students a choice of topics.
  - Remind students to use the Writing Strategy Ladder and the genre elements and materials.
  - Keep the planning materials on display (FTAP, Ideas/Brainstorm, GO), but ask students to draw them instead of using printed copies.
  - As students work, conference with them about how they are using the strategy and the process of writing.
  - Conduct self-evaluations and peer review. You can collaboratively review a paper prior to students' self-evaluation and peer review step to remind them of the importance of giving honest feedback and detailed suggestions. Monitor students' suggestions during the self-evaluation and peer review period to ensure that their comments are productive.
  - Remind students to edit using SCIPS and to remember their editing goals. (At this point in the lesson sequence, we recommend that you do not teach a new editing skill.)
  - Plan for sharing. Students prepare their papers for publishing.
  - Students write a journal entry and reflect on their growth. They can respond to the questions, "How did my writing improve? What worked for me as a writer?"
- During guided practice, repeat modeling of a task for students if needed and/or provide another mini-lesson to a small group of students or the whole class. Remember that the goal is mastery.
- Once students have completed the second paper, you can proceed with an extension activity (e.g., writing of book reviews or persuasive essays with opposing positions) or ask students to write a third opinion paper.

EXTENSION ACTIVITIES

Book Reviews

One of the specific instructional challenges that the CCSS pose to teachers is the provision of lessons that promote reading and writing connections. In this approach, we first support students in writing opinion essays, and then we suggest that teachers work with students to write book reviews.

There are specific similarities and differences between the writing of an opinion paper and a book review. In both types of papers, the writer needs to provide information about the topic, state an opinion, provide convincing reasons and sufficient evidence, and conclude with a restatement of the opinion and a message to the reader. One difference between opinion papers and book reviews is in the introduction of the paper. In a book review, the writer needs to provide information about the book, including the title and author, as well as a brief summary of the plot, to capture the reader's interest. Another difference is the nature of the evidence provided to support the reasons. In a book review, the writer uses specific information from the book to support any claims. For instance, if the writer argues that the school library should purchase a book because it is funny, the writer would need to offer humorous examples from the book as evidence. The elements of book reviews can be found in Handout 5.11.

Book reviews also are based on the assumption that the writer has read and understood the book being reviewed. Comprehension can be challenging to students, and some students may have difficulty understanding the content of a book. The inclusion of read-alouds in your instruction can support students' reading comprehension and thereby help them when they write book reviews.

To prepare students to write book reviews, teachers can choose just about any book they wish. During or immediately after reading, teachers can lead a discussion about what students liked and disliked about the book. It is important to have students identify specific information from the book, including quotes, to support their reasons. Teachers can take notes about students' reasons and evidence on a chart that lists positive reasons on one side and negative reasons on the other. This chart would be much like the Ideas/Brainstorming chart used in the persuasive strategy. Note taking is helpful in two additional ways. First, it allows students to observe and participate in taking notes on specific ideas from a book instead of attempting to record all the details. Second, it exposes all of them to the same text and same information. Students can then collaborate during planning to examine the clarity of their ideas.

In preparation for teaching book review writing, you should introduce students to the elements of the genre and the evaluation process through the application of the elements in a good and a weak example (see Handouts 5.12 and 5.13). You will also need to collect preassessment data to monitor student growth. Then you will model the writing of a book review and give students evaluation opportunities in preparation for peer review. The process of developing your own lessons on any of the extension activities can be found in Chapter 7.

Writing Short, Argumentative Responses to Texts

Another good way to introduce students to writing persuasively based on texts is to begin with short responses to texts that they read. In this way, students get practice using information from texts as part of persuasive writing, but without having to integrate too much information or write a full essay. Students are asked to write a short response that gives their opinion related to the text and that uses specific evidence from the text. These short responses are a natural follow-up activity to read-alouds, and they can also be used to spark discussion of ideas related to the read-alouds.

Either fiction or nonfiction texts can be used for this approach. As an example for fiction, after reading the book *The Cow Who Wouldn't Come Down* by Paul Brett Johnson, you might ask students to respond to the questions, "Do you think that Gertrude was a stubborn cow? What evidence does the author give to show that she was or was not stubborn?" Or, after reading the book *Chicken Sunday* by Patricia Polacco, you could ask, "Why do you think Miss Eula said that Mr. Kodinski 'has suffered so much in his life'? What evidence does the author give to help the reader understand this line?" Many good questions can be generated about whether characters should have done what they did. Nonfiction texts could be used also. For example, after reading the book *Owen and Mzee: The True Story of a Remarkable Friendship* by Isabella Hatkoff, Craig Hatkoff, and Paula Kahumbu, you could ask, "Do you think that Owen was fortunate even though he faced a great challenge? What information from the text makes you think that he was fortunate?" Learning how to make short, argumentative responses to texts effectively is likely to contribute to learning in literature and content areas and also likely to prepare students for assessments based on the CCSS.

Using Sources to Support an Opinion on a Topic

As students move into upper elementary and middle school, they are increasingly asked to use ideas from their reading in their writing. The Standards suggest that fifth-grade students should be able to explain how reasons and evidence are used to support points in informative text. Using sources in persuasive writing can be challenging. However, students who already have some experience with persuasive writing may be ready for this challenge. This task requires students to justify their opinions on a topic using information from readings. The elements for this writing task are the same as for opinion essays. However, this task requires the writer to comprehend a text well enough to identify the reasons and the evidence used to support opinions in the text and to take notes on that information. In terms of instruction, the teacher would first model and support students in taking notes from the text using the same T-chart they used to plan opinion essays. The only difference would be that on each side of the chart students would include information from their readings. Second, the teacher would model for students how to include this information in the GO for their own opinion essay. Students can be asked to state their opinion on a topic and to use information from their readings to support it. Finally, the teacher would model how to write a basic reference for the paper. A sample of a good paper that might be used is included in Handout 5.14. This is a writing task that can take place in social studies and science.

Opposing Position

The writing of an opposing position is a challenging task for most students. One of the main challenges students face is the consideration of an opinion different from the one they hold. This is difficult because students must shift their perspective. In addition, writers must then explain the flaws in the opposing position, which is the rebuttal. Creating a rebuttal is challenging even for middle school writers. However, when students are taught how to write an opposing position through a genre approach, they are better able to understand its purpose and organization and to develop clear opposing positions and rebuttals. The process of developing lessons for persuasive writing with an opposing position will include read-alouds, introduction, and application of genre elements in good and weak examples (see Handouts 5.15, 5.16, and 5.17), teacher modeling, collaborative practice, and practice applying evaluation criteria. The process for developing lessons on an opposing position can be found in Chapter 7. You can use the evaluation rubric (Form 5.4), the memorization sheet for the elements (Form 5.5), and the transition words/sentence frames (Handout 5.18) for the genre of persuasive writing with opposing position.

Materials for Extension Activities

- Form 5.4. Rubric for Self-Evaluation and Peer Review of Persuasive Writing with Opposing Position
- Form 5.5. Memorization Sheet for Persuasive Writing with Opposing Position
- Handout 5.11. Book Review Elements
- Handout 5.12. A Well-Written Book Review, "Why Everyone Should Read the Book *Number the Stars* by Lois Lowry"
- Handout 5.13. A Weak Book Review, "*Number the Stars* by Lois Lowry"
- Handout 5.14. A Well-Written Opinion Essay with Sources, "The Brain: A Wonder"
- Handout 5.15. A Well-Written Paper with Opposing Position, "Pets in the Classroom: Say Yes!"
- Handout 5.16. A Weak Paper with Opposing Position, "Saturday: This Is Our Day!"
- Handout 5.17. Chart with Elements of Opposing Position
- Handout 5.18. Transition Words for Opposing Position

Sample Think-Aloud for Persuasive Writing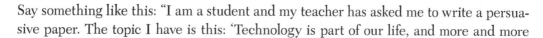

Say something like this: "I am a student and my teacher has asked me to write a persuasive paper. The topic I have is this: 'Technology is part of our life, and more and more

DEVELOPING STRATEGIC WRITERS THROUGH GENRE INSTRUCTION

young children use technology. For example, they play videogames. Some parents say that children should not play videogames. Others say that videogames are good for young children. Write a paper saying whether you think that children should be allowed to play videogames for a long time or not. Give reasons and support them with examples.

"Okay. What type of writing is this? Well, I am writing a paper/essay, not a letter. I think I should write a persuasive paper, but I will not know for sure before I do all my planning. Hmmmmmmm . . . I like to write, but writing is hard! However, I know I can write a great paper if I try my best and use my strategy.

"What do I need to do first? Okay, my strategy ladder says that I need to plan. I know that I need to do three things when I plan: I need to FTAP, generate ideas, and complete my GO. What shall I do first? I know, I will start with FTAP!"

Write *FTAP* on the board vertically, with one letter underneath the other.

Say, "*F* stands for *Form*. I am writing an essay. Okay!

"*T* stands for *Topic*."

Write *Topic* next to *T*.

"So, what is my topic? My topic is 'videogames.' Well, What about videogames? Okay . . . [Underline], it says 'if you think that children should play videogames or not.' So my topic can be a question: 'Should children play videogames or not?' That would be my topic.

"What do I need to do next? I need to say who my audience is, because *A* is for *Audience*."

Write *Audience* next to *A*.

Say, "Well, the prompt I read does not say who will read this paper, but it can be the parents and students from my school. So I will write *parents* and *students*. I can even write *teachers*, because they are parents, too, and they will read this paper as well."

Write *teachers*, *parents*, and *students* next to audience.

Ask, "What is my next step? *P* is for *Purpose*, so I need to tell why I am writing this essay. Well, it asks me to say what I think about the topic of videogames, so since it asks me to state my opinion and support it with reasons, the purpose is to persuade. I need to convince the reader that what I say is the truth to convince the reader to agree with me. Okay! I will write *convince* and *persuade* next to *Purpose*."

Write *convince/persuade* next to purpose.

Ask, "What have I done so far? I finished the Topic, Audience, and Purpose part of my planning. Great Job! I should give myself a pat on the back for doing this part so far! What do I need to do next? I need to generate ideas. Well, in order to do that, I will need to have a belief. In this topic I know I have a clear belief. Let me see what the question is in the topic. Well, I think that children should not be playing videogames. I now need to come up with ideas. Let's see. . . ."

Write the word *Ideas/Brainstorm* on the board.

Say, "Let me think! I will come up with everything I know about this topic and my belief about it. I will come up with at least five ideas." [Feel free to adjust this based on your needs.]

Say, "Let me draw the box with the two sides. I think I know what my opinion is, but I may come up with more ideas if I think both sides. One side says 'IN FAVOR—YES,

THEY SHOULD PLAY VIDEOGAMES.' The other side says, 'AGAINST—NO, THEY SHOULD NOT PLAY VIDEOGAMES.' I will now come up with ideas for the YES side."

Say, "Videogames are fun and entertaining. This is true." Write those ideas on the YES side.

Say, "They can make you **dizzy** if you play for a long time. They can make you **spend time alone** instead of spending time with friends! You may also spend more money on those games instead of books. Oh! They also **do not help you learn anything**."

Write these on the NO SIDE.

Say, "How many ideas do I have so far? I have a good amount for the AGAINST/ NO side and one for the YES/IN FAVOR side. I need to come up with more. . . . This is hard . . . what else do I know about videogames? Well . . . I can think of what they can do to people . . . they **can make them stay on their couch more** instead of playing outside. If they do that, they will **be less healthy**. These are AGAINST, so I will put them on the AGAINST/NO SIDE."

The completed form would look like this:

Plan
FORM: What is it that I am writing? <u>Essay</u>
TOPIC: Should children play videogames for a long time?
AUDIENCE: Parents, children, teachers
PURPOSE: To convince/to persuade (topic, opinion, reasons two to four, examples, restate opinion, and leave reader thinking!)

Ideas/Brainstorm	
IN FAVOR/YES: Children should play videogames for a long time	AGAINST/NO: Children should not play videogames for a long time
entertaining	dizzy
	spend time alone, not with other children
	spend more money on games than books
	do not help you learn
	can make them stay on their couch more . . . be less healthy

Ask "What have I done so far? I came up with ideas, and I think I did a pretty good job! I think that my belief is that NO, CHILDREN SHOULD NOT PLAY VIDEO-GAMES.

"What do I need to do next? The next step in my strategy ladder says that I need to organize my ideas. How do I do that? Oh, yes! I need to use my GO that has the parts of persuasion. What are those again? Topic, my opinion, reasons, examples, saying my belief again, and saying something for the reader to think at the end."

Draw the drafting GO on the board or on a transparency and say, "I will draw the GO because the goal is for me to know the elements and structure of persuasion and to organize my ideas even when I do not have a printed GO with me. I know I need to learn it, so I will try my best!" Complete the GO using the information from the Ideas/Brainstorm form. The completed GO will look like the one in Figure 5.7.

Say, "I think I did a great job! I like the information on my GO. I think my belief is clear and my reasons are convincing. I am sure I will convince my reader! Now I need to start my paper. Well, the truth is that writing the topic part of the paper is challenging, and I have a hard time doing this. For now, I will start with my opinion and the reasons, examples, and restatement of my opinion. Then I will work on my introduction and on how to leave the reader with something to think about. Finally, I will include my title!"

Look at your GO. Say what your opinion is and then state it clearly. Then write, "**I think that children should not be allowed to play videogames for a long time.**"

Say, "I think this is a clear opinion. Now, I need to say what my first reason is. Okay. I have this in my GO. My first reason is 'Videogames can make children unhealthy.'"

Write, "**One reason against videogames is that they can make children unhealthy.**"

Say, "Now, I need to add the examples. I could say what will happen to children if they play videogames for a long time."

Write, "**If children play videogames for a long time, they will spend a lot of time sitting instead of moving. If they do not move, they will gain unneeded weight and this may affect their health. They may end up having a serious illness such as diabetes.**"

Say, "I think that this is a good example.

"Now I need to look at my second reason. My GO says, 'Children do not know how to be social.' Okay, I will write, '**A second reason against videogames is to be social.**' I will now give examples. I think I can use the same ones I did earlier and say that if this . . .

Beginning	Topic: *Children spend a lot of time playing games. Parents are worried . . .*
	Opinion: *Children should not play videogames for a long time.*
Middle	Reason 1: *Videogames can make children unhealthy.*
	Evidence: *Sit on couch, no exercise—gain weight.*
	Reason 2: *Children do not know how to be social.*
	Evidence: *Do not play with other children—learn only about games.*
	Reason 3: *Distraction from true learning.*
	Evidence: *No reading (example).*
End	Restate Opinion: *I think that children should not . . .*
	Think: *Reading and math should be the goal—playing with other children and learning how to be a social person.*

FIGURE 5.7. Example of a completed GO for persuasion.

then that. Okay! 'If children spend a lot of time inside with a machine, then they do not speak with others. If they do that for a long time, then they may not learn how to properly act around other people.' Now I can give an example: 'For example, if a child does not know how to act around others, he may say something hurtful to a friend, or he may not have anything to talk about except the videogame he played.'"

Say, "I like this reason and example! I think I did a good job! Two completed—one more to go!

"The third reason is about the distraction from true learning. I will write, 'A final reason against videogames is that children are distracted from learning important things.' I can surely say if . . . then, and give examples and some personal examples. I will write, 'If a child has a videogame, then the child will be tempted to spend more time playing it than reading. For example, my nephew this summer was addicted to his videogame and would spend all his time playing it. He would stay for 5 hours in front of the machine instead of reading books like he used to do. However, he was not learning anything with the videogame, but he would have learned a lot about life if he was reading.'

"Okay! What have I done so far? I finished the opinion, the three reasons, and now I need to do my conclusion. Well, for the conclusion first I need to restate my opinion. I will use the transition words, 'In conclusion. . . .' Now I need to restate my opinion. Okay, I will write, 'In conclusion, children should not spend time playing videogames.'

"Okay. That was easy! I should give myself a pat on the back for doing all these so far and for following my GO! What do I need to do now? Well, I need to write my introduction and the "Think" part of my conclusion. I think that for the introduction, I should explain what the problem is. I will not start with a question, because a question can be boring to the reader. I will just say what the problem is."

Say, "The problem is that children spend a lot of time on their computers and stay home inside a room playing videogames instead of going out and playing with friends or reading. This is what I will say and I will also say that this is something that happens more and more. I will write, 'Children spend a lot of time at home in front of a computer or a game console playing videogames. A lot of parents and teachers are concerned about the time that children spend in front of a screen. I think. . . .' Great. This is fine!

"Now the 'Think' part of my conclusion. What did I say before? 'In conclusion, children should not be allowed to play videogames.' What do I have in my GO? [read Ideas]. I can say what the children's goal should be. You know, that children should learn and be ready to succeed in school so that they can go to college. Great! I will write, 'Children's goal should not be to become experts in playing a game, but they should learn about the real world. They should practice how to read and answer challenging questions, not how to eliminate the mean people in a game. Also, children should play with other children and learn how to be social, not how to be alone. They should speak and laugh and talk. This is what makes them children and not machines!'"

Say, "I like this! I am so happy I did it! My GO helped me so much to organize my ideas and then put them on my draft! Great!

Children spend a lot of time at home in front of a computer or a game console playing videogames. A lot of parents and teachers are concerned about the time that children spend in front of a screen. I think that children should not be allowed to play videogames for a long time.

One reason against videogames is that they can make children unhealthy. If children play videogames for a long time, they will spend a lot of time sitting instead of moving. If they do not move, they will gain unneeded weight and this may affect their health. They may end up having a serious illness such as diabetes.

A second reason against videogames is to be social. If children spend a lot of time inside with a machine, they do not speak with others. If they do that for a long time, they do not learn how to properly act around other people. For example, if a child does not know how to act around others he may say something hurtful to a friend or he may not have anything to talk about except the videogame he played.

A final reason against videogames is that children are distracted from learning important things. If a child has a videogame, the child will be tempted to spend more time playing it than reading. For example, my nephew this summer was addicted to his videogame and would spend all his time playing it. He would stay for 5 hours in front of the machine instead of reading books like he used to do. However, he was not learning anything with the videogame, but he would have learned a lot about life if he was doing his reading.

In conclusion, children should not spend time playing videogames. Children's goals should not be to become experts in playing a game, but they should learn about the real world. They should practice how to read and answer challenging questions, not how to eliminate the mean people in a game. Also, children should play with other children and learn how to be social, not how to be alone. They should speak and laugh and talk. This is what makes them children and not machines!''

Ask "Did I finish? No, I did not! I need to complete my rubric and see how I could make my paper better and what goals I could set to improve my writing in general."

Display the rubric or draw it on the board, but keep the paper on the board as well. Read each part of the rubric and highlight or underline the information on the paper. Mark your score on the rubric. Do that for each one of the elements. Then answer the questions at the end of the rubric and explain what changes should be in your revision goals.

The completed rubric and comments would look like the one in Figure 5.8.

Select and make a revision (e.g., develop a clearer second reason). Think out loud as you make the correction.

One revision could look like this:

> **Revision of reason 2:** A second reason against videogames is that they cause students to spend time alone.

Comment on your general performance and on how the Writing Strategy Ladder and the elements of persuasion helped you write a clear paper. Finally, edit your work!

		0 Not there	1 Could be better	2 Great!
Beginning	**Topic**: What is the topic and why should the reader care about it?			✓
	Opinion: Is the writer's opinion clear?			✓
Middle	**Reason 1**: Is the first reason connected to the opinion and is it clear and convincing to the reader?			✓
	Evidence: Is there enough evidence to support the reason? Is the evidence explained?			✓
	Reason 2: Is the second reason connected to the opinion and is it clear and convincing to the reader?		✓	
	Evidence: Is there enough evidence to support the reason? Is the evidence explained?			✓
	Reason 3: Is the third reason connected to the opinion and is it clear and convincing to the reader?			✓
	Evidence: Is there enough evidence to support the reason? Is the evidence explained?			✓
End	**Restate Opinion**: Did the writer restate his or her opinion?			✓
	Think: Did the writer leave the reader with a message to think about the topic?			✓
Other Considerations!	Is there a title that clearly refers to the information in the paper?	✓		
	Is the paper's tone appropriate for the audience? Was the writer respectful to the reader?			✓
	Are there clear and appropriate transition words used throughout the paper?			✓

Reviewer/Writer as Reader

- **Was the paper overall convincing? Why?** *Overall, yes. I had convincing reasons and supported them with examples. For example, I said, ". . . ."*
- **What revisions should be made?** *I should improve my second reason, add a title.*

Goals

- **What should be the writer's current and future goals?** *Add a title, perhaps "Videogames: The Danger of Machines." Also, make a revision to the second reason. I should continue using my elements and remember to use the writing process! I did well because I did not skip planning and when I wrote, I used my planning carefully and always thought of the elements. I should set as a goal to work on my reasons, though! They could be more convincing!*

FIGURE 5.8. Example of a completed rubric with comments.

Chart with Persuasive Elements

Beginning	**Topic:** What is the topic and why should the reader care about it?	
	Opinion: Is the writer's opinion clear?	
Middle	**Reasons (two to four):** Are the reasons connected to the opinion and are they clear and convincing to the reader?	
	Evidence: Is there enough evidence to support the reasons? Is the evidence explained?	
End	**Restate Opinion:** Did the writer restate the opinion?	
	Think: Did the writer leave the reader with a message to think about the topic?	

Saturday: This Is Our Day!

Students spend a great amount of time in schools. They are in school 180 days every year. From Monday to Friday, every week of a month, students wake up in the morning and spend more than 6 hours in a classroom. But some grown-ups think that children should spend more time in the classrooms in order to improve students' performance in math and reading. In my opinion, there should not be any school on Saturday.

One reason to not have school on Saturday is that more money will be spent for supplies, for paying teachers, and for utilities. If students come to school during the weekend, school bus drivers will need to be paid. Also, teachers' pay will need to be increased and more money will be spent on electricity and gas, too. More money will need to be given to schools to cover these expenses, and this means that taxpayers will pay more taxes.

Another reason against Saturday classes is that this is a day that students need in order to develop other interests and relax. During the weekend a lot of students participate in sports and other recreational activities. For example, I play tennis, and I am on a team playing competitively. If we have school on Saturdays, I will need to drop my team or try to find time during the school week to play. This may affect my schoolwork, and in the end, I may not be a good student or a good athlete. Also, Saturday is the day that students can relax and sleep in a bit longer. This is necessary for our development while we are still growing.

In addition, school on Saturdays may affect students' and even teachers' motivation. For five days, students and teachers wake up and come to school. Saturday and Sunday are the only days they can spend time with their families and friends. If they need to come to school for an extra day, then they may react negatively and may lose interest in schoolwork.

In conclusion, five days of school is more than enough for students' learning, and there is no need to have more time in class to make students better. More time in school can make students less motivated and may also cost more money. Students should be happy to go to school and should have the energy to participate in classroom activities. If one more day is added, students might be so unhappy that their schoolwork suffers.

Vending Machines in Cafeterias: Not for the Best but for the Worst

In our school we have cafeteria food, and it is the best. We have salads and fruits, and we get pizza every Friday. In general, we have healthy options and everyone supports a healthy lifestyle. Say no to vending machines!

One reason is that if vending machines are in schools, students will be tempted to buy unhealthy snacks. Most snacks contain saturated fats that can increase the levels of cholesterol in the blood, and then increase the risk for a heart attack. In general snacks and unhealthy options do not contain the vitamins and nutrients that young bodies need to develop.

Vending machines contain snacks that cost far more than in a supermarket. Have you seen the price of chocolates and potato chips in vending machines?

In conclusion, vending machines should not be allowed in schools because they can cause more harm than good. If people want to eat vending-machine snacks, they could bring their own unhealthy food.

Vending Machines: Why Not?

Vending machines can be found in all public places and spaces. My brother is a college student, and sometimes I go with him to his school. In that building you will find three vending machines. One has drinks, and the other two have a lot of snacks. I think that we should have a vending machine in our school, too.

A vending machine is necessary because not everyone likes the cafeteria food. Sometimes you may not want to eat a salad or chicken fingers and you may want to have a treat instead. If you have a vending machine, you will have more options.

Everyone is responsible for his or her choices. So, if someone wants to eat food from a vending machine, that someone should be free to do so. This is a free country and everyone has the right to do as he or she pleases.

Our school should consider bringing vending machines and installing them in the cafeteria. That way we can choose something from there and eat, and still be with our friends.

Vending Machines: Necessary

Did you ever visit our cafeteria? You will find that for every meal we have a salad and a fruit. Of course, we do not need to eat those and if we do not, we will be hungry later, and it is difficult to stay in school for so many hours without eating.

Vending machines are great to have in schools because we can get something else to eat at lunch. Personally, I do not like eating salads.

Another reason why our principal should consider bringing vending machines to our school is because that way the school will make more money. If vending machines are in school, students will buy their products and the school will get a percent of those profits. That way more books can be bought for students' classrooms and the school library.

Also, vending machines are everywhere else but our school. Even grocery stores have vending machines even though they have packages of the same products on their shelves. Vending machines are even in hospitals. There is no reason to not have them in our school.

Transition Words

Beginning—for writer's opinion

- I think that _____ should/should not _____
- From my perspective _____
- It is important for _____ to _____

Middle—for reasons

- One reason that _____
- A first reason that supports _____
- A second reason _____
- An additional reason _____

Middle—for added information

- Also, _____
- In addition, _____
- Furthermore, _____

End—for conclusion

- In conclusion, _____

Reasons for the Topic on Field Trips

In Favor

1. One reason to continue having field trips is to help us have a hands-on experience.
2. In addition, field trips help us learn. OR if we had field trips we would have more learning experiences.
3. Third, field trips are fun.
4. Also, field trips are a way to get out of the class.
5. Another reason is that if we have field trips, we would breathe fresh air!
6. Still another reason to have field trips is to learn more about what we learn at school.
7. If we had field trips, teachers would have a chance to relax away from classrooms.

Against

1. One reason to cancel field trips is that they cost a lot of money.
2. Second, field trips may lead to student injuries.
3. Another reason against field trips is that they may trigger student allergies.
4. In addition, field trips can be boring.
5. A fifth reason against field trips is that they are taking away from our classroom learning.
6. If we did not have field trips, we would not have school accidents.
7. Finally, field trips should be cancelled because they require a lot of chaperones.

No School on Saturdays

The other day in our classroom, our teacher said that there would be a change in our schedule. She said that for one month we would try to have school on Saturdays to only work on math and reading. She said that this is a pilot and it will not be forever. This was the most upsetting news I ever heard since the decision to have uniforms. We should all say no to this!

One reason to not have school on Saturdays is because we are kids and we want some time for ourselves. We come to school from Monday to Friday. Five days are more than enough to teach us about reading and math. Some of us have other things to do on the weekends.

Also, not everyone may need additional help with reading and math. For example, I have straight As in both. Why would I need to spend more time in the classroom? The school may have this rule for students whose parents and teachers think that they need additional help.

School on Saturdays is the most unreasonable decision. Children need time for themselves, too.

No Uniforms

Our school has recently made a change to our dress code. Our teachers decided that we should wear uniforms to school. I think that this is wrong.

One reason why we should not have a uniform policy is because uniforms do not let students express themselves. Young children are creative. This is clear from the way they write and think about the world. One way to express our creativity is through our clothes. Uniforms are a blah way of expression, and they suppress our creative natures.

Also, uniforms cost a lot of money. I did a search on the Internet, and they cost more then $100.00. Not all families can afford that. Also, we are growing, and our parents will have to buy different sizes during the year. This may lead to spending much more money than if we were allowed to wear regular clothes.

No uniforms!

School in June and July? Why Not?

One reason that we should have school in the summer months is so we can improve our grades. The United States is left behind compared to China and Finland. If more time is spent in school, students will be able to be better in math and reading comprehension. For example, during June and July we may only work on math in preparation for the next grade and on how to respond to questions from what we read.

During the summer months not everyone goes on vacation or the vacation time is limited to a few weeks. For example, my family goes away only for two weeks. The rest of the time for us is leisure time. Children like me may play videogames or they may watch T.V. However, those activities will not prepare them or me for the competitive world.

Finally, three months away from school is a long time. Students forget what they learned during the week on the weekend; won't they forget a lot during the three months of summer? If we have school, though, not only will they remember the information better, but they will also be prepared for the next grade.

Book Review Elements

Beginning	**Book Information:** What is the book and is there a preview to interest the reader?	
	Opinion: Is the writer's opinion about the book clear?	
Middle	**Reasons (two to four):** Are the reasons connected to the opinion and are they clear to the reader?	
	Evidence: Are there specific examples or quotes from the book to support the reasons? Are the examples explained clearly?	
End	**Restate Opinion:** Did the writer restate his or her opinion?	
	Think: Did the writer leave the reader with a message to think about the topic?	

Why Everyone Should Read the Book *Number the Stars* by Lois Lowry

A book that I recently read with my reading group is *Number the Stars* by Lois Lowry. This is a fictional book that tells the story of two friends, Annemarie Johansen and Ellen Rosen. They live in Copenhagen, Denmark, during World War II. German soldiers gather Jewish families and remove them from Denmark. Annemarie's family decides to help their friends and bring Ellen, who is Jewish, to their house, pretending to be their daughter. The same night Ellen comes home, the Nazis search the apartment, but do not find anything. Annemarie's family and the Johansens are very inventive as they try to stay safe and save their friends. This book is a great book that our school library should buy.

One reason our library should buy it is because it has received national recognition. The book is a Newberry winner. This is an award that is given to great books for children. That medal of recognition on the cover means that the book has excellent plot, characters, and writing style.

A second reason is because students can relate with the characters and through them they can understand better what Nazi occupation means. For example, in the first chapter, the reader joins Annemarie and Ellen as they play and when they are stopped, interrogated, and scolded for running and "looking like hoodlums." The reader can see that even basic freedoms were taken away. Later, the reader can feel the worry of Annemarie's mother who looks out the window after young Kristy's description of the events. The reader can understand the fear of the times by the fear the characters feel.

The book is also informative and describes the Danish resistance and the "tricks" that simple everyday people thought of to save Jewish people. Several of these tricks were dangerous for them all, but it was more important to save lives. One of those was the decision that Annemarie's family took to hide Ellen and pretend she was their daughter. Another one was Henric's secret compartment on his boat where he hid escaping Jews. Another one was the special drug they had created to destroy the dogs' sense of smell, so they could not detect the smell of humans and find where they were hiding.

The book teaches that simple people can be heroes and shows what it means to fight for what you know is right. Toward the end of the book the reader learns that Annemarie's older sister was run over by a military car when she and her fiancé, Peter, were running away from a raid. This did not stop Peter, though, who continued his resistance and gave his life for freedom.

Overall, this is a great book that is written nicely and can help students understand a time that scarred the lives of many people and many nations. It is a book that should be in our school library for everyone to read. Perhaps it can be in our summer reading list, too.

Number the Stars by Lois Lowry

Two friends are in Denmark during the German occupation. One of them is Jewish and she is hiding. Her friend and her family are helping Jewish people get away. Every library should have this book.

One reason why every library should have this book is because it has great descriptions. Students are learning how to write papers with good descriptions and this book can help them.

Another reason is a book that teaches students about the German occupation without showing the bad things that Germans did. The author lets the reader understand things without describing in great detail the deaths. For example when the death of the girl and her fiancé is described, it is done in a way that does not make you cry.

Finally, the book has some funny moments.

In conclusion, this is a great book that all fourth graders should read and all libraries should have.

The Brain: A Wonder

The human body consists of many different systems and all of them need to be in good health for someone to be healthy. However, I find the brain to be by far the most unique, important, and fascinating human organ. As Seymour Simon says in his book *The Brain: Our Nervous System,* "The brain is really what makes you, You."

One reason that the brain is the most fascinating human organ is because it directs your actions and reactions. For example, when you touch something that is hot, your brain interprets the level of heat and tells you whether you should move your hand or not. Your brain also tells you whether you should close your eyes and cover your face when you see a volleyball coming at you, for example. This is because your brain tells your body to react through a series of neurons.

A second reason is because the brain is where all your memories are stored. Short- and long-term memories are carefully stored in the cerebral cortex. Without the presence of memories, humans would not be able to function in society. Imagine someone teaching and not having any memory about what to teach and what he or she read. It would be impossible to have a job without the ability to memorize information or learn information.

Also, the brain is fascinating because of its complexity. As Seymour Simon says, "Each second, millions of signals pass through your brain, carrying all kinds of messages. They bring news about what your body is doing and feeling. Your brain examines the messages, produces thoughts and memories, and then plans what to do next" (p. 2). The brain is surely the conductor in the human body and the "maestro" of all we do. If one of the pathways for those signals is interrupted, specific human actions may not be possible any more.

Finally, the brain is fascinating because it is so small, but also so powerful. As Seymour Simon says, the brain is "no larger than a grapefruit." However, even though it has such a small volume, it can control your actions, reactions, and form your personality.

In conclusion, the brain is a powerful organ, and we should appreciate its complexity. The next time that you are reacting to something, or you remember something from a book you read, or you hum a song you like, thank your brain.

Reference

Simon, S. (2006). *The brain: Our nervous system.* Washington, DC: Smithsonian Collins.

Pets in the Classroom: Say Yes!

When you visit an elementary classroom, you may see in the corner of the room a cute little creature. In my classroom for example, we have a hamster. Classroom pets are an excellent addition to classrooms.

One reason that pets are an excellent addition to classrooms is because they help students develop caring skills and respect for others. For example, in my classroom we all learned how to take care of our hamster. This helped us be responsible. We all learned that if we did not feed our pet, it would starve and suffer. We also learned how to be sensitive to its needs, and in a way we learned how to be better people. We are far quieter in my fourth-grade classroom compared to how we were in second and third grade. We all use a quiet voice and try not to disturb our pet as we live with it, and it deserves our respect.

Also, pets can support students' science learning. Having pets allows students to learn about the pet's habitat and ways of living. In my classroom, our teacher taught us about hamsters' cycle of life, their diet, and their habits. We could have learned this information from a book, but we were much more interested to learn this information because we were learning about our hamster.

Having pets also can improve students' writing skills. Students can write interesting reports about the classroom pet, and they may learn in an engaging way to take observation notes. In my class, our teacher gave us science journals and we observed the pet's behaviors to better understand the ways that our behavior affected its behavior. We also wrote a daily journal where we recorded its daily consumption of food and water.

Some people are scared of having pets in the classrooms. They say that pets may carry diseases, and young children may get infected. If you care for your pet and you want it to live many years, you should visit the vet so it stays healthy. There is no fear of infections if precautions are taken.

In conclusion, having pets in the classrooms can benefit all students and can make them even better people. If children learn to care for and respect a pet, they may also care for and respect their classmates and everyone else. Why shouldn't we have them in our classrooms? "Scratch, scratch!" This is our hamster calling. It is time for feeding!

Saturday: This Is Our Day!

Students spend a great amount of time in schools. To be exact, students spend 180 days in school every year, and this is a long time. From Monday to Friday, every week of a month, students wake up in the morning and spend more than 6 hours in a classroom. There is no need to spend more time in the classrooms in order to improve students' performance in math and reading. From my perspective 5 days are more than enough for students' learning and there should not be any class on Saturdays.

One reason to not have school on Saturdays is that more money will be spent for supplies, teachers' salaries, and utilities. If students need to come to school during the weekend, school buses will need to be paid for this. Also, teachers' salaries will need to be increased and more money will be spent on electricity and gas, too. More money will need to be given to schools to cover these expenses and this means that more taxes will need to be paid by taxpayers. However, not everyone will agree to this.

Another reason against Saturday classes is that this is a day that students need to develop their other interests. During the weekend a lot of students participate in sports and other recreation activities. For example, I play tennis, and I am on a team playing competitively. If we have school on Saturdays, I will need to drop my team or try to find time during the school week to play. This may affect my schoolwork, and in the end, I may not be as good of a student or as good of an athlete. Losing the chance to play sports would be a real loss because sports and other activities are necessary for our development while we are still growing.

In addition, school on Saturdays may affect students' and even teachers' motivation. For five days students and teachers wake up and come to school. Saturday is the only day they can spend time with their families and friends. If they need to come to school that day, then they may react negatively and may lose interest in schoolwork.

Some people say that school on Saturday is necessary in order to increase students' performance at a national level. That is so wrong! Five days of school are more than enough for students' learning and there is no need to increase the time spent in school in order to increase students' academic performance. More time in school can affect students' motivation to learn and can also cost the state and the taxpayers more money. Students should be happy to go to school and should have the energy to participate in class-room activities. If one more day is added perhaps there will be negative effects instead of positive ones in their performance.

Chart with Elements of Opposing Position

Beginning		**Topic:** What is the topic and why should the reader care about it?	
		Opinion: Is the writer's opinion clear?	
Middle	ME	**Reasons:** Are the reasons connected to the opinion and are they clear and convincing to the reader?	
		Evidence: Is there enough evidence to support the reasons? Is the evidence explained?	
	OTHERS	**Opposing Position:** Is there a clear opposing position that states what others who do not agree with the writer think?	
		Reasons: Are the reasons connected with the opposing position and are they clear?	
		Evidence: Is there enough evidence to support the reasons? Is the evidence explained?	
		Rebuttal: Does the rebuttal prove that what others say is wrong and the writer is right?	
End		**Restate Opinion:** Did the writer restate his or her opinion?	
		Think: Did the writer leave the reader with a message to think about the topic?	

Transition Words for Opposing Position

Middle—for opposing position

- On the other hand, _____
- Others suggest/claim/assert/think/believe that _____
- On the other side of the controversy, X suggests that _____

Middle—for opposing reason

- A first reason _____
- One reason, _____

Middle—for rebuttal

- Even though X is _____, this suggestion is not _____, because
- This is an interesting/important perspective/idea/suggestion; however, it is _____

Planning Materials

PLAN

Form: What am I writing?   Essay   Paragraph   Letter   Other _____

T

A

P

Ideas

Brainstorm

In Favor (YES . . .)	Against (NO . . .)

(continued)

Graphic Organizer (GO) for Persuasive Writing

Beginning	Topic:
	Opinion:
Middle	Reason 1:
	Evidence:
	Reason 2:
	Evidence:
	Reason 3:
	Evidence:
End	Restate Opinion:
	Think:

Rubric for Self-Evaluation and Peer Review of Persuasive Writing

Date: _____

Writer's Name: _____ Reviewer's Name: _____

		0 Not there	1 Could be better	2 Great!
Beginning	**Topic:** What is the topic and why should the reader care about it?			
	Opinion: Is the writer's opinion clear?			
Middle	**Reason 1:** Is the first reason connected to the opinion and is it clear and convincing to the reader?			
	Evidence: Is there enough evidence to support the reason? Is the evidence explained?			
	Reason 2: Is the second reason connected to the opinion and is it clear and convincing to the reader?			
	Evidence: Is there enough evidence to support the reason? Is the evidence explained?			
	Reason 3: Is the third reason connected to the opinion and is it clear and convincing to the reader?			
	Evidence: Is there enough evidence to support the reason? Is the evidence explained?			
End	**Restate Opinion:** Did the writer restate his or her opinion?			
	Think: Did the writer leave the reader with a message to think about the topic?			
Other Considerations!	Is there a title that clearly refers to the information in the paper?			
	Is the paper's tone appropriate for the audience? Was the writer respectful to the reader?			
	Are there clear and appropriate transition words used throughout the paper?			

(continued)

Rubric for Self-Evaluation and Peer Review of Persuasive Writing *(page 2 of 2)*

Reviewer/Writer as Reader
• Was the paper overall convincing? Why?
• What revisions should be made?
Goals
• What should be the writer's current and future goals?

Memorization Sheet for Persuasion

Writer's Name: _____   Date: _____

Beginning	
Middle	
End	
Other Considerations!	

What did I miss? _____

_____

_____

What should be my study goals? _____

_____

_____

Rubric for Self-Evaluation and Peer Review of Persuasive Writing with Opposing Position

Date: _____

Writer's Name: _____ Reviewer's Name: _____

		0 Not there	1 Could be better	2 Great!
Beginning	**Topic:** What is the topic and why should the reader care about it?			
	Opinion: Is the writer's opinion clear?			
Middle ME	**Reasons (two to four):** Are the reasons connected to the opinion and are they clear and convincing to the reader?			
	Evidence: Is there enough evidence to support the reasons? Is the evidence explained?			
OTHERS	**Opposing Position:** Is there a clear opposing position that states what others who do not agree with the writer think?			
	Reasons and Evidence: Are the reasons connected with the opposing position and are they clear?			
	Rebuttal: Does the rebuttal **prove that what others say is wrong** and the writer is right?			
End	**Restate Opinion:** Did the writer restate his or her opinion?			
	Think: Did the writer leave the reader with a message to think about the topic?			
Other Considerations!	Is there a title that clearly refers to the information in the paper?			
	Is the paper's tone appropriate for the audience? Was the writer respectful to the reader?			
	Are there clear and appropriate transition words used throughout the paper?			

(continued)

Reviewer/Writer as Reader

- Was the paper overall convincing? Why?

- What revisions should be made?

Goals

- What should be the writer's current and future goals?

Memorization Sheet for Persuasive Writing with Opposing Position

Writer's Name: _____   Date: _____

Beginning		•
		•
Middle	**ME**	•
		•
	OTHERS	•
		•
End		•
		•
Other Considerations!		

What did I miss? _____

_____

_____

What should be my study goals? _____

_____

_____

Chapter 6

Compare–Contrast Writing

People frequently make comparisons in everyday life, for example, when choosing which car or television to purchase, which movie to see, or which candidate to support. To make such choices, they gather information and consider the similarities and differences in order to evaluate which is the best choice. They might use written comparisons—for example, comparisons of consumer products or independent comparisons of the records of politicians. Compare–contrast writing is also common in school, but in school it is most often used to help students learn and understand content and ideas. For example, in science, students might compare and contrast reptiles and amphibians to get a better understanding of classes of animals. In literature, students might compare two characters in a book as a part of learning to interpret fiction.

Compare–contrast writing can be very challenging both for students and teachers (Englert & Thomas, 1987). First, like most informative writing, comparisons require students to gather information, usually from reading as well as class activities. Students need to read and comprehend texts, take notes on the most important information, (often) integrate information from more than one text, organize the information, and write using their own words. Thus, in this chapter, the Ideas step in the strategy is expanded to include reading and note taking. The GO is used to take notes as well as to plan the final paper.

Second, compare–contrast writing can be challenging because it requires students to group information both by categories and by similarities and differences. Students need to learn how to group information into categories, which involves grouping ideas from their brainstorming or notes and generating superordinate category labels. The GO is designed to support this organization by categories.

The CCSS for reading and writing call for students to write in order to inform (CCSS, 2010). Information should be factual, accurate, and well explained for the reader to learn about a topic (see Table 6.1). Overall, students are expected to present organized ideas, provide supporting details, use transition words that support the transition from one idea to the next, and conclude with a section that brings an ending to their analysis. Compare–contrast is mentioned specifically in response to reading informative texts and also literature.

These lessons are slightly different from the lessons of the previous instructional chapters. One main difference is that in this chapter students learn to write using sources, and we directly integrate reading and writing. As in other chapters, the compare–contrast genre is introduced through read-alouds, and the teacher and students take notes using the GO. The modeling lesson is done without the use of sources. In the collaborative lesson, the teacher models note taking on one topic and works with students to take notes on the second topic, complete the GO, and draft a paper following the guide of the Writing Strategy Ladder. Because there are two equally demanding objectives (to use the new elements for the genre and to use note taking), we decided to show students how to write using the new elements for the new genre first and then to work with them on note taking. After collaborative practice, students work on their own papers with or without sources. The decision to use sources is one that you will need to make based on the capabilities and needs of your students. We encourage you to use readings from social studies, science, and literature to make the task authentic and engaging to students.

A second difference is that in this chapter, we could not use trade books for the read-alouds. This is because it is rather difficult to find trade books with an explicit compare–contrast structure; usually comparison is part of a larger text. Therefore, the introduction to the genre begins with a read-aloud of a well-written paper. We encourage you, though, to read additional compare–contrast papers using online sources (e.g., *www.diffen.com*) to discuss their organization and the purpose of the genre. After your students are introduced to the genre and have practiced writing from sources, you could expand to include websites (e.g., *http://kids.nationalgeographic.com*).

The next section includes the writing lessons and materials. At the end of all writing lessons, we include two additional activities that you could use in small-group instruction or as mini-lessons (creating a reference list and developing categories and topic sentences). Also, at the end of the chapter, you will find some extension activities and pertinent resources. The most direct extension of the lessons is to use them with topics that students are learning in science and social studies. However, these lessons could also be used with literature. For instance, as part of an author study, students can be asked to write a paper comparing and contrasting two books written by the same author, or students can compare and contrast characters or other literary elements.

The rest of this chapter includes (1) a lesson outline that provides information about the read-aloud tasks and a synopsis of each writing lesson, (2) sample writing prompts that you could use for assessment and instruction, (3) detailed writing lessons on compare–contrast with ready-to-use materials, (4) extension activities for additional genres, (5) resources for the teaching of additional genres, and (6) forms that are used in more than one lesson and can be displayed in your classroom. The lessons are based on the Strategy for teaching strategies (see Figure 3.1). You may want to review the instructional procedures in Chapter 3. Also, you may want to review the Writing Strategy Ladder and the Be Strategic! strategy in Chapter 2.

TABLE 6.1. Informative Writing and Reading Standards on Compare–Contrast for Grades 3–5

Grade 3	Grade 4	Grade 5

Writing

Write informative/explanatory texts to examine a topic and convey ideas and information clearly.

Grade 3	Grade 4	Grade 5
1. Introduce a topic and group related information together; include illustrations when useful to aiding comprehension. 2. Develop the topic with facts, definitions, and details. 3. Use linking words and phrases (e.g., *also, another, and, more, but*) to connect ideas within categories of information. 4. Provide a concluding statement or section.	1. Introduce a topic clearly and group related information in paragraphs and sections; include formatting (e.g., headings), illustrations, and multimedia when useful to aiding comprehension. 2. Develop the topic with facts, definitions, concrete details, quotations, or other information and examples related to the topic. 3. Link ideas within categories of information using words and phrases (e.g., *another, for example, also, because*). 4. Use precise language and domain-specific vocabulary to inform about or explain the topic. 5. Provide a concluding statement or section related to the information or explanation presented.	1. Introduce a topic clearly, provide a general observation and focus, and group related information logically; include formatting (e.g., headings), illustrations, and multimedia when useful to aiding comprehension. 2. Develop the topic with facts, definitions, concrete details, quotations, or other information and examples related to the topic. 3. Link ideas within and across categories of information using words, phrases, and clauses (e.g., *in contrast, especially*). 4. Use precise language and domain-specific vocabulary to inform about or explain the topic. 5. Provide a concluding statement or section related to the information or explanation presented. *Draw evidence from literary or informational texts to support analysis, reflection, and research.* Apply grade 5 reading standards to literature (e.g., "Compare and contrast two or more characters, settings, or events in a story or a drama, drawing on specific details in the text [e.g., how characters interact]").

Reading literature

Grade 3	Grade 4	Grade 5
1. Compare and contrast the themes, settings, and plots of stories written by the same author about the same or similar characters (e.g., in books from a series). 2. With prompting and support, compare and contrast the adventures and experiences of characters in familiar stories.	1. Compare and contrast the treatment of similar themes and topics (e.g., opposition of good and evil) and patterns of events (e.g., the quest) in stories, myths, and traditional literature from different cultures. 2. Compare and contrast the adventures and experiences of characters in stories.	1. Compare and contrast stories in the same genre (e.g., mysteries and adventure stories) on their approaches to similar themes and topics. 2. Compare and contrast two or more versions of the same story (e.g., Cinderella stories) by different authors or from different cultures.

Reading informational text

Grade 3	Grade 4	Grade 5
1. Compare and contrast the most important points and key details presented in two texts on the same topic.	1. Integrate information from two texts on the same topic in order to write or speak about the subject knowledgeably.	1. Integrate information from several texts on the same topic in order to write or speak about the subject knowledgeably.

LESSON OUTLINE

Read-Aloud Lesson(s)

Introduction to the Genre

Students are introduced to the purpose of compare–contrast writing and the elements of the genre during the reading of a well-written paper.

Preassessment

Students write in response to a compare–contrast writing prompt on a familiar topic (see sample topics).

Compare–Contrast Writing Lessons

Lesson 1: Introduction—Evaluation of Good and Weak Examples and Self-Evaluation

Students review the purpose and elements of the compare–contrast genre. They evaluate good and weak papers applying evaluation criteria, and they evaluate their own papers and set personal goals for improvement.

Lesson 2: Modeling How to Write a Compare–Contrast Paper

Students review the compare–contrast elements and observe the teacher during think-aloud modeling of planning, drafting, evaluating to revise, and editing of a compare–contrast paper without the use of sources.

Lesson 3: Self-Regulation and Note Taking (Modeling and Collaborative Planning)

Students reflect on the application of the writing strategy, review the use of the self-regulation strategies, and make revisions on their self-talk sheets. The teacher models note taking on one topic; students and teacher collaboratively take notes on a new topic, review ideas, and complete the GO by identifying categories.

Lesson 4: Collaborative Drafting of a Compare–Contrast Essay Using Sources

Teacher and students collaboratively use the plan from Lesson 3 to draft, evaluate to revise, and edit a compare–contrast paper using sources. During collaborative writing, the teacher scaffolds students' application of the strategy and does the writing as the students provide the ideas and sentences.

Lesson 5: Students Plan and Draft Their Own Compare–Contrast Papers

Students begin working on their own papers, using the planning strategy, including taking notes from sources and drafting their papers. The teacher monitors use of the strategy and provides support as needed.

Lesson 6: Preparation for Peer Review and Self-Evaluation

Students practice evaluating compare–contrast papers, making suggestions and revisions. Students self-evaluate their papers, using evaluation criteria, and set goals for revision.

Lesson 7: Peer Review and Revision

Students peer-review in pairs or small groups, applying the evaluation criteria. Students compare their self-evaluations with the comments of their peers, set goals for revision, and make revisions.

Lesson 8: Editing

Students examine their papers for editing errors. By using the editing strategy (SCIPS), students identify surface-level errors and correct them. Teachers can choose to teach a specific grammatical/editing skill, practice it with students, and ask students to make changes to their essays. Additionally, students set editing goals and reflect on their performance and progress.

Publishing Guidelines

It is important for students to share some of their work with a larger audience. See Chapter 3 for a discussion of ideas about opportunities for publishing. These guidelines do not comprise a specific lesson, but rather present ideas for discussing publishing options with your students. The specifics will depend on what sort of publishing you have chosen.

Guidelines for Continuous Guided Practice to Mastery

It is important for students to write more than one paper in a genre to develop mastery of that genre. As students write a second paper and more, they typically work more quickly and feel much more competent. Teachers can then focus their attention on students who need more support.

Read-Aloud Lesson(s)

INTRODUCTION TO THE GENRE

Students are introduced to the purpose of compare–contrast writing and the elements of the genre during the reading of a well-written paper.

Lesson Objectives

By the end of this lesson, students will be able to:

- Explain the meaning of compare–contrast and discuss why, when, and where people compare and contrast in everyday life and in school.
- Identify the elements of compare–contrast in a compare–contrast essay.
- Recall the elements of compare–contrast.
- Explain the meaning of categories.

Materials for Introduction to the Genre Lesson

- Form 6.1. Planning Materials—use only the GO section
- Handout 6.1. Chart of Elements of Compare–Contrast
- Handout 6.2. A Well-Written Paper for Introduction to the Genre, "Sharks and Dolphins"

Notes

- In the subsequent days, you could read papers online that compare and contrast topics (e.g., *www.diffen.com*), using the GO (as you do in this introductory class) to record the information from the reading. If you choose to use the suggested website, you should know that the provided topics discuss differences, but at the end of your work with students, you could also discuss similarities. Overall, this practice can help students (1) review and learn the elements of the genre; (2) discuss, with your support, the importance and use of categories; and (3) discuss the importance of clear and well-developed GOs when drafting papers. For example, if a paper does not have categories or sufficient ideas, you could point out the limited information on the GO. Of course, this will be a valuable discussion once you have modeled the writing process and students have seen the use of the GO when drafting their papers. As we noted, the papers on the suggested website do not have similarities; however, it is easy to identify similarities once you have completed the GO. For example, if you are reading about alligators and crocodiles (see *www.diffen.com/difference/Alligator_vs_Crocodile*), you could discuss with students what is similar between the two topics and what type of animal the two are. You could even work with students to develop a topic sentence and a paragraph using this information.

  o It is essential that you visit the site and review its information before meeting with the students. This is a wiki, and the accuracy of information may be something that you need to examine. You could discuss issues of accuracy concerning online sources and wikis with your students, too.

- Categories are an essential feature of compare–contrast writing. At the end of the lessons, we provide an activity on understanding and identifying categories. The discussion about categories of similarities and differences can be also included during read-alouds.

- We encourage you to use readings from social studies and science, but we also provide sample books for your reference (see Figure 6.1).

Procedures

Discussion of Compare–Contrast

- Explain to students that people often compare and contrast two things and think about them to make a decision. *Compare* means to look for similarities, and *Contrast* means to look for differences. You can give an example (e.g., comparing and contrasting two cars before making a purchase). Ask students if they have heard the term *compare and contrast* and if they have ever used it. Support them in making connections to personal experiences (e.g., two movies, two outfits, two sports, two athletes).

- Explain that in school students are asked to write compare–contrast papers in order to

• *Jupiter* by Seymour Simon	• *Destination: Mars* by Seymour Simon
• *Tornadoes* by Seymour Simon	• *Hurricanes* by Seymour Simon
• *Cats* by Seymour Simon	• *Dogs* by Seymour Simon
• *Earth* by Seymour Simon	• *The Moon* by Seymour Simon
• *First on the Moon* by Barbara Hehner	• *Columbus* by Edgar Parin D'Aulaire
• *Dolphins* by Seymour Simon	• *Sharks* by Seymour Simon
• *Bill Clinton* by Michael Benson or • *Abraham Lincoln* by George Sullivan	• *Obama: A Promise of Change* by David Mendell
• *The Orphan: A Cinderella Story from Greece* by Anthony L. Manna & Soula Mitakidou	• *The Egyptian Cinderella* by Shirley Climo
• *The Three Little Wolves and the Big Bad Pig* by Eugene Trivizas	• *The Three Pigs* by David Weisner
• *The Three Pigs* by David Weisner	• *The Three Little Aliens and the Big Bad Robot* by Margaret McNamara

FIGURE 6.1. Sample pairs of books for read-alouds on compare–contrast.

learn information. For example, they may be asked to compare and contrast the eyes and the ears in order to better understand the way they work in the human body and what functions they perform in humans. Explain that compare–contrast is used to: evaluate and make a decision, or help learn and understand information.

Introduction of Compare–Contrast Elements

- Ask students to tell you what elements they think that a compare–contrast paper would have, based on what they have learned from the previous genres. Display the elements' chart (Handout 6.1) and discuss it with the students. Explain that when working on compare–contrast papers, it is important for writers to clearly answer these questions:

  1. What is the topic and what is compared to what?
  2. What is the purpose of the comparison?
  3. What are the similarities? How do you know?
  4. What are the differences? How do you know?

- Explain that the "How do you know?" question is answered by citing evidence. Discuss the meaning of evidence, using what students learned in the persuasion genre lessons.
- Point out the differences and similarities between this genre and persuasion. For example, you can point out that this genre also has a Beginning, Middle, and End, but in the middle the writer will include similarities and differences instead of reasons.

Read-Aloud

- Explain to students that you will display and read a well-written paper aloud. Read a small section of the paper at a time and stop to discuss the elements of compare–contrast and the information. Record the key information on the GO in Form 6.1 (a completed example is shown in Figure 6.2).
- For the introduction, discuss the purpose for the comparison. In the case of sharks versus dolphins, the purpose is to learn more about both kinds of sea creatures.
- For each paragraph, discuss what category of information is presented. Be sure to discuss the information in the paper and how the comparisons and contrasts help readers understand the topic. Talk about unfamiliar vocabulary and ideas as well.
- For the conclusion, discuss how the author brings the paper to a close.
- After completing the read-aloud and note taking, briefly review the notes and discuss what you learned.

End of Lesson

- Explain to students that in the next weeks they will learn how to write compare–contrast papers.

Beginning	**Topic:** Sharks and Dolphins		
	Purpose: to learn about them		

Middle	How are they **similar**?	**Similarities**	
	Creatures of the sea	Live in oceans, and some can be in freshwater, too, have streamline bodies	
	What they eat and how	Eat fish, they swallow it whole—sharks may cut it in pieces with razor-sharp teeth	
	How are they **different**?	**Differences**	
		Unique features of Topic A: Sharks	**Unique features of Topic B: Dolphins**
	Different type of animal	Fish, have gills, may lay eggs on ocean floor	Mammals, breathe air (blowhole), give birth to babies
	How they care for their young	Do not care for their babies	Mother dolphin cares for calf for a year and a half
	Intelligence	Predators	Can learn tricks and communicate with each other with sounds

End	**Restate purpose:** important to learn about them so we can understand them better
	Leave a message to the reader: keep oceans clean

FIGURE 6.2. Example of a completed chart to introduce the compare–contrast genre (for your reference).

SAMPLE TOPICS FOR WRITING ASSESSMENT/INSTRUCTION

Note: The topics included in this list should not limit your choices. Consider developing authentic, engaging topics.

1. Pets can be found in people's homes and often in school classrooms. Write a paper comparing and contrasting two pets of your choice.

2. A lot of people go on vacation. Depending on their destination, they may use different means of transportation. Write a paper comparing and contrasting traveling by airplane or by car.

3. Write a paper comparing and contrasting two of your favorite superheroes (e.g., Wolverine vs. Iron Man).

4. Bees and ants are insects that have both similarities and differences. Write a paper comparing and contrasting bees and ants.

5. Sharks and dolphins are part of the oceanic life. Write a paper comparing and contrasting sharks and dolphins.

6. Sports can be entertaining and you can spend your free time either participating in one, attending a game, watching it on TV. Write a paper comparing and contrasting two sports about which you know a lot.

7. We make music when we whistle, when we clap, and even when we walk. Music is entertaining and relaxing. Write a paper comparing and contrasting two musical instruments, two musicians, or two musical groups you like.

8. Technology has really changed the way we write. Write a paper comparing and contrasting typing and writing using a paper and pencil.

Compare–Contrast Writing Lessons

LESSON 1: INTRODUCTION—EVALUATION OF GOOD AND WEAK EXAMPLES AND SELF-EVALUATION

Students review the purpose and elements of the compare–contrast genre. They evaluate good and weak papers, applying evaluation criteria. They also evaluate their own papers and set personal goals for improvement.

Lesson Objectives

By the end of this lesson, students will be able to:

- Recall the elements of compare–contrast.
- Apply the evaluation criteria to score and comment on a paper.
- Evaluate their own papers and set specific goals for personal improvement.

Assessment Information

The teacher informally assesses whether students can (1) recall the compare–contrast elements, (2) apply the evaluation criteria to score papers, and (3) set personal goals for improvement.

Notes

- Students will self-evaluate their preassessment paper. You can also score students' papers using the evaluation rubric (see Form 6.2).
- We provide sample papers for this lesson; however, you may decide to use different samples on topics drawn from your subject areas.
- We provide more than one well-written paper. You could review more than one well-written paper or you could use those additional papers for read-alouds.

- During practice applying the evaluation criteria, students also evaluate a paper in small groups. You may want to assign students to groups ahead of time, using the information from the preassessment. It is usually a good idea to mix better and weaker writers in a group.

- During students' self-evaluations, you can also evaluate a paper you have written. It is important for students to see you as a writer, too.

Materials for Lesson 1

- Form 6.2. Rubric on Self-Evaluation and Peer Review
- Form 6.2 (copies for students' self-evaluation and small-group evaluation)
- Handout 6.1. Chart of Elements of Compare–Contrast
- Handout 6.3. A Well-Written Paper for Evaluation, "A Cat or a Dog?: This Is the Question"
- Handout 6.4. A Well-Written Paper for Evaluation, "Sparta and Athens: Where Would You Live?"
- Handout 6.5. A Well-Written Paper for Evaluation, "Tornadoes and Hurricanes"
- Handout 6.6. A Weak Paper for Evaluation, "Jupiter and Mars"
- Handout 6.7. A Weak Paper for Evaluation, "Where Would You Like to Wake Up, by the Beach or in a Mountain Cabin?"
- Handout 6.8. A Weak Paper for Evaluation, "Writing on a Computer or Using a Paper and a Pencil to Write"
- Handout 6.9. A Weak Example for Evaluation, "Eyes and Ears"
- Students' preassessments (see sample topics for writing assessment/instruction, pp. 180–181)

Procedures

Review

- Review the elements and purposes of compare–contrast writing.

Identification and Evaluation of Compare–Contrast Elements in a Well-Written Paper and a Weak Paper

- Explain that in order to tell whether a paper is well written, it is important to know the genre elements and their organization. In the introduction of a compare–contrast paper, readers would expect to read which two things are being compared and for what purpose. In the body, readers would expect to read about the similarities and differences between the two topics, organized by categories. Finally, a conclusion should return to the purpose.

- Explain that students can develop their "critical reading skills" by reading well-written papers and weak papers. They can then look for the elements and evaluate them, using a rubric. Finally, students should record suggestions for improving each paper. Explain that this process will help students learn the elements, develop their critical reading and evaluation skills, and learn how to apply evaluation criteria to their own writing.

- Present and explain the elements and scoring system of the rubric for evaluation (see Form 6.2). Point out that the rubric contains the elements of compare–contrast and that students will use it when they evaluate the work of their peers during peer review and when they evaluate their own work during self-evaluation. Also explain the information in the section of the rubric called "Other Considerations."

Evaluation of a Well-Written Paper

- Explain that you will first read and examine the elements of a well-written paper.
- Display for students and read out loud a well-written paper (you could choose from Handouts 6.3–6.5). Then discuss students' general impressions of the paper. Explain that even though this is a well-written paper, they should still look for the elements and score them using the rubric (Form 6.2). Tell students that they can help you find each element.
- Read each evaluation question from the rubric and invite students to locate that element in the paper. Underline each element, turn to the rubric, assign a score, and explain your thinking. Students can participate, but you should lead the process. Refer to the elements when you decide the next step to take. Complete the rubric and follow-up questions.
- Review the information on the rubric and discuss what would be the writer's goals.
- You may repeat the task with an additional well-written paper or use the second well-written paper on a different day during read-aloud time.

Evaluation of a Weak Paper

- Briefly review the elements of compare–contrast in Handout 6.1. Explain that you will read a second paper (see Handout 6.6) out loud and evaluate it together (see Figures 6.3 and 6.4 for your reference).
- Display the paper for students and read it out loud. As you did earlier, ask students their general impressions of the paper. Then explain that you will evaluate the paper together using the evaluation rubric (Form 6.2). Think out loud as you look for each element, underline it, and score it. Explain your reasoning for your scoring. Also, take some notes about things the writer could do to improve a specific element. When you record your suggestions, use the phrase "Perhaps the writer could say. . . ." This will help students develop a model about how to make constructive suggestions. You can invite students to help you identify each element, but the goal is for you to model and explain the process of scoring and giving detailed suggestions to the writer.
- Finally, discuss the goals that the writer should set and explain the importance of honest evaluation and goal setting.

Jupiter and Mars

Space has always been a place that scientists have wondered about. The stars fascinated a lot of ancient civilizations like the Assyrians, Greeks, and the Romans. The Romans also named many planets after their Gods! The discovery of the telescope and the ways that our technology advanced helped us learn more about space and the planets. Two exciting planets are Jupiter and Mars [TOPIC].
    [PURPOSE?]
    [TRANSITION? CATEGORY OF SIMILARITIES?] Mars and Jupiter are both named after ancient Roman gods. Mars was the god of war, and the Romans named the planet that because its red color made them think of blood and warfare. Jupiter was the king of the Roman gods, and Jupiter is the biggest planet in our solar system [EVIDENCE].
    [TRANSITION? CATEGORY OF SIMILARITIES?] Both of the planets also orbit the sun, just like Earth. They also both have moons: Mars has two small moons, and Jupiter has at least sixteen. Mars's moons are called Phobos and Deimos and in the Greek mythology they were twin brothers and sons of Ares, the Greek god of war [EVIDENCE].
    [TRANSITION? CATEGORY OF DIFFERENCES?] Mars is much smaller than Earth. In fact, Mars could fit inside the Earth seven times. Meanwhile, Jupiter could fit 1,300 Earths inside. That's enormous! They also have different surfaces. As Seymour Simon says in his book *Mars,* Mars has many land formations, like craters, mountains, volcanoes, plains, and valleys. Jupiter, however, is completely covered by clouds and the surface is one big ocean of liquid hydrogen. Seymour Simon in the book *Jupiter* says that the clouds are not made of water like on Earth, but they are made of many gases, like helium and hydrogen [EVIDENCE].
    [TRANSITION?] These planets are also different because humans have been able to explore them in different ways [CATEGORY OF DIFFERENCES]. Jupiter is much harder to explore because the clouds that surround it have very high winds. The winds have destroyed a probe that was sent inside and this is why no one has ever seen the surface of the planet. Mars, on the other hand, has had spaceships and robots explore the surface of the planet and send back images to Earth. Seymour Simon in the book *Mars* explains that the *Pathfinder* is one rover that has sent back thousands of images and analyzed the rocks and weather on the surface to give us a lot of data about Mars [EVIDENCE].
    [CONCLUSION?]

FIGURE 6.3. Example of a weak paper, "Jupiter and Mars," with elements identified (for your reference).

Discussion

- Ask students why and how you evaluated the papers. Make a connection between the elements and the evaluation criteria of the rubric.

Collaborative Evaluation of a Weak Paper

- Explain to students that you will read papers and use the evaluation rubric to score them and set goals for the writers. Explain the purpose of setting clear goals for revisions.

- Display one of the weak papers (from Handouts 6.7–6.9) and, with students' input, evaluate it. (Note: Your role during this activity is to scaffold students' application of evaluation criteria. Therefore, it is best to ask them process questions [e.g., "What should we do next?"], ask them to find the elements for you to underline, and ask them to tell you a score per element with explanations for you to record the information on the rubric. Also ask students to give you suggestions for improvement. If students are challenged or if their responses are not accurate, reassume control of the activity.)

		0 Not there	1 Could be better	2 Great!
Beginning	**Topic**: Is it clear what is compared and contrasted?			✓
	Purpose: Why are the topics compared and contrasted?	✓		
Middle *Similarities*	**Similarity 1**: Is the 1st category of similarities clear to the reader?	✓		
	Evidence: Is the evidence clear and accurate? Is the evidence explained?			✓
	Similarity 2 and more: Is the second and the rest of the categories of similarities clearly stated?	✓		
	Evidence: Is the evidence clear and accurate? Is the evidence explained?			✓
Differences	**Difference 1**: Is the 1st category of differences clear to the reader?	✓		
	Evidence: Is the evidence clear and accurate? Is the evidence explained?			✓
	Difference 2 and more: Is the 2nd and the rest of the categories of differences clear to the reader?		✓	
	Evidence: Is the evidence clear and accurate? Is the evidence explained?			✓
End	**Restate Purpose**: Did the writer restate why the topics are compared and contrasted?	✓		
	Think: Did the writer leave the reader with a message to think about?	✓		
Other Considerations!	Is there a title that clearly refers to the information in the paper that relates to the purpose?			✓
	Are there appropriate transition words used throughout the paper?	✓		
	If the writer used sources, are ideas and details appropriately drawn from the text?			✓
	If the writer used sources, are they accurately referenced at the end of the paper?			✓

Reviewer/Writer as Reader
- Is the paper informative? Why? *Yes, I learned a lot of information about the two planets. The writer overall had a lot of evidence and used a lot of information from the readings.*
- What revisions should be made? *The paragraphs did not have categories and transitions. Also, the writer did not have a conclusion!*

Goals
- What should be the writer's current and future goals? *Add categories and a conclusion. In the future always make sure to have clear categories and include transitions to introduce them. Always have a clear conclusion that restates the purpose and leaves the reader with something to think about.*

Suggested Revision of "End": *In conclusion, Mars and Jupiter are amazing planets that have a lot of similarities and differences that we should know in order to learn about them and the conditions on their surface. They both have moons and like all planets they orbit the sun. However, they have different sizes and surfaces. Perhaps additional ways can be found to explore them and find out about those planets that fascinated the ancients many years ago and us today.*

FIGURE 6.4. Example of a completed rubric of a weak paper (for your reference).

Small-Group Evaluation of a Weak Paper

- Ask students to work in groups to read a different paper (you can choose from Handouts 6.7–6.9), identify the elements, and complete the rubric (copies of Form 6.2). Ask students to follow the same procedures you followed earlier. Discuss students' scoring and suggestions as a group.

Self-Evaluation of Students' Papers and Goal Setting

- Review the importance of goal setting. Discuss the undesirable results of recording inaccurate scores and assigning high scores on elements that the writer needs to improve. Stress the importance of honesty in evaluation and goal setting.

- Ask students to read their own preassessment papers, evaluate them using the rubric for compare–contrast (copies of Form 6.2), and set goals for their own writing. Ask them to be specific about the goals they set and congratulate honest evaluations.

Differentiation

- During small-group practice, you can work with a group of students that is having difficulty locating the elements and scoring them using the rubric or making suggestions. Similarly, during students' self-evaluation time, you can work with individuals or a small group of students to guide them in the process of developing realistic goals for improvement.

Reflection Activity

- **Journal writing.** You can ask students to write a journal entry in response to the following questions:
  1. What did I learn about *my* compare–contrast writing?
  2. What should be my goals for improvement? What could I do to reach those goals?

End of Lesson

- Review the elements of compare–contrast and discuss why writers should always make sure to include them. Review the importance of honesty in evaluation and goal setting.

LESSON 2: MODELING HOW TO WRITE A COMPARE–CONTRAST PAPER

Students review the compare–contrast elements and observe the teacher during a think-aloud modeling of planning, drafting, evaluating to revise, and editing of a compare–contrast paper without the use of sources.

Lesson Objectives

By the end of this lesson, students will be able to:

- Recall the elements of compare–contrast.
- Recall the steps of the Writing Strategy Ladder and explain their components.

Assessment Information

The teacher (1) informally assesses whether students understand the steps of the Writing Strategy Ladder and its components and (2) uses students' written responses to identify those who may need assistance learning the elements.

Notes

- Even though the ultimate goal of the chapter is to support students writing from sources, the teacher does not model using sources in this lesson. This decision was made for two reasons:

  ○ First, because we judged that students would be overwhelmed by a lesson that included note taking and the use of the new procedures for planning, drafting, and evaluating to revise for the new genre, we decided to break the task into two parts. In the first part students learn about the genre and how to write without sources. In the second part, during collaborative work, they learn how to take notes and write from sources.

  ○ Second, if some teachers choose to write without using sources throughout this chapter, they could use this lesson as a guide.

- During review, you can ask students to complete Form 6.3, Memorization Sheet for Compare–Contrast Writing, or you can ask them to write the elements on a blank sheet. You can repeat this memorization task across several lessons to see how students progress over time.

- It is very likely that students will participate more during the modeling of this genre compared to the previous ones. This is expected; students know a lot about the lesson sequence compared to the beginning instructional chapters (e.g., the meaning of FTAP). You could use students' input; however, you should be in control of the modeling. If you have not taught another genre and this is the first, please read the modeling lessons and think-aloud from Chapter 4 or 5.

- The lesson uses a comparison of baseball and basketball as the topic for the think-aloud. We chose this topic because it is familiar to most students. You can use this example if you like or choose your own topic based on what your students know. If you do use our topic, the completed planning materials and essay can be found in Figure 6.5.

- The introduction to the Writing Strategy Ladder will be shorter if you have taught the lessons in the previous chapters.

- If you have taught Chapters 4 and 5, then students have been introduced to the Be Strategic! strategy, and they have had practice in developing self-talk. In this lesson, you can choose to briefly review the meaning of self-regulation at the end of your modeling and give students the opportunity to revisit their self-talk sheets and make revisions. For this task, you could use Form 2.2 or use a blank sheet. By doing this, you will have more time to devote to note taking in Lesson 3.

Materials for Lesson 2

- Form 6.1. Planning Materials (FTAP, Ideas, GO)
- Form 6.2. Rubric on Self-Evaluation and Peer Review
- Form 6.3. Memorization Sheet for Compare–Contrast Writing
- Handout 2.1. Writing Strategy Ladder (from Chapter 2)
- Handout 2.2. SCIPS Editing Guide (from Chapter 2)
- Handout 6.10. Transition Words and Sentence Starters

Procedures

Review

- Ask students to write the elements of the compare–contrast genre. Hold a class discussion about the importance of each element. You might spend some time working on memorization techniques or games.

Introduction to the Writing Strategy Ladder

- Explain to students that you will teach them how to apply the strategy to writing compare–contrast papers. Remind them that the strategy is useful because it helps them stay on track and not skip a step.

- Display the Writing Strategy Ladder, point, read, and explain each one of the steps (see Handout 2.1). (Note: The lesson steps below assume that you have already taught the strategy for narrative and/or persuasive writing, so the emphasis is on parts that are different for compare–contrast writing.)

PLAN

Form: What am I writing? (Essay) Paragraph   Letter   Other _____

Topic: *Compare–contrast baseball and basketball*

Audience: *Young children who want to join a sport*

Purpose: *To learn about them and decide which one to watch or join*

IDEAS

Brainstorm   **Reading** *and* **Note Taking**

Unique features of Topic A: Baseball		Unique features of Topic B: Basketball
cleats long pants a cap protective gear glove bat baseball bases Canceled if weather is bad World Series 9 players	**Similarities between Topics** Great players (Michael Jordan in basketball and Derek Jeter in baseball)—players retire early Highly paid players (Jeter with more than 10 million contract with Yankees) Injuries (Boban Jancovič in basketball and Ray Chapman in baseball) Entertaining Popular Have fans Players' signatures can be worth millions after years	NBA 5 players shoes (flat) shorts and shirts basketball and hoops/goal post court Players play in a covered space protected from weather Ball bounces Need to dribble when walking on court

Completed GO for modeling (for your reference; draw the GO on the board)

<table>
<tr><td rowspan="2">Beginning</td><td colspan="2">Topic: Baseball versus basketball</td></tr>
<tr><td colspan="2">Purpose: To learn about the game and perhaps decide what game to watch when both play on TV.</td></tr>
<tr><td rowspan="4">Middle</td><td>How are they similar?</td><td align="center">Similarities</td></tr>
<tr><td>They are sports</td><td>Entertaining, popular, fans, people watch them</td></tr>
<tr><td>Players well paid</td><td>More than $10,000,000 in contracts (Jeter with Yankees)</td></tr>
<tr><td>Injuries to end career</td><td>Injuries (Boban Jancovič in basketball—hit his head on concrete post reacting to the referee's decision to give him his fifth foul; Rudy Tomjanovich hit by Kermit Washington during a fight—stayed out of a game for 5 months; and Ray Chapman in baseball who died in 1920 hit by pitch on the head).</td></tr>
</table>

(continued)

FIGURE 6.5. Example of a completed Planning Materials for modeling and sample essay (for your reference).

	How are they **different**?	**Differences**	
		Unique features of Topic A: Baseball	**Unique features of Topic B:** Basketball
Middle	Uniforms	Cleats, long pants, a cap, protective gear	Shoes (flat), shorts, and shirts
	Equipment and regulations	Glove, bat, baseball, bases, 9 players, throw ball, use bats	Basketball and hoops/goal post, 5 players, dribble ball, fouls
	Where they are played	Field (dirt)	Court with lines and markings—made of polished maple wood
End	**Restate purpose:** By comparing and contrasting you can decide which one to watch		
	Leave a message to the reader: Let your brother change the channel!		

Basketball and Baseball: Two amazing Sports

"Do not change the channel! I am watching the game!" Isn't this something you have said or have heard others saying? It is annoying when you are watching a game and you are interrupted. There are a lot of different sports, but basketball and baseball are two sports that are very popular in the United States. By comparing and contrasting the two, you may decide which one you should join, or which one you like the most and which one you should definitely watch when it is on TV.

One way that basketball and baseball are similar is that they are both sports. Both are popular American sports with a lot of fans. There are also fan clubs that plan trips for the fans to watch the games up close and support their teams and their players.

Another similarity is that in both sports players are very well paid. Some players' contracts have astronomical numbers. For example, a yearly contract signed during their careers by the baseball player Derek Jeter and the basketball player LeBron James were more than $10,000,000. This is an unbelievable number if you compare it to the salary of a teacher, firefighter, or a police officer.

Also, in both sports players can get seriously or fatally injured and end their career. For example, Ray Chapman, a baseball player, died in 1920 after a pitch hit him on the head. Boban Jancović, a Serbian player on a Greek team, was paralyzed after a game when he received his last foul and reacted by hitting his head on the goal post. He immediately collapsed and was never able to play again. Injuries can happen because of fights, too. Rudy Tomjanovich, for example, was hit and was injured seriously by Kermit Washington during a basketball game.

In baseball, players wear caps and their shoes, called cleats, have grips, so the players can run well on the field. Basketball players wear shorts and their shoes do not have grips. In baseball, players need a glove, a baseball ball, a bat, bases, and protective gear, but in basketball, the only thing needed is a basketball and two hoops on posts. Also, in baseball there are nine players, but in basketball there are five.

Also, basketball is played on a court, but baseball is played on a field.

In conclusion, they are both recreational sports and a lot of people watch them. Even though they have similarities, they also differ in the equipment they need, and where they are played. By comparing and contrasting them, it is easier to decide which one to watch or join. So, next time, when someone tries to change the channel, think what is playing and how interested you are in that game.

FIGURE 6.5. (continued)

Plan

- Ask students why writers always need to start by planning. Give an example of the importance of planning (e.g., preparing to go on vacation).
- Explain that in the planning section they will follow specific steps: FTAP, generate Ideas, and organize ideas with a GO. You can display Form 6.1 and write each component on the board.

FTAP

- Write each letter, say what it stands for, and discuss why it is important.
  - **F** stands for *Form*.
  - **T** stands for *Topic*.
  - **A** stands for *Audience*.
  - **P** stands for *Purpose*. Explain that in compare–contrast writing, the purpose is to make a decision or to learn information.

IDEAS

- Point to Ideas and explain that the next step is to come up with as many ideas as possible about the topic. Ideas, in this lesson, now includes a choice between two strategies depending on whether students will be using sources. They can still *Brainstorm* ideas based on what they already know, but if they are also supposed to get information from reading, they will *read and take notes* from that reading source. Point to the three-column chart in Form 6.1 or draw the chart on the board. Explain that writers will fill in information for each topic in the two outside columns and in the middle column they will note the similarities between the topics. (Note: If you have used a Venn diagram in the past, you could explain that this chart resembles a Venn diagram, but uses columns instead of circles.)

GRAPHIC ORGANIZER

- Display the GO (see Form 6.1) and point out that it has the elements of compare–contrast as they appear on the elements chart (Handout 6.1). Explain that the goal is to group ideas and identify categories. Discuss what "good" categories are. These will be "big ideas" or "umbrella terms" for a number of ideas that have similar content. Discuss the importance of coming up with good categories. Explain that they could draw the GO on blank paper when planning and not even use this printed version. Add that when they draw the GO, the lines do not need to be perfect! (Note: Students will be familiar with this from the read-aloud sessions.)

Draft

- Point to the second step of the Writing Strategy Ladder and explain that good writers make sure to use their plan to write a first draft. Discuss the reasons for this. Explain how the GO, with its organization, helps a writer write a clear paper. Also, explain that good writers use transition words; display and briefly discuss the chart with the transition words and sentence starters (see Handout 6.10).

Evaluate to Revise

- Point to the Evaluate to Revise step of the ladder and say that good writers always revisit their work to make changes to improve it. For this step they will use the evaluation rubric that contains the evaluation elements (if you have it on display, point to Form 6.2). Point out that the elements of compare–contrast writing are the ones used in the GO and on the evaluation rubrics. Explain that you could write the elements and assign a score next to them instead of using the rubric. Briefly comment on the importance of remembering information instead of relying on printed documents and forms.

Edit

- Pointing to Edit (if you have Handout 2.2 on display), explain that good writers also check for errors that could affect the quality of the paper (e.g., spelling, indentation, grammar).

Publish

- Finally, point to *Publish* and explain that writers should celebrate their work and share it with others!

Modeling of Compare–Contrast Writing

- Explain that you will write a paper to show students how they should work when they are asked to write a compare–contrast paper. Say that you have been reading about the topics and now have enough information about them to begin. State clearly that you will not use sources, only information you already know about the topic. Add that if you are not sure about some information, though, you will look for confirmation by reading. Explain that you will think out loud, so students can hear and see how you think and how you solve challenges. (Note: See Figure 6.5 for a sample of completed materials and essay.)

Plan

- Explain that you are a student and were asked to write a compare–contrast paper about basketball and baseball. Display the topic on the board. The topic states, **"Write a paper comparing and contrasting basketball and baseball to decide which one to watch or join."**

- Think out loud and ask yourself what are the steps of the strategy you need to follow. Write the steps of the ladder at the side of the board. Underline *Plan*.

FTAP

Ask yourself what is the first part of planning. Write each letter of *FTAP* on the board vertically and complete each section.

IDEAS/BRAINSTORM

Ask what would be next. Say, it would be Ideas. Circle the word *Brainstorm* and repeat that you will not be using sources. Draw a three-column chart and develop ideas about each topic, including their similarities. Ask yourself questions about each topic and explain that this process helps you develop ideas (e.g., "What is X? Where is it played? How is it played?").

GRAPHIC ORGANIZER

- Once you have completed this step, review the ideas and explain that you will need to look for categories of similarities and differences and to organize those ideas on the GO. Display or draw the GO and begin to transfer your ideas and cross them out from the Brainstorm chart.

- Make sure to use self-talk to ask what you have done and where you are in the process and to encourage yourself to continue, even though the task is challenging.

Draft

- Ask what you should do next. Place a checkmark next to the word *Plan* that you had underlined earlier. Point to steps of the Writing Strategy Ladder and underline *Draft*. Explain that you will draft your paper and then do so. In this process, consult the chart with the transition words (Handout 6.10) and think out loud as you use them. (Note: In case you run out of time, make a plan to review the strategy and the information from the GO before writing.)

Evaluate to Revise

- Ask what would be the next step. Point to the Writing Strategy Ladder and explain that now you will need to evaluate and revise your paper. In order to do that, you will use your rubric with the elements (see Form 6.2). Point out the similarities between the elements, the GO, and the rubric.

- Apply the rubric to the paper. Identify the areas that need to be improved and set goals for the next paper. Make at least one revision.

Edit

- Explain that for editing you have a helpful technique (SCIPS), but for now you will reread and look for spelling, punctuation, or other errors that may disrupt the meaning of the paper.

Publish

- Explain that you could share this paper with another class or with another teacher, but you would first need to make all revisions and carefully edit.

Discussion of the Modeling and Self-Regulation

- Discuss with students what you said to yourself as you wrote. Lead students to talk about some of the self-regulation talk you used. Record students' responses and explain that this talk helped you complete your writing without experiencing stress. Explain that you will discuss this self-talk with the students in the next class.

Optional Commitment

- Students make a commitment to learn the strategy and the elements (you can use procedures described in previous chapters).

Additional Activity

- Students can work with you or in small groups to make additional revisions to the paper.

Reflection Activities

- **Journal entry.** You can ask students to write a journal entry and explain how they think the strategy will help them with their own writing. They could revisit the goals they had set in the previous lesson to explain how the strategy could help them achieve those goals.
- **Class discussion.** You could discuss as a group the benefits of using the Writing Strategy Ladder.

End of Lesson

- Review the steps of the Writing Strategy Ladder and the elements of the genre.

LESSON 3: SELF-REGULATION AND NOTE TAKING (MODELING AND COLLABORATIVE PLANNING)

Students reflect on the application of strategies, review the use of the strategy on self-regulation, and make revisions on their self-talk sheets. The teacher models note taking on one topic; students and teacher collaboratively take notes on a new topic, review ideas, and complete the GO by identifying categories.

Lesson Objectives

By the end of this lesson, students will be able to:

- Develop their own self-talk.
- Demonstrate that they know the meaning of the strategy steps and can contribute appropriately to planning.
- Read and take notes using the planning sheet.
- Develop categories and complete the GO.

Assessment Information

The teacher informally assesses whether students can (1) develop self-statements, (2) take notes, and (3) develop categories and complete the GO.

Notes

- This is the beginning of collaborative work. Because note taking is necessary for writing from sources, we decided to divide the task into (1) modeling on note taking and (2) collaborative completion of note taking. In Lesson 4, students and their teacher collaboratively draft a paper using the planning from this lesson.

- In this lesson we use the book *Big Cats* by Seymour Simon. This book begins with information about the similarities among big cats and includes separate sections on lions and tigers. Sample FTAP and Ideas are provided in Figure 6.6 for your reference. We encourage you, though, to use readings from your social studies and science curricula.

- If you chose to work on different topics and use two books, you could model the note taking process on one book, completing one of the columns on differences, and collaboratively take notes on the second book, completing the second column on differences from the planning chart. Finally, you would review the information with students and identify similarities, completing the middle column of the chart. For this task, you would need more time; therefore, you could work on one book during the reading time and on the second book during the writing time, or you could work on the tasks across 2 days if the books are lengthy.

- If you think that writing from sources is too challenging for your students, in this lesson you could instead work on collaborative planning using two topics that require general information (e.g., two restaurants, two sports, being a baby and being a 10-year-old). You could proceed with collaborative drafting in Lesson 4.

PLAN

What am I writing? (Essay) Paragraph   Letter   Other _____

Form:

Topic: *Tigers and Lions*

Audience: *Teacher and classmates*

Purpose: *to learn about those topics (use of purpose, similarities, differences, restatement of purpose, and a message to reader)*

IDEAS

Brainstorm   Reading *and* Note Taking

Unique features of Topic A: *Tigers* *Seymour Simon (book: Big Cats)*		Unique features of Topic B: *Lions* *Seymour Simon (book: Big Cats)*
<u>*Tigress raises cub alone*</u>	**Similarities between Topics**	<u>*Called king of beasts*</u>
Striped—helps them blend in with grass and forest and attack prey	*Big cats roar*	*Adults have manes, can be 9–10 feet long, and weigh more than 400 pounds*
Larger cat	*Heavy and long bodies*	
Solitary hunter	*Carnivores—part of cat family (Felidae)*	*Sociable (live in prides from 3 individuals to 35; the number of females is double the number of males)*
Seven to eight different kinds of tigers	<u>*Razor-sharp claws and sharp teeth*</u>	
When it kills a large animal, it hides it and eats it for 3–4 days	*Excellent senses (whiskers, ears that turn in different directions, moist nose, eyes far apart to see widely and even at night due to a special lining at the back of their eyes)*	*Lioness raises cubs with the male lion*
<u>*Good swimmers*</u>		<u>*Females hunt and care for each other's cubs*</u>
	Mammals—give birth to live babies	*Pride successful in hunting due to the large group*
	Cubs are blind—litters of two or three	*Live in wide-open plains*
	Cubs grow fast and can weigh 40 pounds within 6 months	

FIGURE 6.6. Example of a completed FTAP and Ideas for collaborative writing on tigers and lions (for your reference).

Materials for Lesson 3

- Form 2.2. Self-Talk Recording Sheet (from Chapter 2)
- Form 6.1. Planning Materials (FTAP, Ideas, GO)
- Form 6.2. Rubric on Self-Evaluation and Peer Review
- Handout 2.3. Be Strategic! (from Chapter 2)
- Handout 6.1. Chart of Elements of Compare–Contrast
- Handout 6.10. Transition Words and Sentence Starters

Procedures

Review

- Review the steps of the Writing Strategy Ladder and the elements of compare–contrast writing.

Self-Regulation and Self-Statements

- (Note: This is a task you have completed in the two previous chapters.) Remind students about the importance of using self-talk and monitoring their progress (see Handout 2.3 and Form 2.2). Refer to the self-talk you used after your think-aloud modeling. Students revisit the self-talk they have done in the previous chapter, make revisions if needed, and save the information for future use.

Introduction to Writing from Sources

- Explain to students that in school they will be asked to write compare–contrast papers on topics they have read about. This task can help them learn and remember information about these topics.
- Remind students that you wrote a paper without using sources and that now you will show them how to take notes when they read. Next they will practice the task, and finally they will complete the GO with your help.
- Discuss with students what they think may be challenging about the process of reading from sources in order to write a compare–contrast paper.
- Acknowledge that reading sources is challenging, but explain that they can take notes and use the strategies they know to be successful.

Collaborative Writing of a Compare–Contrast Paper

- Explain that you will model how to write a paper comparing and contrasting tigers and lions. First you will read a book together that contains information on big cats (*Big Cats* by Seymour Simon). (Note: See completed sample in Figure 6.6 for your reference.)

Plan

- Ask students what is the first thing they need to do (they should respond, planning with FTAP and Ideas).

FTAP and Ideas

- Write *FTAP* and *Ideas* on the board. Under the Ideas label, write *Brainstorm* and *Reading and Note Taking*.

- Ask students what FTAP means and why is it important. As they tell you the information, you can record it on the board.

- Turn to the Ideas. Explain that your primary source of information this time will be reading and note taking. Circle the Reading and Note Taking labels.

- Draw the three-column chart on the board. With students' feedback complete the headings per topic and also record the information about the author and book title. In this case the author is the same. Explain that when you are writing from sources, it is important to record this information because you may refer to the author when you write and you need to be accurate. (Note: Of course in this example, the topics are covered in the same book, but in future tasks, students may need to use different books.)

- Explain that you know some information about the topic and that you could also brainstorm, but the information may not be accurate. Underline <u>Brainstorm</u> and explain that you will generate some ideas and underline them to signal that you will need to verify them from the reading. Explain that often you may know some information about a topic, but you need to be accurate, and this is why you will also try to confirm those ideas when reading (or even look in other sources).

- You can ask some questions about each topic (e.g., "What is a lion? Where is it found? What does it look like? What does it eat?").

Modeling of Note Taking

- Explain that note taking requires reading information, understanding it, and taking notes without copying everything students read. Add that if they copy information, they should put the material in quotes and use it word for word; otherwise they would be stealing the author's ideas and presenting them as their own.

- The first section of the book discusses information about big cats. Read this part aloud and stop as you read to explain, in your own words, what you read. Then take notes in the middle column of the chart. This is the process to follow for note talking:

  ○ Read the information.

  ○ Look away from the book and explain the information in your own words.

  ○ Take notes.

Collaborative Note Taking

- Explain to students that you will read the information and they will help you take notes. Read the information on tigers, stop, and ask students to tell you what the information is and what notes to take. Continue with the section that discusses lions.

- When you have completed the reading, review the information in the two columns about differences and identify any additional information that should appear in the middle column of similarities.

Collaborative Completion of the GO

- Ask what the next step of the Writing Strategy Ladder is. With students' assistance, draw or display the GO.

- Review the information in the "different" columns of the Ideas chart and begin collaboratively to identify "things that go together" to form categories.

Reflection Activities

- **Journal entry.** You can ask students to write a journal entry and explain what steps and components of the writing strategy seem challenging to them and what they could do to be successful.

- **Class discussion.** Discuss what students find challenging in the process of taking notes from readings. Use this information to consider ways to differentiate instruction depending on how much help individual students need.

End of Lesson

- Review with students the importance of self-talk, the information from note taking, the accurate use of information from reading, and the use of quotes when using direct information from the text.

LESSON 4: COLLABORATIVE DRAFTING OF A COMPARE–CONTRAST ESSAY USING SOURCES

Teacher and students collaboratively use the plan from Lesson 3 to draft, evaluate to revise, and edit a compare–contrast paper written using sources. During collaborative writing, the teacher scaffolds students' application of the strategy and does the writing as students provide the ideas and sentences.

Lesson Objectives

By the end of the lesson, students will be able to:

- Demonstrate that they know the meaning of the strategy steps and can contribute appropriately to drafting, evaluating to revise, and editing.

Assessment Information

The teacher informally assesses whether students (1) know the meaning of the strategy steps and (2) can apply them as a group to draft, evaluate to revise, and edit.

Notes

- Drafting using sources presents some new challenges. First, one must refer to sources, providing the author, book title, and information. The sentence starters (see Handout 6.10) may help. Second, paragraph topic sentences have to include both categories and whether they are similarities or differences. We suggest that you do most of the collaborative drafting as a whole group, and use sentence starters. Also, we suggest that you explain that at the end of the paper students should include information about the sources they used, so readers could also find them (author's last name, initial of first name, year of book's publication, *book's title*, city, publisher). Composing collaboratively with the whole group lets all the students see your suggestions and how to use the sentence starters.

Materials for Lesson 4

- Form 6.1. Planning Materials (FTAP, Ideas, GO)
- Form 6.2. Rubric on Self-Evaluation and Peer Review
- Handout 2.1. Writing Strategy Ladder (from Chapter 2)
- Handout 6.1. Chart of Elements of Compare–Contrast
- Handout 6.10. Transition Words and Sentence Starters
- Students' completed self-talk sheets (Form 2.2) from Lesson 3 (or Lesson 2, depending on your decision)

Procedures

Review

- Review the elements of compare–contrast writing and the steps and components of the Writing Strategy Ladder. You may ask students to write down the information and check its accuracy with a partner. Then they can set goals for learning the information they missed.

- Review the information on the GO.

Draft

- Ask students what the next step would be. They should answer, "To write the paper using the information on the GO." Use the transition words and/or sentence starters in Handout 6.10 to jumpstart the process. Using student input, write the paper.

- An important part of modeling this drafting component is working from the notes on the GO. Resist any urge to look back at the source book; learning to write from their notes will help students avoid plagiarism.

- Drafting using sources presents some new challenges for composing sentences. See the notes above. You might draft the introduction, one body paragraph, and all the topic sentences as a whole class and then let small groups work on the content of different paragraphs.

    - **Introduction.** Start by asking the students for ideas about how to introduce the topic. What could they say to interest the reader without giving away the comparisons? Then ask for a sentence that says what is being compared and why. You can get a couple of suggestions and then choose one or parts of both.

- **Referring to the source(s).** For the lions and tigers topic, you might refer to the book, *Big Cats*, in the introduction. Use the sentence starters and ask students to generate a sentence.

    - **Body paragraphs.** Follow the GO and use the transition words for reference. One way to prompt students to get them started in suggesting a sentence is to tell them which transition words to use.

- Do one full paragraph together. Then decide whether to continue together or divide up the paragraphs among groups. If groups work on different paragraphs, then come back as a whole class and write their suggested paragraphs on the group paper, making suggestions and changes as you write it. You could group students using your preassessment data or you could use flexible grouping.

    - **Conclusion.** Work on the conclusion together. Then remember to add the reference at the end.

Evaluate to Revise

- Ask what the next step would be and refer students to the Writing Strategy Ladder. After they respond, collaboratively use the evaluation rubric (see Form 6.2) to evaluate the paper and make at least one revision.

Edit

- Ask what the next step is and explain that students will be learning a general approach for editing. At this point you could reread for spelling errors and make corrections.

Reflection Activity

- **Class discussion.** Discuss any comments that students have about writing from sources. Emphasize the importance of mentioning the authors when you are using direct information from the books.

End of Lesson

- Review with students the process followed for writing from sources and discuss the difference between brainstorming and reading and note taking during planning.

LESSON 5: STUDENTS PLAN AND DRAFT THEIR OWN COMPARE–CONTRAST PAPERS

Students begin working on their own papers, using the planning strategy, including taking notes from sources, and drafting their papers. The teacher monitors use of the strategy and provides support as needed.

Lesson Objectives

By the end of this lesson, students will be able to:

- Apply the planning and drafting steps of the strategy to take notes and organize ideas appropriately.
- Write a compare–contrast paper that includes the compare–contrast elements.

Assessment Information

The teacher informally assesses whether (1) students are using the strategy appropriately, (2) their writing includes the elements and is generally well written, and (3) students take notes from sources and use them appropriately in their essay.

Notes

- This is the beginning of guided practice.
- This lesson will probably take more than one session, especially if students write from sources. If students write using sources, they will need to go to the library and find books on the topics they chose unless you provide them. Set expectations for when students should finish.
- If you have decided not to work on writing from sources, provide students with general-information topics (e.g., compare–contrast swimming at a pool and at the ocean; compare–contrast computers and iPads; compare–contrast typing and writing with paper and pencil).
- Suggestions about topic selection are provided in the Procedures section below.
- We encourage you to plan and write your own paper. It is important for your students to also see you writing. Furthermore, writing the paper will give you insight into some of the difficulties that students experience.

Materials for Lesson 5

- Form 6.1. Planning Materials (FTAP, Ideas, GO)
- Form 6.3. Memorization Sheet for Compare–Contrast Writing
- Handout 2.1. Writing Strategy Ladder (from Chapter 2)
- Handout 6.1. Chart of Elements of Compare and Contrast
- Completed self-talk sheets (Form 2.2) from Lesson 3 (or Lesson 2, depending on your decision)
- Sample Topics for Writing Assessment/Instruction (see pp. 180–181)

Procedures

Review

- Review the steps of the Writing Strategy Ladder and the elements of compare–contrast writing.

Choosing Topics

- If you choose not to work on topics that require sources, you could display the sample list of topics we provide at the beginning of the chapter (see pp. 180–181) and let students select one. Help individual students choose topics for which they have some prior knowledge. For this, you may complete the FTAP and Ideas/Brainstorm for two or more topics before making a final choice. This practice will help students select a topic that they can develop sufficiently in their writing.
- If students write using sources, you will need to give careful thought to the range of topics offered. We recommend that you have students write on different but related topics. For example, all students could compare two animals, but choose the animals themselves. We recommend against having all students write on the same topic; it's too

boring and may lead to copying. We also recommend against completely open choice; by restricting choices to a set of related topics, many of the categories will be the same, and students can learn more from collaboration.

- An important consideration is whether to connect the topic to something that students are learning in science or social studies. If you do this, it's probably a good idea to make sure that the topics are not too complicated and do not rely too much on the learning in that content area. For the first attempt at the compare–contrast genre, the topic should be relatively easy.

- Regardless of the topic, you will need to decide whether to have students work individually throughout or to work in groups to gather information, take notes, and then write individually.

- You also need to plan for access to reading materials. The availability of books or other sources may affect your choice of topic.

- If you work on writing papers from sources, you could assign several students the same topic, but different readings according to their reading level. In this case, you would need to provide the reading sources for each group.

Guiding Practice

- As students work, you can monitor their progress and conduct brief conferences. In conferencing, you can support students in note taking, talk to them about how they planned, and look at their planning sheets and developing papers. This type of feedback helps students understand that using the strategy is important to improving their writing and that you value the process they follow to complete their paper.

- For the Ideas step, remind students to take notes from the readings. For the GO, check that students have identified categories and also confirm that ideas underneath a category belong together.

- Remind students to use self-talk as they work independently.

Differentiation

- Based on your informal assessment, you might plan to work with small groups of students that need additional help. You may also plan to work with a small group of students to support them as they take notes, complete the GO, and/or draft.

Reflection Activity

- **Class discussion.** Discuss with students how the Writing Strategy Ladder helped them complete their writing.

End of Lesson

- Review with students the elements of compare–contrast.

LESSON 6: PREPARATION FOR PEER REVIEW AND SELF-EVALUATION

Students practice evaluating compare–contrast papers, making suggestions and revisions. Students self-evaluate their papers, using evaluation criteria, and set goals for revision.

Lesson Objectives

By the end of this lesson, students will be able to:

- Apply the evaluation rubric to evaluate papers written by others.
- Use their evaluations to make revisions and suggestions for revision.
- Self-evaluate their own papers and set revision goals.

Assessment Information

The teacher informally assesses whether students can (1) apply the evaluation criteria, (2) make revisions using the evaluation results, and (3) self-evaluate their own papers and set revision goals.

Notes

- In this lesson we provide a choice of papers for evaluation (see Handouts 6.11–6.15). You can choose to use papers that refer to sources or not.

- The procedures followed in this lesson do not differ from the ones in the previous chapters. For a description of the procedures, you can refer to a previous chapter (see Chapter 4 or 5, Lesson 6). An outline of the lesson's content is provided below.

  ○ Review
  ○ Discussion of the Importance of Evaluation and Revision and the Role of Peer Review
  ○ Modeling of Evaluation for Peer Review
  ○ Collaborative Practice of Evaluation
  ○ Small-Group Practice of Evaluation
  ○ Students Work on Their Own Papers to Self-Evaluate

Materials for Lesson 6

- Form 6.2. Rubric on Self-Evaluation and Peer Review
- Form 6.2 (copies for students' small-group and self-evaluations)
- Form 6.3. Memorization Sheet for Compare–Contrast Writing
- Handout 2.1. Writing Strategy Ladder (from Chapter 2)
- Handout 6.11. A Weak Paper for Evaluation, "Polar Bears and Penguins"
- Handout 6.12. A Weak Example for Evaluation, "Earthquakes and Volcanoes: Which One Would You Rather Experience"

- Handout 6.13. A Weak Paper for Evaluation, "Traveling by Plane or Car"
- Handout 6.14. A Weak Paper for Evaluation, "The Earth and Mars"
- Handout 6.15. A Weak Paper for Evaluation, "Bees and Ants: Hardworking Little Creatures"
- Students' completed self-talk sheets (Form 2.2) from Lesson 3 (or Lesson 2, depending on your decision)

LESSON 7: PEER REVIEW AND REVISION

Students peer-review in pairs or small groups, applying the evaluation criteria. Next, students compare their self-evaluations with the comments of their peers, set goals for revision, and make revisions.

Lesson Objectives

By the end of this lesson, students will be able to:

- Apply the evaluation criteria to give specific feedback to peers.
- Make revisions to their own essays.

Assessment Information

The teacher informally assesses whether students can (1) apply the evaluation criteria and give feedback to peers and (2) make revisions to their essays.

Notes

- The procedures for peer review do not differ from those in the previous chapters (see Chapter 4 or 5, Lesson 7). The outline of the lesson follows:
  - Review
  - Peer Review
  - Peer Review Procedures
  - Completing Peer Review
  - Revision(s)
  - Reflection Activities

Materials for Lesson 7

- Handout 2.1. Writing Strategy Ladder (from Chapter 2)
- Form 6.2. Rubric on Self-Evaluation and Peer Review

- Form 6.2 (copies for peer review)
- Students' completed self-talk sheets (Form 2.2) from Lesson 3.

LESSON 8: EDITING

Students examine their papers for editing errors. By using the editing strategy, students identify surface-level errors and correct them. Teachers can choose to teach a specific grammatical/editing skill, practice it with students, and ask students to make changes to their essays. Additionally, students set editing goals and reflect on their performance and progress.

Lesson Objectives

By the end of this lesson, students will be able to:

- Set goals for improving their editing.
- Apply editing procedures to make changes.

Assessment Information

The teacher informally assesses whether students (1) apply previous editing goals to make editing changes and (2) use the taught skills to edit their work.

Notes

- The editing procedures are identical to those used in Chapters 4 and 5 (see Lesson 8). The outline of the lesson can be viewed below:
  - Review
  - Editing
  - Editing Mini-Lesson
  - Reflection Activity

Materials for Lesson 8

- Handout 2.1. Writing Strategy Ladder (from Chapter 2)
- Handout 2.2. SCIPS Editing Guide (from Chapter 2)
- Form 2.1. Editing Goals for Improvement (from Chapter 2)
- Your choice of materials for a specific editing and grammatical goal

PUBLISHING GUIDELINES

It is important for students to share some of their work with a larger audience. See Chapter 3 for a discussion of ideas about opportunities for publishing. These guidelines do not comprise a specific lesson, but rather present ideas for discussing publishing with your students. The specifics will depend on what sort of publishing you have chosen.

Review

Review the elements of compare–contrast writing, the steps of the Writing Strategy Ladder, and the importance of sharing/publishing. Discuss the importance of publishing to the motivation of the writer and to the distribution of information.

Publishing

- Students prepare their papers for sharing. Besides general approaches to publishing (see Chapter 3), some specific approaches for publishing compare–contrast papers could be to create a Glogster (*http://edu.glogster.com/?ref=com*) where students post their work. They could also include pictures about the topics or even video. They could finally share this information with students from other classrooms and grades.
- After students have some experience writing general compare–contrast papers, they could start writing papers related to content learning in science, social studies, and literature. Then sharing among peers takes on new meaning: They can learn from each other about the content. This is another important type of sharing/publishing.

GUIDELINES FOR CONTINUOUS GUIDED PRACTICE TO MASTERY

It is important for students to write more than one paper in a genre to develop mastery of it. As students write a second paper, they typically work more quickly and feel much more competent. Teachers can then focus their attention on students who need more support.

Mastery Objectives

By the end of all compare–contrast lessons, students will be able to:

- Apply the planning and drafting steps of the writing strategy to take notes (or generate) and organize ideas appropriately.
- Identify and record main ideas from readings (if they write using sources).
- Write a compare–contrast paper that includes the elements.
- Write a compare–contrast paper with clear categories for similarities and differences.

Assessment Information

The teacher informally assesses whether students can (1) apply the Writing Strategy Ladder to plan, draft, and evaluate to revise; (2) provide topic sentences with clear categories of comparison and contrast; and (3) accurately apply the evaluation criteria to give suggestions and make revisions. *Mastery instruction* means that instruction should continue until all students can use the strategy to write a paper that includes at least all the basic elements.

Notes

- You could provide a mini-lesson on creating a basic reference list before students work on this next paper (see end of this section). Also, you could teach a mini-lesson on categories and practice how to identify categories in a group of ideas with small groups or a larger group of students (see end of this section).
- Students work on a new paper using sources.
  - Give students a choice of topics (see sample topics or develop additional ones) and readings.
  - Remind students to use the Writing Strategy Ladder and the genre elements and materials.
  - Keep the planning materials on display (FTAP, Ideas, GO), but ask students to draw them instead of using printed copies.
  - As students work, conference with them about how they use the strategy and how their writing is progressing.
  - Conduct self-evaluations and peer reviews. You can collaboratively review a paper prior to students' self-evaluations and peer reviews to remind them of the importance of giving honest feedback and detailed suggestions. Monitor students' suggestions at the self-evaluation and peer review stage.
  - Remind students to edit using SCIPS and to remember their editing goals (do not teach a new editing skill).
  - Plan for sharing. Students prepare their papers for publishing.
  - Students write a journal entry and reflect on their growth. They can respond to the questions, "How did my writing improve? What worked for me as a writer?"
- Remember that the goal is mastery. You should support students as needed.
- Once students have completed the second paper, you can proceed with an extension activity or ask students to write a third paper.
- Remember to use the evaluation rubric to assess students' writing and monitor their progress. Also, remember to administer and score the postassessment so that you can compare students' performance with their preassessment results. You can ask students to evaluate their postassessment and to assess their own growth from the preassessment. They can use the experience to write a reflection in their journal on their progress and their learning.

ADDITIONAL MINI-LESSON: CREATING A BASIC REFERENCE LIST

Students develop a reference list that includes information about the books used in their essays (author's name, year of publication, title of book, city, and publisher).

Mini-Lesson Objectives

By the end of this lesson, students will be able to:

- Create a reference list that includes information about the author, the year of publication, the title of the book, the city, and publisher.

Assessment

The teacher informally assesses whether students can create a reference list for sources used in papers.

Discussion

- Explain to students that when readers read compare–contrast essays, they may also want to read the books the students used as sources of information in their papers.

Creating a Reference List: Teacher Practice

- Explain that a reference list needs to have information that will help other readers find the books. Have a discussion with students about what this information might be (e.g., title of the book).
- Explain that in order for someone else to locate sources used in an essay, the writer will need to include the title of the books, the year that each book was published, and the names of the authors.
- Write on the board or on a chart that you will keep on display the format: author's last name, initial of first name, (year), *title of book*, city, and publisher.
- Using the information from the book you used during collaborative planning (e.g., *Big Cats*), record the information for it. This would be: Seymour, S. (1991). *Big Cats*. New York: HarperCollins.

Creating a Reference List: Student Practice

- Ask students to revisit their papers and add a reference list at the end of their work.
- Remind them to include this information in the next paper they write.

ADDITIONAL MINI-LESSON: DEVELOPING CATEGORIES AND WRITING TOPIC SENTENCES

Students practice grouping ideas into categories and writing a topic sentence using this information.

Mini-Lesson Objectives

By the end of this lesson, students will be able to:

- Develop categories for groups of ideas.
- Write a topic sentence for each category of ideas.

Assessment Information

The teacher informally assesses whether students can (1) develop categories and (2) write topic sentences using the completed GO.

Materials for Developing Categories

- Form 6.1. Planning Materials (only the GO)
- Handout 6.16. Practice Developing Categories

Discussion

- Explain that one main challenge with compare–contrast writing is the identification of categories. A category is a main idea, an umbrella term under which similar details and ideas can be found. You could use a brief example to make this concept clearer. For instance, if the topic is to compare and contrast food groups, cucumbers, onions, broccoli, and lettuce would be together in one category as vegetables.
- Explain that the identification of categories is tricky and that it is often a challenge to decide how ideas should best be grouped. Suggest that a student you know is currently working on a paper and has developed the ideas about the topic but has not yet organized or determined the categories—and that you and your students are going to help.

Collaborative and Small-Group Application

- Display for students the brainstorming sheet (see Handout 6.16) and explain that you will all work as a group to organize ideas on the GO, decide the category, and write a topic sentence.
- Work with your students as a group and then ask them to continue the task in small groups. You can ask them to write the paragraph, too, after writing the topic sentence.

Differentiation

- You can work with a small group of students that needs more guidance during the small-group practice.

Reflection Activity

- **Class discussion.** Discuss with students why the use of categories is important in compare–contrast writing.

EXTENSION ACTIVITIES

Author Study

An author study exposes all students to the same information and allows them to conduct research on an author and also reflect on what they read. After students have read books by the same author, you can ask them to compare and contrast two books in order to comment on the author and his or her style, and in general explain in their critique what they learned about that author (see Handout 6.17). They could refer to themes that appear throughout readings, comment on the art used in the book, or explain how the author describes a common theme.

Response to Literature

Compare–contrast writing can be very useful in understanding literature. Note that any of the examples here could be written as an essay or as a short response. After reading two versions of Cinderella, for example, students could write an essay comparing and contrasting the two books (see Handout 6.18). The knowledge they have acquired from Chapter 4 on story elements can help them identify similarities and differences across those topics.

Also, students could compare and/or contrast characters in a book. The purpose of the analysis is to understand characters' intentions or explain their answers; consequently, the conclusion of the essay is an explanation, and the evidence students provide can be based on written information and on inferences that they made when reading the book. For example, the book may not state that a character is unfortunate (e.g., Marcel in the book *The Sweetest Fig* by Chris Van Allsburg), but the reader could infer that information from the character's actions and interactions with other characters. Finally, students could compare and/or contrast two different types of books (e.g., a mystery book and a biography). This will help them better understand the characteristics of the genre.

Writing in Science and Social Studies

The most common purpose of compare–contrast writing in school is to learn information in the content areas. Once students have some practice writing about general topics (e.g., animals), they can start writing papers related to content learning in science, social studies, and literature. The strategies and instructional procedures explained in the detailed lessons can be adapted quite directly for use in science and social studies.

A good example of content-area writing comes from a research project on the development of a history curriculum for fifth-grade students (Okolo, Ferretti, & MacArthur, 2002; MacArthur, Ferretti, & Okolo, 2002). The curriculum included a unit of instruction on westward expansion in the years prior to the Civil War. During that period, multiple groups of American settlers migrated to the West and, in the process, interacted with different groups of Native Americans. The curriculum developers designed inquiry projects in which students learned about the settlers and Native Americans by comparing and contrasting the various groups. In the process, they learned categories of reasons for migration (push and pull reasons) and categories for ways of life (economy, beliefs, daily life, etc.). Students worked in groups to read and take notes and prepare reports on individual groups and then to compare them. Meanwhile, other groups investigated different Native American tribes. Eventually, students studied how the groups came into conflict because of differences in ways of life and competition for resources. Importantly, before students engaged in these extensive investigations, they were taught how to write compare–contrast papers based on common topics. Creating such units of instruction takes time and effort, but students can learn a great deal by applying critical thinking processes such as comparison and contrast to their studies.

Materials for Extension Activities

- Handout 6.17. Author Study: Comparing and Contrasting Books by the Same Author, *The Butterfly* and *The Blessing Cup* by Patricia Polacco
- Handout 6.18. Response to Literature: Comparing and Contrasting Characters from Books That Have the Same Plot, *The Salmon Princess: An Alaska Cinderella Story* by Mindy Dwyer and *Prince Cinders* by Babette Cole

Chart of Elements of Compare–Contrast

Beginning		**Topic:** What are the topics that are compared and contrasted?	
		Purpose: Why are the topics compared and contrasted?	
Middle	Similarities	**Similarities:** Are the categories of similarities clear to the reader?	
		Evidence: Is the evidence clear and accurate? Is the evidence explained?	
	Differences	**Differences:** Are the categories of differences clear to the reader?	
		Evidence: Is the evidence clear and accurate? Is the evidence explained?	
End		**Restate Purpose:** Why are the topics compared and contrasted?	
		Think: Did the writer leave the reader with a message to think about?	

Sharks and Dolphins

Sharks and dolphins are fascinating creatures of the sea. You may have seen them on a trip to the beach or a visit to an aquarium. You probably have seen them on television or in the movies, for example, the shark in *Finding Nemo* and the dolphin in *Dolphin Tale*. But how much do you really know about sharks and dolphins? By looking at the similarities and differences between sharks and dolphins, you can fully understand how wonderful they are.

On the one hand, both sharks and dolphins are creatures of the sea. They have streamlined bodies with fins and tails made for swimming. They both eat fish and other sea animals like squid, swallowing small fish whole. However, some sharks can eat larger fish, using their razor-sharp teeth to take huge bites. Some dolphins, like the Amazon River dolphin, can be found in freshwater. Similarly, a few sharks, like the bull shark, can be found in rivers.

On the other hand, sharks and dolphins are different types of animals. Dolphins are mammals, but sharks are fish. Like all mammals, dolphins are warm-blooded and have lungs to breathe air. Dolphins have to come to the surface to breathe through a blowhole, which is an opening on top of their head. Sharks are cold-blooded like all fish and breathe using their gills, getting oxygen directly from the water.

In addition, sharks and dolphins differ on how they give birth and care for their young. Mother dolphins give birth to live babies and nurse them for many months, up to a year and a half. The baby dolphin, called a calf, can eat fish after four months, but the mother continues to nurse it. Some sharks lay eggs like other fish, but many give birth to live babies. However, sharks do not care for their babies at all once they are born.

Further, sharks and dolphins have different levels of intelligence and social behaviors. Dolphins are highly social animals that live in groups and are able to communicate by a variety of whistling sounds. They communicate well enough to hunt collaboratively, herding small fish into small areas so they are easier to catch. Sharks may swim in large groups called schools, but they do not communicate or cooperate in hunting. Another kind of behavior that shows intelligence is that dolphins have been observed to play with each other and with objects. Sharks do not show play behaviors. In captivity, dolphins can also learn commands from humans to do tricks, but this is not possible with sharks.

In conclusion, sharks and dolphins are both well adapted to the sea with streamlined bodies that enable them to swim fast and catch fish. However, dolphins are mammals while sharks are fish. They differ greatly in their social behavior and child rearing, communication, and intelligence. They are both part of our environment, and we should do the best we can to protect them and keep our oceans clean for them.

References

Simon, S. (2006). *Sharks*. Washington, DC: Smithsonian Collins.
Simon, S. (2009). *Dolphins*. Washington, DC: Smithsonian Collins.

A Cat or a Dog? This Is the Question

Cats and dogs are both popular pets and are found in many households. Also, they both have starred in movies. You may have seen dalmatians playing in *101 Dalmatians*, or Tom, the cat, chasing Jerry, the mouse, around in old cartoons. By comparing and contrasting cats and dogs, a future pet owner can learn about them and also decide which animal would be best to bring home.

One similarity between cats and dogs is that they are both domesticated animals. This means that many years ago they were in the wild. For example, dogs are thought to derive from wolves, but thousands of years ago they approached humans and became their friends. Cats were also domesticated, and scientists say that cats may have lived with humans many thousand years ago.

Another similarity between those two animals is that they are both intelligent. Dogs can learn tricks and are easy to train. Even though cats do not learn tricks, they are intelligent, too. As Seymour Simon says in his book *Cats,* cats remember and do things that are important to them, not to humans. Therefore, they will continue to scratch furniture, even though you try to teach them not to do that.

In addition, cats and dogs are similar in the ways they reproduce and care for their young. They both can give birth to babies in the first year of their life. Also, both animals can have more than one baby, which is called a litter. Both puppies and kittens are helpless, cannot hear or see when they are born, and they depend on their mothers for food. However, within three to four weeks they can open their eyes and by the end of two months they stop nursing.

One difference between cats and dogs is what they eat. Dogs can eat anything and will not mind eating dog food or even human food. Cats, though, are picky eaters. As Seymour Simon says, they will not eat food that is stale because it has an odor and cats, with their sensitive sense of smell, will refuse to eat spoiled food.

Also, cats and dogs differ in how they interact with humans. Dogs are playful and will be around humans. Dogs want human company, but cats are quieter and they can be independent. Cats can also disappear for long times and they return to their owner when they please, not when their owner wants them.

In conclusion, cats and dogs are both wonderful pets, and they have a number of similarities and differences that someone who is going to get one of the two should know about ahead of time. You may choose one or the other based on your preference for a companion or for an independent animal friend, who may scratch the furniture or be found in the most unexpected places in your room.

References

Simon, S. (2009). *Cats*. New York: HarperCollins.
Simon, S. (2009). *Dogs*. New York: HarperCollins.

Sparta and Athens: Where Would You Live?

During ancient times, Sparta and Athens were well-known enemies. There are many ways that Sparta and Athens are similar and different, and if you know those similarities and differences, you can decide where you would like to live if you were an ancient Greek.

Both Sparta and Athens were ancient Greek cities that can still be found in Greece. They were both independent cities with their own government, their own citizens, and their own customs and educational systems. If you visit Greece, you can visit ruins of those ancient cities.

One main difference between the two city-states was in their government. Sparta was an oligarchy, and this means that few people had power. Athens was a democracy, and this means that elected people had the power. It is actually said that Athens was the city that created democracy and shared it with the world.

Another difference is in their way of living. Spartans lived without luxuries and were trained under harsh conditions in the art of war. They were actually known to be great warriors, and other cities admired them and feared them. On the contrary, Athenians were philosophers and were more interested in politics and the arts. Also, in Sparta from as early as 7 years of age, all Spartan boys lived in barracks by the river Evrotas and were trained to be obedient soldiers. They also learned to endure pain and be proud to protect their land. In Athens, though, Athenians did not have to go to the army if they did not want to go.

Another difference between the two was in their education system and the position of women. In Athens, women did not have any rights. They could not vote, they were not educated, and they were expected to stay at home and have children. In Sparta, women had the same rights as men. They were taught how to read and write, they trained in sports, could own land, and have money.

In conclusion, there are a number of similarities and differences between ancient Sparta and Athens. They had different systems of government, expectations for male citizens and for women. If you are a woman, you may have wanted to live in Sparta, but if you are a man, you may have preferred to live in a city that would let you be a philosopher.

Tornadoes and Hurricanes

Tornadoes and hurricanes are some of nature's scariest events. Everyone saw the pictures on the news showing the destruction after Hurricane Sandy and the Oklahoma tornadoes in 2012 and 2013. By understanding how tornadoes and hurricanes are similar and different, we can prepare ourselves in case one of them ever threatens to hit our area.

One thing in common between hurricanes and tornadoes is powerful winds. Tornadoes are twisting columns of air that make contact with the ground. Winds can reach up to 300 miles per hour, and can throw cars around. In a hurricane, high-speed winds spin around the eye of the storm. They get so strong, they can rip pieces off the roof or siding off of houses! Hurricane winds are so powerful they can even produce dozens of small tornadoes.

Tornadoes and hurricanes also both come in different levels of intensity. Both of them are measured based on how strong the winds are, and the type of damage they can do. Seymour Simon in the books *Hurricanes* and *Tornadoes* explains that for hurricanes, the "Saffir–Simpson Hurricane Scale" is used, whereas for tornadoes the "Fujita–Pearson Tornado Intensity Scale" is used. Each of these has five levels, called "categories" for hurricanes and "F-scale" for tornadoes. For example, a weak hurricane is called a "Category 1," and a weak tornado is an "F1." Both scales go up to level 5.

There are some major differences, however, between tornadoes and hurricanes. One major difference is how much warning you get before one happens. As Seymour Simon says, the National Weather Services uses radar to try to predict when a tornado will happen so that it can warn people. This can really only happen 15 to 20 minutes before a tornado forms. However, satellites, planes, radar, and computers are all equipped to track hurricanes as they form, allowing for hurricane watches to be issued up to 36 hours before one forms in a particular area.

Another difference is when and where each of these usually happens. Hurricanes most often hit the East Coast of America between June and November. Tornadoes are most common in the eastern two-thirds of the country during the spring months.

It is important to know all about the similarities and differences in hurricanes and tornadoes, so everyone can be prepared and know what to do if one hits the area. We need to know about when to look for warnings, when they are likely to happen, and what causes all that damage during a tornado or hurricane. By learning about them, lives can be saved.

References

Simon, S. (2007). *Hurricanes.* New York: Smithsonian Collins.
Simon, S. (1999). *Tornadoes.* New York: HarperCollins.

Jupiter and Mars

Space has always been a place that scientists have wondered about. The stars fascinated ancient civilizations like the Assyrians, the Greeks, and the Romans. The Romans also named many planets after their Gods! The discovery of the telescope and the ways that our technology advanced helped us learn more about space and the planets. Two exciting planets are Jupiter and Mars.

Mars and Jupiter are both named after ancient Roman gods. Mars was the god of war, and the Romans named the planet that because its red color made them think of blood and warfare. Jupiter was the king of the Roman gods, and Jupiter is the biggest planet in our solar system.

Both of the planets also orbit the sun, just like Earth. They also both have moons: Mars has two small ones and Jupiter has at least sixteen. Mars's moons are called Phobos and Deimos and in the Greek mythology they were twin brothers and sons of Ares, the Greek god of war.

Mars is much smaller than Earth. In fact, Mars could fit inside the Earth seven times. Meanwhile, Jupiter could fit 1,300 Earths inside of it. That's enormous! They also have different surfaces. As Seymour Simon says in his book *Destination: Mars,* Mars has many land formations, like craters, mountains, volcanoes, plains, and valleys. Jupiter, however, is completely covered by clouds and the surface is one big ocean of liquid hydrogen. Seymour Simon in the book *Jupiter* says that the clouds are not made of water like on Earth, but they are made of many gases, like helium and hydrogen.

These planets are also different because humans have been able to explore them in different ways. Jupiter is much harder to explore because the clouds that surround it have very high winds. The winds have destroyed a probe that was sent inside and this is why no one has ever seen the surface of the planet. Mars, on the other hand, has had spaceships and robots explore the surface of the planet and send back images to Earth. Seymour Simon in the book *Mars* explains that the *Pathfinder* is one rover that has sent back thousands of images and analyzed the rocks and weather on the surface to give us a lot of data about Mars.

References

Simon, S. (2000). *Destination: Mars.* New York: HarperCollins.
Simon, S. (1998). *Jupiter.* New York: HarperCollins.

Where Would You Like to Wake Up, by the Beach or in a Mountain Cabin?

During breaks and holidays when we have time to go on vacation, it can be difficult to decide where to go. In my family, we are divided between my brother and my mother who prefer the mountains and my father and me who prefer the beach. Thinking about the similarities and differences between the two, we can make the best decision.

One way that a vacation at the beach or a mountain cabin is the same is that they are both done for the same reason.

Also, both places are dangerous and can get you hurt. If you are at a mountain, you may fall, or a bear may attack you.

One way that vacationing at a beach or a mountain is different is the activities you can do. If you are at a mountain cabin by a lake, you can go fishing, or if they have canoes, you can go canoeing with your family. Also, you can go mountain climbing. However, at the beach you can swim, go canoeing, fish on a boat, and build sand castles. If you get hot or you feel sweaty, you can dive in the sea, but in the mountain, you will have to go take a shower.

Another way that vacationing at a cabin on a mountain or a beach is different is the packing you need to do. When you go on vacation at a mountain, you need to carry boots and even some sweaters, but when you go to the beach, you do not need a lot of clothes. If you have to bring bulky clothes and boots, you may need a lot of luggage. If you travel by plane, some airlines do not let you have a lot of bags, and if you need to have more, you will need to pay a fee. In conclusion, going on vacation at a mountain or a beach have similarities and differences that people should know before they choose where they will spend their vacation.

Writing on a Computer or Using a Paper and a Pencil to Write

Writing is difficult and sometimes if your handwriting is not good, other people may not be able to read your papers and you may get a bad grade. In my school we learn how to write on a computer in fourth grade. Until then, we write using a paper and a pencil. By comparing and contrasting writing on a computer and writing with a paper and a pencil, our school can decide if we should continue to learn typing in fourth grade or do that earlier.

With both you can write letters to communicate with people, you can write a journal with your ideas, and write poems.

Also, both have rules you should follow. For example, when you type, in both you need to keep spaces between words and you should spell words correctly.

If you write on a computer, you can see green lines under words you have misspelled. Also, if you do not know how to correct the spelling, if you click on the word, you will see different words in a list and you can choose which one you want. However, when you write with a paper and a pencil, you need to find out the mistakes on your own and you have to remember how to spell a word, or you need to look at a dictionary or ask someone.

Also, writing on a computer and using a paper and a pencil are different on the time it takes to finish a paper and get it ready for publishing.

Finally, writing on the computer and on paper differs on the possibilities the writer has to get a good grade. When you write on the computer, you do not have to worry about the size of letters, the spaces, or your handwriting. Everything will be the same, but when you write you may make mistakes. Also, if you have bad handwriting, your paper may not be readable, but on a computer it would be.

If we need to do projects and write papers in middle school and college, we may start practice early on.

Eyes and Ears

Did you ever stop and think about your senses? How would we get around without eyesight or hearing? Can you imagine what it would be like to be deaf or blind?

Eyes and ears both use waves to see and hear. Eyes use light waves. And ears use sound waves. Cells in our eyes see the light waves that bounce off objects. Cells in our ears sense the vibrations from sound waves. Our eyes and ears communicate with our brains to make sense of the light and sound waves.

Some people may need glasses because they are nearsighted or farsighted. Nearsighted means that they cannot see things that are far away clearly, but they can see things that are near. Farsighted means that they can see things that are far but not things that are close to them. Similarly, some people may need a hearing aid.

Ears also can help you keep balance. When you move your head in different directions, fluid moves around in your ears and the nerves tell your brain if you are sitting, standing, or moving around. Ears have two jobs, while eyes only have one. Your eyes help you see objects that are far away and near by.

Eyes and ears work in the same way, but also do different things. It's important to think about how our senses work and what's different about them to understand sight and sound.

Reference

Simon, S. (2003). *Eyes and Ears*. New York: HarperCollins.

Transition Words and Sentence Starters

Beginning—purpose

- By comparing and contrasting X and Y, _____
- An examination of the similarities and differences between X and Y will _____

Middle—for similarities

- One way that X and Y are similar is _____
- On the one hand, _____
- A second point of comparison between X and Y is _____
- Another similarity between X and Y is _____

Middle—for contrasts

- On the other hand, _____
- On the contrary, _____
- An additional difference between X and Y is _____

Transition words—for adding information

- Also, _____
- In addition, _____
- Furthermore, _____

End—for conclusion

- In sum, _____
- In conclusion, _____

When Using Sources

- The book _____ written by _____ says, "_____"
- The author [author's name] writes [explains] that _____
- _____ [author's name], in her book _____ [name of book], explains [gives information, writes] _____

Polar Bears and Penguins

By comparing and contrasting polar bears and penguins, we can learn more about them and their habits.

One way that polar bears and penguins are similar is in the use of camouflage for protection and in the case of polar bears for hunting. Similarly, polar bears' white color helps them blend with their surroundings. That is how they can approach a seal and attack it without being seen.

Another way that they are similar is in the way they protect themselves against cold. They both have blubber, which is a layer of fat under their skin. This works as an insulation. Polar bears have a thick, short coat of hair that traps heat while the penguins have a thick, soft, coat layer next to their skin that traps warm air. Polar bears have an outer coat of guard hairs that are like a raincoat. Penguins also have a raincoat, but they have feathers instead.

Penguins are great divers and this is because their bones are solid. In the water they swim very fast and can quickly move to different directions. They also breathe air and when they swim and hunt, they come back to the surface to take a breath. Polar bears are also great swimmers and can swim for many hours and long distances.

Polar bears live in the Arctic, on the North Pole, and can be found in Alaska, Canada, and Norway, for example. Penguins live in the southern hemisphere, at the Antarctic. Polar bears and penguins will live their lives without seeing each other.

A main difference between polar bears and penguins is that they are different types of animals. Polar bears are mammals and like all mammals they give birth to live babies that the mother bear called the sow feeds milk. Penguins are birds and they lay eggs. Most penguins lay two eggs, but the King and the Emperor penguin lay one egg.

In conclusion, polar bears and penguins have many similarities and differences.

References

Switzer, M. (1988). *Penguins.* In series *Getting to know nature's children: Penguins & elephants.* Danbury, CT: Scholastic.

Greenland, C. (1997). *Polar bears.* In series *Getting to know nature's children: Polar bears & skunks.* Danbury, CT: Scholastic.

Earthquakes and Volcanoes:
Which One Would You Rather Experience?

Earthquakes and volcano eruptions are scary events that can seriously hurt people. Seymour Simon in his books *Volcanoes* and *Earthquakes* says that one earthquake in 1985 in Mexico killed 10,000 people, and a volcano eruption of Mount St. Helens in 1980 killed 60 people. Both of those also destroyed parts of cities and entire forests.

Volcanoes erupt and earthquakes happen in places where two of the Earth's plates meet. Plates are different sections of the Earth's crust that move around and cause these problems when they move apart or hit each other.

They are different, too. Volcanoes can explode and erupt constantly, like in the Hawaiian islands. These volcanoes have been going for millions of years, actually forming the islands once the lava cooled. Earthquakes, however, can last several minutes for a major one, with aftershocks only lasting on and off for a few weeks at the most.

Earthquakes are measured using the Richter scale by scientists so they know how strong it was. Volcanoes, however, are not measured by any scales.

Earthquakes are scary, but they do not last very long. On the other hand, volcanoes can erupt for many years. Which would you rather experience?

References

Simon, S. (2006). *Volcanoes*. New York: HarperCollins.
Simon, S. (1988). *Earthquakes*. Washington, DC: Smithsonian Collins.

Traveling by Plane or Car

Look up in the sky and for sure you will see a plane. Look out your window and on the street you will see cars. People come and go and travel at all times. By comparing and contrasting traveling by plane or traveling by car, you may decide which one is best for you.

One way that traveling by plane and car is the same is that they both take you to places. Both cars and planes are means of transportation and are used every day by millions to get them to their destinations.

Also, they both have space for you to put your things.

They are different in how comfortable they are. In a car no one serves you juice and food, but in a plane they do.

In order to travel on a plane, you need to find an available flight and seat. You also need to have documentation and a ticket. When you travel with your car, you only need to have someone who can drive it, and you can go.

The Earth and Mars

During a dark night if you look up in the sky, you can see stars, and if you have a telescope, you can see planets. Two planets in our solar system are the Earth and Mars. We live on Earth but could you dream of living on Mars?

The Earth is bigger than Mars and farther away from the Sun. Seymour Simon in his book *Destination: Mars* explains that seven planets like Mars could make one Earth. Also, Mars has two moons, called Phobos and Deimos, while Earth just has one moon.

On our planet, there are many types of features: oceans, mountains, volcanoes, plains, deserts, and glaciers. Believe it or not, Mars also has many of those things! All around Mars, there are craters, mountains, plains, and valleys. And at the north pole of Mars, there is an ice cap. Also, scientists think that Mars had an ancient ocean, but now either it is below the surface, or it was lost into space. There is also a giant valley called Valles Marineris. It is like the Grand Canyon on Earth, except it is four times as deep.

Earth is full of life and humans live on Earth as well as many little and big animals. So far, scientists are still trying to figure out if there was ever life on Mars. There may have been microscopic life many years ago. Now, there is no water on the planet, it gets very hot during the day, and freezing cold at night. Humans definitely could not live on Mars.

There are some similarities between Earth and Mars, but humans cannot live on Mars without the help of technology. There is no water and we would need spacesuits to breathe and to maintain livable temperatures. Earth is still the best place for humans!

References

Simon, S. (2003). *Earth: Our planet in space.* New York: Simon & Schuster Books for Young Readers.
Simon, S. (2000). *Destination: Mars.* New York: HarperCollins.

Bees and Ants: Hardworking Little Creatures

Bees and ants have many similarities and differences, and it is important to know what they offer to our natural world and even to us.

On the one hand, bees and ants are members of the same family and have similar body parts. They are both insects and like all insects they have six legs, and three body parts: an antennae, thorax, and abdomen. Also, they both have two stomachs and a hard exoskeleton that protects their small bodies. Bees have wings and can fly and even though not all ants have wings, some do.

They both live in well-organized colonies that have a hierarchy. This means that different members of the colony perform different tasks. Both colonies can only have one queen.

Also, bees and ants share the same cycle of life. They both start from tiny eggs. Then, eggs turn to grubs, called larvae, and they eat a lot of food. Then, they form cocoons. When they come out, they look like the bees and ants we know.

Finally, they are both very useful creatures. Ants make tunnels and turn the dirt. That helps the dirt be healthy. Also, they prey on the larvae of other pests like aphids.

On the other hand, ants and bees have some differences in their senses. Even though they both feel with their antennae and sense the world with the hair found on their exoskeleton, ants do not have good vision, but bees do. They have two really big eyes, one at each side of their body, that help them see the world.

In conclusion, bees and ants have many similarities and few differences. They are both useful to humans and humans should protect them. Therefore, the next time you see a bee buzzing on top of a flower, let it do its work, and the next time you see a little ant on your balcony, step away to let it continue its hard labor.

References

Greenland, C. (2000). *Ants*. In series *Getting to know nature's children: Gorillas & ants*. Danbury, CT: Scholastic.

Kelsey, E. (1998). *Bees*. In series *Getting to know nature's children: Turtles & bees*. Danbury, CT: Scholastic.

Practice Developing Categories

PLAN

Form: What am I writing? (Essay) Paragraph   Letter   Other _____

Topic: Compare and contrast first grade and fourth grade

Audience: young children

Purpose: to decide which one offered you the most in your learning

IDEAS

Brainstorm   **Reading** *and* **Note Taking**

Unique features of Topic A: Grade 1		Unique features of Topic B: Grade 4
Groups—buddy reading, home help from parent and sister to read and practice Learned how to read and write, do basic calculations—add, subtract, and a bit of multiplication Wrote little stories and read short books to practice reading and learn the letters and the alphabet Little homework—practice writing or reading, one spelling test every Friday	Similarities between Topics School—wake up early, take bus, be at school by 8:00 Rules for sitting, playing, talking, participating in class, permission to leave classroom Teacher explained everything many times	Multidigit subtractions, subtraction of numbers with decimals, equations, compare and order fractions, angles/geometry, division Reading of chapter books and book reports and research projects Homework and online projects Group work in and out of school (now food chains and food webs of oceanic ecosystem) Independent work, parents check my work A lot of tests

The Butterfly and *The Blessing Cup* by Patricia Polacco

Patricia Polacco is a great author, and I think that her books are masterpieces. Her stories always have a message, and they make you think more. The books *The Butterfly* and *The Blessing Cup* are two good examples of how good of an author she is. By comparing and contrasting them, you can better see how Polacco does her stories.

In both books Polacco draws excellent pictures. The pictures have a lot of details that help you, as a reader, understand the time and place. Also, the pictures help you better understand the stories. For example, in the book *The Blessing Cup*, all pictures are black and white and only the china set has color. This is because the china set in a way is the main character of the story.

In both those books Polacco describes horrible times for Jewish people. Jewish people were taken away from their homes and were treated poorly by people who did not want them because they were Jewish. In the book *The Butterfly*, through the eyes of Sevrine and Monique, the reader can see the fear that both children had because of the Nazis. Also, in the book *The Blessing Cup*, when the czar ordered Jews to leave Russia, their Temple was burned and they had to leave their homes.

Polacco always uses dialogue and great descriptions so you see the characters. When you read a dialogue from Polacco, you see through the character and you feel the pain, fear, or happiness the character feels. When Anna and her family are chased away from their home and they stay in a cold barn the first night, the descriptions let you be the characters and feel their fear and understand how grateful they were to be together and alive.

Polacco shows in both books how kind people can be. In *The Blessing Cup*, uncle Genya takes in Anna and her family risking his life, sells the most valuable item in his home, buys them tickets, and helps them escape. In the book *Butterfly*, Marcel risks her life and the life of her family to help innocent refugees who are in danger from the Nazis.

What is different about those books is the time of events. In the book *The Blessing Cup*, Russian Jews are chased out of Russia, and they are mistreated. In *The Butterfly*, Servine and her family are in France, and they are trying to escape from the Germans during the Second World War. Polacco knows well the history behind those times, and she can describe those times. Even though there are so many years apart, those events are connected with hatred to Jewish people.

Overall, Patricia Polacco is a great storyteller. She draws very detailed pictures and her descriptions let you connect with the characters. Her writing takes you to places and you can better understand what it meant to be a Jew when the czar or the Nazis were in power. Her books can make you laugh or even cry. But her books can make you understand what good stories are.

The Salmon Princess: An Alaska Cinderella Story by Mindy Dwyer and *Prince Cinders* by Babette Cole

Cinder and Cinders

The story of Cinderella is one that can be read in books and can be watched in movies. There are a lot of different versions of this story. By comparing and contrasting the character of Cinderella in the books *The Salmon Princess: An Alaska Cinderella Story* and *Prince Cinders,* you can better understand the characters, the plot, and even write your own version.

One similarity between the two characters is that they are both unfortunate. Prince Cinders is skinny and while his strong brothers were at a disco having fun, he would stay behind and clean up the house. Cinder, the salmon princess, had lost her mother, and her stepmother forced her to clean fish and this was a stinky job.

Also, they are both "saved" and recognized by the savior using a specific item. For example, the wealthy Princess Lovelypenny saves Prince Cinders who can fit into a pair of trousers that was left behind. In the story of Cinder, an industrialist, whose father has a cannery company called "King of Salmon," searches for a woman who has lost winning raffle tickets and also her boot. After she wears the boot and it fits, she collects the prize and marries the prince.

Another similarity between the two characters is that they are both "saved" by someone other than themselves. For example, the wealthy Princess Lovelypenny saves Prince Cinders and the industrialist saves Cinder.

In addition, someone who has magical powers helps them both. In the case of Cinders, a clumsy fairy tries to help him, even though her magic turns him into a big and hairy monkey. Cinder is helped by an eagle who talks like a human and gives her a shiny dress to wear to the festival.

A final similarity is that in the end they both "punish" those who mistreated them even though they chose different ways to do that. Prince Cinders asked the fairy who protected him to turn his brothers into house fairies to do all the housework. Cinder's mother ended up being the one to clean up salmon, and her brothers were working at the cannery for many hours cleaning slimy fish.

A main difference between the two characters is in their gender. Prince Cinders is a man, but Cinder in the story "The Salmon Princess" is a girl. As a result, a female princess saves Cinders and a male prince saves Cinder.

(continued)

An additional difference between the two characters is what they choose to do after their life is changed. Prince Cinders just enjoys a life of luxury. On the contrary, Cinder uses the silver she won to buy a homestead, and she farms prizewinning cabbages with her husband and children.

In conclusion, the story of Cinderella has a number of variations, but by comparing and contrasting these two versions, you can better understand the characters, the plot, and the variation in the main story. This understanding can help you write your own version of a story. Perhaps now you can write a story where Cinderella is an alien.

FORM 6.1

Planning Materials

PLAN

Form: What am I writing?   Essay   Paragraph   Letter   Other _____

T

A

P

IDEAS

Brainstorm   Reading *and* Note Taking

Unique features of Topic A:		Unique features of Topic B:
	Similarities between Topics	

(continued)

Planning Materials *(page 2 of 2)*

Graphic Organizer for Compare–Contrast Writing

<table>
<tr>
<td rowspan="2">Beginning</td>
<td colspan="3">Topic:</td>
</tr>
<tr>
<td colspan="3">Purpose:</td>
</tr>
<tr>
<td rowspan="9">Middle</td>
<td>How are they similar?</td>
<td colspan="2" align="center">Similarities</td>
</tr>
<tr>
<td></td>
<td colspan="2"></td>
</tr>
<tr>
<td></td>
<td colspan="2"></td>
</tr>
<tr>
<td>How are they different?</td>
<td colspan="2" align="center">Differences</td>
</tr>
<tr>
<td></td>
<td>Unique features of Topic A:</td>
<td>Unique features of Topic B:</td>
</tr>
<tr>
<td></td>
<td></td>
<td></td>
</tr>
<tr>
<td></td>
<td></td>
<td></td>
</tr>
<tr>
<td></td>
<td></td>
<td></td>
</tr>
<tr>
<td rowspan="2">End</td>
<td colspan="3">Restate purpose:</td>
</tr>
<tr>
<td colspan="3">Leave a message to the reader:</td>
</tr>
</table>

Rubric on Self-Evaluation and Peer Review

Date: _____

Writer's Name: _____ Reviewer's Name: _____

		0 Not there	1 Could be better	2 Great!
	Beginning **Topic:** Is it clear what is compared and contrasted?			
	Purpose: Why are the topics compared and contrasted?			
Middle / **Similarities**	**Similarity 1:** Is the first category of similarities clear to the reader?			
	Evidence: Is the evidence clear and accurate? Is the evidence explained?			
	Similarity 2 and more: Are the other categories of similarities clearly stated?			
	Evidence: Is the evidence clear and accurate? Is the evidence explained?			
Differences	**Difference 1:** Is the first category of differences clear to the reader?			
	Evidence: Is the evidence clear and accurate? Is the evidence explained?			
	Difference 2 and more: Are the other categories of differences clear to the reader?			
	Evidence: Is the evidence clear and accurate? Is the evidence explained?			
End	**Restate purpose:** Did the writer restate why the topics are compared and contrasted?			
	Think: Did the writer leave the reader with a message to think about?			
Other Considerations!	Is there a title that clearly refers to the information of the paper and relates to the purpose?			
	Are there appropriate transition words used throughout the paper?			
	If the writer used sources, are ideas and details appropriately drawn from the text?			
	If the writer used sources, are they accurately referenced at the end of the paper?			

(continued)

Rubric on Self-Evaluation and Peer Review *(page 2 of 2)*

Reviewer/Writer as Reader
• Is the paper informative? Why?
• What revisions should be made?

Goals
• What should be the writer's current and future goals?

Memorization Sheet for Compare–Contrast Writing

Student's Name: _____   Date: _____

Beginning		
Middle		
End		

What did I miss? _____

_____

_____

What should be my study goals? _____

_____

_____

Chapter 7

How to Plan Your Own Genre-Based Strategy Instruction Lessons

INTERVIEWER: I know you have been working on your new lessons. What genre did you choose?

MR. SAVVAS [a fifth-grade teacher]: We are working on biographies.

INTERVIEWER: How did you work with your team to develop the lessons?

MR. SAVVAS: We worked as a group, as you all suggested, getting the materials together. And after we got down the elements—you know, the elements' chart and the planning sheets—and they made sense, each one of us did a different thing. Ms. Johnson, Mr. Friedman, and I were in charge of good and weak examples, Mr. Peters did the evaluation rubric, and Mr. Knowles with Ms. Elias worked on some mini-lessons. Mr. Peters, Mr. Knowles, and Ms. Elias got together to add some parts to the rubric later, too.

INTERVIEWER: Where did you find the good and weak examples?

MR. SAVVAS: Mr. Peters and Ms. Elias are new here, but the rest of us have been working in this school for a while. So we had samples from previous years, and Ms. Johnson also had samples from earlier this year, so she gave us the papers.

INTERVIEWER: How did you prepare the papers?

MR. SAVVAS: Well, first of all we took out all students' names and then we looked for papers that had or didn't have the elements. We also ended up fixing the good example to be, you know, good.

INTERVIEWER: What did you find most challenging in the process?

MR. SAVVAS: The first part. We spent time thinking about those elements and the planning sheets. I think that after we had everything in place, it was easy for us to do the lessons. We just followed the sequence of instruction. We all had a good number of biographies in class, and this helped, too, because we didn't have to go out and look for books.

238

DESIGNING ADDITIONAL LESSONS

In Chapter 1, we explained that our goal was for teachers to use this book as a professional development guide and resource. As a preservice teacher, you could increase your knowledge about writing, and as an inservice teacher, you could use the approach to help plan your writing instruction within your grade level or even across grades. Now that we have reached the end of the book and you have had the opportunity to teach at least three genres, we describe how you can become the architects of genre-based writing instruction and develop your own lessons. Designing your own lessons will be easier once you have familiarized yourselves with the lesson structure and strategies for writing and self-regulation.

Genre

- **Select the genre.** Which genres you choose will be something you can decide in relation to the needs of your students and your grade-level colleagues. You might choose genres that will fit into your content-area instruction; for example, an explanation of a process in science or an analysis of character traits in literature.
- Create the elements' chart for that genre and questions that accompany each element. This chart will be used to develop your planning materials.

Materials: Part 1

- **Develop the planning materials.** Depending on the genre you select, you may use a different approach to generate Ideas. For example, in persuasion we included *brainstorm*, but in compare–contrast writing with sources, we worked on *reading and note taking*. Also, we used different charts that reflected the core components of each genre. For example, in persuasion, the brainstorm component has a two-column chart with ideas *in favor* and *against*.
- Using the elements' chart, create a GO that follows the structure of the genre, is memorable, and is not too complicated. Also, create the evaluation rubric that will be used for self-evaluation and peer review. Besides the genre elements, think of additional questions that you can add in the "Other Considerations!" section of the rubric and that can perhaps lead to mini-lessons. You could complete this section, too, after you have determined the mini-lessons.

Application (Caution)

- **Try out the strategy as a student.** Before you proceed with the development of any other piece of material, practice the strategy as a student. Use a topic that you would ask your students to write about, then plan, draft, and revise your paper using the materials. This is an opportunity to check that all the components make sense and, if necessary, make revisions.

Materials: Part 2

- **Select good and weak examples for evaluation.** You could collaborate with your colleagues and share papers across your classes. If you do, remove students' information, so they will be "papers written by unknown students." In case you do not have papers that are good examples, you can write your own or revise a paper written by a student. The *good example* should represent the paper you would like your students to compose at the end of your instruction.

- **Create a chart of transition words.** Think of essential transition words for the genre and whether they would appear in the Beginning, Middle, or End of the paper. Organize them in a chart and consider keeping them on display for students.

Read-Alouds

- **Select books.** Depending on the genre you choose, you will need to select books to introduce it. If you are working on a genre that does not appear in the literature, you will need to develop more than one good example.

Mini-Lessons

- **Design mini-lessons.** The mini-lessons will need to connect with the elements of the genre. For example, if you were developing lessons on biographies, you might have a mini-lesson on looking for online sources and evaluating them. You might discuss with students what would be an effective and reliable source and what would be an ineffective and unreliable one. Or you might include a lesson on interviewing, and discuss whom to interview and what types of questions to ask. If you were working on cause-and-effect relationships, you might want to include a mini-lesson on fact and opinion.

Topics

- Develop topics for assessment and instruction. If you use sources, the topics could connect to the subject areas.

Differentiation

- **Think about different learners' needs.** Your differentiation will be based on your informal assessments, and you can then address students' needs in mini-lessons and small-group meetings. However, if your lessons also include sources, you may want to differentiate the readings. For instance, if you are working on scientific explanations, and your students are writing to explain natural phenomena (e.g., earthquakes), you may choose to use a selection of books that has a range of Lexile measures (*www.Lexile.com*). For instance, you could use *Earthquakes* by Seymour Simon (1010L), *Earthquakes* by Sally Walker (640L), *Earthquakes* by Ker Than (890L), or *Earthquakes!* by Cy Armour (490L).

• **Use the sequence of genre-based writing instruction (Chapter 3) to design each lesson.** When you develop your lessons, also include clear objectives and the assessment information. At the end of each lesson, you can take notes about areas that you would change when you teach the lesson the next time or variations to the lesson that you had not thought of previously. If in your grade you have different times that you start teaching, one colleague can teach a lesson first and then share notes and observations with other teachers.

CLOSING THOUGHTS

Writing is a challenging task for students and adults. We anticipate that through this approach teachers will be able to design instruction that will be methodical and systematic. Through this instruction, students will learn not only to be good writers, but also good learners. In addition, teachers will work more strategically and collaboratively. Teachers can work with colleagues to discuss their instruction, develop additional minilessons for the three instructional chapters, and design future lessons. This collaboration can help the school develop its own writing program for grades 3–5.

We have enjoyed working with teachers during the development of this approach. We learned a lot about writing instruction with them and from them. Something that was clear during our interactions was teachers' zeal to learn more about writing and their dedication to their students' growth. We hope that this book will be helpful to all teachers, and that it will help them make a difference in their students' writing and learning.

Study Guide

This study guide is meant to support your meetings and discussions in your professional learning communities (PLCs) and/or in your independent reading of the book. We hope these questions will get you started, but we expect you will add questions to make your discussions meaningful and responsive to your specific instructional needs. Each section includes a reading guide with questions about the chapter and activities you might use during meetings, in preparation for meetings, or before teaching. We hope that you will find this helpful as you plan your writing instruction independently or in your PLCs.

CHAPTER 1

Reading Guide

1. What are some challenges that teachers face with writing instruction?

2. What are the guidelines in the Common Core State Standards (CCSS) for writing instruction?

3. What are the research recommendations on writing instruction?

4. How does the genre-based strategy instruction connect to research recommendations and the CCSS guidelines?

Activities and Discussion

1. Review Mr. Tragas's comments about his day and classroom. What are your instructional challenges (in your classroom or your grade)?

2. Download and review the CCSS for your grade. Create a list of the specific recommendations for writing genres, purposes, and editing goals for your grade.

3. Record how much time you devote to the teaching of writing and how much time students write within a week. Based on the recommendations in the chapter, is the time sufficient? How could you give students more writing opportunities?

CHAPTER 2

Reading Guide

1. What are the principles of genre-based strategy instruction in writing? Explain the origin and meaning of each one. How is this approach different from the one you already use?

2. What is the Writing Strategy Ladder? What are its components and what is the meaning of each one?

3. What is the meaning of *self-regulation*? What is the Be Strategic! strategy? Why do students need to set goals? How does the Be Strategic! strategy support students' self-regulation?

4. How does this approach connect reading and writing?

5. Why is it important to learn evaluation criteria? How can this knowledge support students' self-evaluation and peer review?

CHAPTER 3

Reading Guide

1. What is the sequence of instruction? Explain the parts of the Strategy for Teaching Strategies (see Figure 3.1).

2. What advice is given about the instructional methods in this approach? What questions do you have about the methods?

Activities

1. **Create posters or select resources for class display.** The forms of the Writing Strategy Ladder, the Be Strategic! strategy, and perhaps the SCIPS checklist could be put on display. You could create posters or draw and write the information on chart paper. If the forms are on display, students can refer to them when writing across subjects.

2. **Journals.** If you do not already use journals, consider adding them to your classroom for students' reflection and overall self-regulation.

ASSESSMENT TASKS FOR CHAPTERS 4, 5, AND 6

Assessment

Preassessment and analysis. After you collect students' preassessments, prepare copies of the evaluation rubric found in that chapter. With your colleagues, review at least two different papers written by students (or you can use the weak papers from the chapter) and then review the papers written by your students. Create a table like the one below and record students' performance.

Using the information, group students based on similar needs as shown in the analysis of the completed sample below. This information can be used to help you determine groupings for mini-lessons.

Completed Sample

	Story Elements							
	Beginning				Middle		End	
Students' Names	Characters	Time	Place	Problem	Events	Complications	Solutions	Emotions
Georgia	2	0	0	1	0	0	0	0
Helena	2	1	0	1	0	0	1	1
Tobias	1	0	1	1	2	1	1	1
Alex	2	2	2	0	1	1	0	0
Peter	2	2	1	1	1	1	1	1
Daniel	2	2	2	0	0	1	1	0

Sample analysis. Students' preassessment information shows that all students will benefit from lessons on how to create a *Problem* in a story and develop *Complications*, *Solutions*, and *Emotions*. All students, except for Tobias, will need instruction on description of *Events*. Finally, Georgia, Helena, Tobias, and possibly Peter will also benefit from instruction on how to describe the elements of *Time* and *Place*.

CHAPTERS 4, 5, AND 6

Reading Guide

1. What are the purposes and elements of the story, persuasion, and compare–contrast genres?

Preparation for Teaching Lessons

1. Create posters/display forms. The genre elements, the planning and evaluation forms, and transition words could be turned into posters or you could draw them on chart paper.
2. Review the lesson outline and discuss the sequence of lessons.
3. Think of additional memorization techniques you could use for students to learn the genre elements.
4. Identify as a group the read-alouds that you will read daily and bring them to your class.
5. With your group, develop a list of potential mini-lessons that you could use during the segment on Continuous Guided Practice to Mastery.
6. If you work on an extension genre, refer to Chapter 7 and its study guide.

Discussion Questions after Instruction

1. What did you find interesting and useful in this lesson? What was different from your previous practice?

2. How did your students respond to instruction? How did your students progress as writers? What evidence do you have? What could you do differently?

3. What questions do you have after trying out the instruction?

4. What did you learn in this chapter that you could now use to design future lessons?

Special Note for Chapter 6

In Chapter 6, you will need to decide if you will use sources. If you do, then you should identify and bring to your classroom the books that you will use for students' reading. One effective approach that would connect reading and writing and content learning would be to include readings from social studies and science. If you choose to use trade books, you should consider students' reading levels.

CHAPTER 7

Reading Guide

1. What is the process of developing lessons for a different genre?

Activities

1. The development of a new set of lessons will not happen in one meeting. Work individually and in small groups to develop additional lessons.

2. You might start by considering the extension activities for related genres in Chapters 4–6.

3. Also, you might consider the types of writing that are included in your curricula for literature, science, and social studies. Or consider the types of writing you have asked students to use in the past.

4. Review what Chapter 7 says about analyzing the elements of the genre and work with your colleagues to define those elements. Then develop the evaluation rubric.

References

Baumann, J. F., & Bergeron, B. S. (1993). Story map instruction using children's literature: Effects on first graders' comprehension of central narrative elements. *Journal of Reading Behavior, 25*, 407–437.

Bruner, J. S. (1986). *Actual minds, possible worlds.* Cambridge, MA: Harvard University Press.

Carter, O. B. J., Patterson, L. J., Donovan, R. J., Ewing, M. T., & Roberts, C. M. (2011). Children's understanding of the selling versus persuasive intent of junk food advertising: Implications for regulation. *Social Science and Medicine, 72*, 962–968.

Cho, K., & MacArthur, C. (2011). Learning by reviewing. *Journal of Educational Psychology, 103*, 73–84.

Coirier, P., & Golder, C. (1993). Writing argumentative text: A developmental study of the acquisition of supporting structures. *European Journal of Psychology of Education, 8*(2), 169–181.

Coker, D. (2007). Writing instruction for young children: Methods targeting the multiple demands that writers face. In S. Graham, C. A. MacArthur, & J. Fitzgerald (Eds.), *Best practices in writing instruction* (pp. 101–118). New York: Guilford Press.

Common Core State Standards Initiative. (2010). *Common Core State Standards for English language arts and literacy in history/social studies, science, and technical subjects.* Washington, DC: National Governors Association Center for Best Practices and Council of Chief State School Officers. Retrieved from *www.corestandards.org/assets/CCSSI_ELA%20Standards.pdf.*

Duke, N. K. (2000). 3.6 minutes per day: The scarcity of informational texts in first grade. *Reading Research Quarterly, 35*, 202–224.

Englert, C. S., Raphael, T. E., Anderson, L. M., Anthony, H. M., & Stevens, D. D. (1991). Making strategies and self-talk visible: Writing instruction in regular and special education classrooms. *American Educational Research Journal, 28*, 337–372.

Englert, C. S., & Thomas, C. C. (1987). Sensitivity to text structure in reading and writing: A comparison between learning disabled and non-learning disabled students. *Learning Disability Quarterly, 10*, 93–105.

Ferretti, R. P., MacArthur, C. A., & Dowdy, N. S. (2000). The effects of an elaborated goal on the persuasive writing of students with learning disabilities and their normally achieving peers. *Journal of Educational Psychology, 92*, 694–702.

Ferretti, R. P., MacArthur, C. A., & Okolo, C. M. (2001). Teaching for historical understanding in inclusive classrooms. *Learning Disability Quarterly, 24,* 59–71.

Fitzgerald, J., & Spiegel, D. L. (1983). The development of knowledge of social intentions, plans, and resolutions as reflected in story production and recall of scrambled stories. In J. A. Niles & L. A. Harris (Eds.), *Searches for meaning in reading/language processing and instruction* (32nd Yearbook of the National Reading Conference, pp. 192–198). Rochester, NY: National Reading Conference.

Fitzgerald, J., & Teasley, A. B. (1986). Enhancing children's writing through instruction in narrative structure. *Journal of Educational Psychology, 78*(6), 424–432.

Gilbert, J., & Graham, S. (2010). Teaching writing to elementary students in grades 4–6: A national survey. *Elementary School Journal, 110,* 494–518.

Golder, C., & Coirier, P. (1994). Argumentative text writing: Developmental trends. *Discourse Processes, 18,* 187–210.

Graham, S. (2006). Strategy instruction and the teaching of writing: A meta-analysis. In C. A. MacArthur, S. Graham, & J. Fitzgerald (Eds.), *Handbook of writing research* (pp. 187–207). New York: Guilford Press.

Graham, S., Bollinger, A., Olson, C., D'Aoust, C., MacArthur, C., McCutchen, D., et al. (2012). Teaching elementary school students to be effective writers. Retrieved from *http://ies.ed.gov/ncee/wwc/PracticeGuide.aspx?sid=17.*

Graham, S., & Harris, K. R. (2005). Improving the writing performance of young struggling writers. *Journal of Special Education, 39,* 19–33.

Graham, S., & Hebert, M. (2011). Writing to read: A meta-analysis of the impact of writing and writing instruction on reading. *Harvard Educational Review, 81,* 710–744.

Graham, S., McKeown, D., Kiuhara, S. A., & Harris, K. R. (2012). A meta-analysis of writing instruction for students in the elementary grades. *Journal of Educational Psychology, 104,* 879–896.

Graham, S., & Perin, D. (2007). What we know, what we still need to know: Teaching adolescents to write. *Scientific Studies of Reading, 11,* 313–335.

Harris, K. R., & Graham, S. (2009). Self-regulated strategy development in writing: Premises, evolution, and the future. *British Journal of Educational Psychology Monograph Series II, 6,* 113–135.

Harris, K. R., Graham, S., MacArthur, C. A., & Santangelo, T. (2018). Self-regulation and writing. In B. Zimmerman & D. H. Schunk (Eds.), *Handbook of self-regulation of learning and performance* (2nd ed., pp. 138–152). New York: Routledge.

Harris, K. R., Graham, S., & Mason, L. (2006). Improving the writing, knowledge, and motivation of struggling young writers: Effects of self-regulated strategy development with and without peer support. *American Educational Research Journal, 43,* 295–340.

Harris, K. R., Graham, S., Mason, L., & Friedlander, B. (2008). *Powerful writing strategies for all students.* Baltimore, MD: Brookes.

Hayes, J. R. (1996). A new framework for understanding cognition and affect in writing. In C. M. Levy & S. Ransdell (Eds.), *The science of writing* (pp. 1–27). Mahwah, NJ: Erlbaum.

Heath, S. B. (1983). *Ways with words: Language, life, and work in communities and classrooms.* New York: Cambridge University Press.

Hillocks, G. (1986). *Research on written composition: New directions for research.* Urbana, IL: National Conference on Research in English and ERIC Clearinghouse on Reading and Communication Skills.

Hyon, S. (1996). Genre in three traditions: Implications for ESL. *TESOL Quarterly, 30*(4), 693–722.

Lewis, W. E., & Ferretti, R. P. (2009). Defending interpretations of literary texts: The effects of topoi instruction on the literary arguments of high school students. *Reading and Writing Quarterly, 25*(4), 250–270.

MacArthur, C. A. (2011). Strategies instruction. In K. R. Harris, S. Graham, & T. Urdan (Eds.),

Educational psychology handbook: Vol. 3. Applications of educational psychology to learning and teaching (pp. 379–401). Washington, DC: American Psychological Association.

MacArthur, C. A. (2016). Instruction in evaluation and revision. In C. A. MacArthur, S. Graham, & J. Fitzgerald (Eds.), *Handbook of writing research* (2nd ed., pp. 272–287). New York: Guilford Press.

MacArthur, C. A., Ferretti, R. P., & Okolo, C. M. (2002). On defending controversial viewpoints: Debates of sixth-graders about the desirability of early 20th century American immigration. *Learning Disabilities Research and Practice, 17,* 160–172.

MacArthur, C. A., & Philippakos, Z. A. (2013). Self-regulated strategy instruction in developmental writing: A design research project. *Community College Review, 41*(2), 176–195.

Martin, J. R. (2009). Genre and language learning: A social semiotic perspective. *Linguistics and Education, 20*(1), 10–21.

Martin, J. R., & Rose, D. (2012). *Learning to write, reading to learn: Genre, knowledge and pedagogy in the Sydney School.* Sheffield, UK: Equinox.

Meyer, B. J. F. (1985a). Prose analysis: Purposes, procedures, and problems. In B. K. Britton & J. Black (Eds.), *Analyzing and understanding expository text* (pp. 11–64, 269–304). Hillsdale, NJ: Erlbaum.

Meyer, B. J. F. (1985b). Signaling the structure of text. In D. H. Jonassen (Ed.), *The technology of text* (pp. 64–89). Englewood Cliffs, NJ: Educational Technology.

National Center for Education Statistics. (2012). *The nation's report card: Writing 2011.* Washington, DC: NCES, Institute of Education Sciences, U.S. Department of Education.

National Commission on Writing in America's Schools and Colleges. (2003). *The neglected "R": The need for a writing revolution.* New York: College Board.

National Institute of Child Health and Human Development. (2000). *Report of the National Reading Panel. Teaching children to read: An evidence based assessment of the scientific research literature on reading and its implications for reading instruction* (NIH Publication No. 00-4769). Washington, DC: U.S. Government Printing Office.

Okolo, C. M., Ferretti, R. P., & MacArthur, C. A. (2002). Westward expansion and the ten-year-old mind: Teaching for historical understanding in a diverse classroom. In J. Brophy (Ed.), *Advances in research on teaching: Vol. 9. Social constructivist teaching: Affordances and constraints* (pp. 299–331). Greenwich, CT: JAI Press.

Persky, H., Daane, M., & Jin, Y. (2003). *The nation's report card: Writing.* Washington, DC: U.S. Department of Education.

Philippakos, Z. A. (2012). *Effects of reviewing on fourth and fifth-grade students' persuasive writing and revising* (doctoral dissertation). Retrieved from WorldCat. OCLC 830832350.

Pressley, M., Mohan, L., Raphael, L. M., & Fingeret, L. (2007). How does Bennett Woods Elementary School produce such high reading and writing achievement? *Journal of Educational Psychology, 99*(2), 221–240.

Saddler, B. (2012). *Teacher's guide to effective sentence writing.* New York: Guilford Press.

Troia, G. A. (2006). Writing instruction for students with learning disabilities. In C. A. MacArthur, S. Graham, & J. Fitzgerald (Eds.), *Handbook of writing research* (pp. 324–336). New York: Guilford Press.

Children's Books

Adler, D. (2004). *Cam Jansen: The mystery of the dinosaur bones.* New York: Puffin Books.

Armour, C. (2012). *Earthquakes!* Huntington Beach, CA: Teacher Created Materials.

Benson, M. (2004). *Bill Clinton.* Minneapolis, MN: Lerner.

Berger, M. (1994). *Oil spill!* New York: HarperCollins.

Blos, J. W. (1990). *Old Henry.* New York: Mulberry Books.

Brett, J. (2005). *Honey, honey—lion!: A story from Africa.* New York: Putnam's.

Climo, S. (1992). *The Egyptian Cinderella.* New York: HarperTrophy.

Cole, B. (1997). *Prince Cinders.* New York: Putnam's.

Cronin, D. (2004). *Duck for president.* New York: Simon & Schuster Books for Young Readers.

Cronin, D. (2011). *Click, clack, moo: Cows that type.* New York: Simon & Schuster.

D'Aulaire, I., & D'Aulaire, E. P. (1983). *Columbus.* Sandwich Village, MA: Beautiful Feet Books.

DePaola, T. (2008). *Brava, Strega Nona!: A heartwarming pop-up book.* New York: Putnam's.

Dwyer, M. (2004). *The salmon princess: An Alaska Cinderella story.* Seattle, WA: Sasquatch Books.

Grambling, L. G. (1995). *Can I have a Stegosaurus, Mom? Can I? Please!?* Mahwah, NJ: Bridge-Water Books.

Greenland, C. (1997). Polar bears. In series *Getting to know nature's children: Polar bears and skunks.* Danbury, CT: Scholastic.

Greenland, C. (2000). Ants. In series *Getting to know nature's children: Gorillas & ants.* Danbury, CT: Scholastic.

Hatkoff, I., Hatkoff, C., & Kahumbu, P. (2006). *Owen and Mzee: The true story of a remarkable friendship.* New York: Scholastic Press.

Hehner, B. (1999). *First on the moon: What it was like when man landed on the moon.* New York: Hyperion Books for Children.

Hoose, P. M., & Hoose, H. (1998). *Hey, little ant.* Berkeley, CA: Tricycle Press.

Johnson, P. B. (1997). *The cow who wouldn't come down.* New York: Orchard Books.

Kelsey, E. (1998). Bees. In series *Getting to know nature's children: Turtles & bees.* Danbury, CT: Scholastic.

Lawson, R. (1988). *Ben and me: A new and astonishing life of Benjamin Franklin as written by his good mouse Amos*. Boston: Little, Brown.

Layne, S. L. (2003). *My brother Dan's delicious*. Gretna, LA: Pelican.

Lehman, B. (2004). *The red book*. Boston: Houghton Mifflin.

Louie, A. L. (1982). *Yeh-Shen: A Cinderella story from China*. New York: Philomel Books.

Lowry, L. (1989). *Number the stars*. New York: Houghton Mifflin Harcourt.

Manna, A. L., & Mitakidou, S. (2011). *The orphan: A Cinderella story from Greece*. New York: Schwartz & Wade.

McNamara, M. (2011). *The three little aliens and the big bad robot*. New York: Schwartz & Wade.

Mendell, D. (2008). *Obama: A promise of change*. New York: Amistad/Collins.

Mochizuki, K. (1993). *Baseball saved us*. New York: Lee & Low.

Orloff, K. K. (2004). *I wanna iguana*. New York: Putnam's.

Orloff, K. K. (2010). *I wanna new room*. New York: Putnam's.

Palatini, M. (2003). *The perfect pet*. New York: HarperCollins.

Polacco, P. (1995). *Babushka's doll*. New York: Aladdin Paperbacks.

Polacco, P. (1997). *Chicken Sunday*. New York: Paperstar.

Polacco, P. (2009). *The butterfly*. New York: Puffin Books/Penguin.

Polacco, P. (2012). *Thank you, Mr. Falker*. New York: Putnam's.

Polacco, P. (2013). *The blessing cup*. New York: Simon & Schuster Books for Young Readers.

Rohmann, E. (1997). *Time flies*. New York: Dragonfly Books.

Rylant, C. (1993). *The relatives came*. New York: Aladdin Books.

Schanzer, R. (2007). *George vs. George: The American Revolution as seen from both sides*. Washington, DC: National Geographic Society.

Simon, S. (1991). *Big cats*. New York: HarperCollins.

Simon, S. (1998). *Jupiter*. New York: HarperCollins.

Simon, S. (1998). *Volcanoes*. New York: HarperCollins.

Simon, S. (1999). *Tornadoes*. New York: HarperCollins.

Simon, S. (2000). *Destination: Mars*. New York: HarperCollins.

Simon, S. (2003). *Earth: Our planet in space*. New York: Simon & Schuster Books for Young Readers.

Simon, S. (2003). *Eyes and ears*. New York: HarperCollins.

Simon, S. (2003). *The moon*. New York: Simon & Schuster Books for Young Readers.

Simon, S. (2006). *Earthquakes*. Washington, DC: Smithsonian Collins.

Simon, S. (2006). *Sharks*. Washington, DC: Smithsonian Collins.

Simon, S. (2006). *The brain: Our nervous system*. Washington, DC: Smithsonian Collins.

Simon, S. (2007). *Hurricanes*. New York: Smithsonian Collins.

Simon, S. (2009). *Cats*. New York: HarperCollins.

Simon, S. (2009). *Dogs*. New York: HarperCollins.

Simon, S. (2009). *Dolphins*. Washington, DC: Smithsonian Collins.

Sullivan, G. (2000). *Abraham Lincoln*. New York: Scholastic Reference.

Switzer, M. (1988). Penguins. In series *Getting to know nature's children: Penguins and elephants*. Danbury, CT: Scholastic.

Teague, M. (2002). *Dear Mrs. LaRue: Letters from obedience school*. New York: Scholastic Press.

Than, K. (2009). *Earthquakes*. New York: Children's Press.

Trivizas, E. (1997). *The three little wolves and the big bad pig*. New York: Aladdin Paperbacks.

Van Allsburg, C. (1993). *The sweetest fig*. New York: Houghton Mifflin.

Van Allsburg, C. (1995). *Jumanji: A storybook*. New York: Scholastic.

Varon, S. (2007). *Robot dreams*. New York: First Second.

Viorst, J. (1990). *Earrings!* New York: Atheneum.

Walker, S. M. (2008). *Earthquakes*. Minneapolis, MN: Lerner.

Weinman Sharmat, M. (1992). *Nate the great and the stolen base.* New York: Random House Children's Books.

Weitzman, J. P. (1998). *You can't take a balloon into the Metropolitan Museum.* New York: Dial Books for Young Readers.

Wiesner, D. (1988). *Free fall.* New York: HarperCollins.

Wiesner, D. (1992). *June 29, 1999.* New York: Clarion Books.

Wiesner, D. (2001). *The three pigs.* New York: Clarion Books.

Wiesner, D. (2006). *Flotsam.* New York: Clarion Books.

Yashima, T. (1983). *Crow boy.* Harmondsworth, UK: Puffin Books.

Websites

Diffen
www.diffen.com

A wiki that includes contrasts between a variety of nonfiction topics.

Glogster
http://edu.glogster.com/?ref=com

A Web 2.0 tool that allows the creation and sharing of virtual posters. Users can embed videos, sound, pictures, and text.

How Stuff Works
www.howstuffworks.com

A website that provides information on a variety of topics. The text is enhanced with pictures.

Lexile
www.lexile.com

A website that allows users to locate information about a book's level of difficulty.

Library of Congress
www.loc.gov/education

The Library of Congress has a website that provides primary historical resources as well as lesson ideas for teachers.

National Geographic for Kids
http://kids.nationalgeographic.com

A website that provides information on scientific topics. The site also includes quizzes and activities.

Voicethread
https://voicethread.com

An interactive and sharing Web 2.0 tool that allows users to communicate in different modalities. Users can respond to information using video, audio, or text.

Index